D1266544

ISRAEL AMONG THE NATIONS

ISRAEL AMONG THE NATIONS

J. L. TALMON

Professor of Modern History,
The Hebrew University of Jerusalem

THE MACMILLAN COMPANY

NEW YORK, NEW YORK

The Macmillan Company
866 Third Avenue, New York, N. Y. 10022

First published in Great Britain in 1971 by
Weidenfeld & Nicolson.

Library of Congress Catalog Card Number: 74-155270

First American Edition 1971

Printed in the United States of America

Contents

Preface

In less than a quarter of a century after the greatest catastrophe followed by the most spectacular achievement in their history, the Jews find themselves again fighting on several fronts – Arabs, Soviet-Russia, other Communist countries, parts of the Old and the New Left, neo-Fascism – for recognition, acceptance and indeed survival, both as a people and as individuals. They are once more reappraising in great anguish the problems of their identity and destiny.

This is the inspiration of and the vantage point for the present attempt to probe into the responses of the Jews to the two vital challenges which have faced them in modern times – Revolution and nationalism. These essays eschew any analysis of the immanent forces and internal developments in Jewish life, and no claim is therefore made for them to offer a complete view of modern Jewish history.

These essays originally appeared in one form or another in the New York City College *Papers*, *Commentary*, *Haaretz*, the *Jerusalem Post* and *Maariv*, and thanks are due to them for permission to reprint them. I wish to express my indebtedness to Mrs Lily Polliack for reading the proofs and preparing the index.

J.L.T.

Jerusalem
5 July 1970

ISRAEL AMONG THE NATIONS

I

Jews Between Revolution and Counter-Revolution

It has for a long time been almost an axiom that The Revolution was the ally, some were even wont to say saviour of the Jews, and that the Jews were the natural standard-bearers of the revolution. Just now, however, only a quarter of a century after the apocalyptic confrontation between revolution and counter-revolution, in the course of which a third of the Jewish people were put to death by the latter as part of its crusade against the former, various upholders of revolution are adopting anti-Jewish attitudes, and yet Jews continue to be taking an active and often leading part in the revolutionary wave of today; although also their social-economic situation should on the face of it be drawing them away from revolution rather than driving them to it.

These developments are a sufficient justification for attempting another look at the now nearly two centuries old association between Jews and revolution, or on a wider canvas – at the problem of Jews between revolution and counter-revolution.

This is not a subject that can easily be treated with lofty detachment.

It is indeed like a foundling, a waif, an abandoned child. No one is willing to claim it for its own sake. Those who should be most interested, revolutionaries of Jewish extraction, or revolutionaries in general, tend to deny the very legitimacy of the juxtaposition, 'Jews and revolution'. It is, they argue, men, classes, peoples who rise in revolt against oppression; that many revolutionaries have

been of Jewish ancestry is quite irrelevant and the very desire to
see it as relevant arises out of a sinister intention to discredit the
cause of revolution itself.

Then there are those Jews who are unable to ignore the intimate
relation between Jews and revolution, but wish they had never
heard of it. They too sense mischievous designs in the raising
of the issue, and they respond by nervously disclaiming any
connection with their distant kinsmen gone astray.

There are Jews, nationalists, usually, who like to dwell on the
subject, but only as a cautionary tale. How fatuous, vain and
perilous it is to wander into alien vineyards: 'Back to your tents,
oh children of Jacob.' This has become also the attitude of the
survivors of those groups in Jewry which in the past desired to
combine revolutionary commitment with a sustained endeavour
to assert some form of national Jewish identity. They feel now
utterly rejected, almost a reproach unto themselves.

It is indeed a charged, infinitely sensitive, not to say explosive
subject, while being at the same time maddeningly vague and
elusive, with no definite structure. The dangers of arbitrary
speculation and unsubstantiated generalisation are calculated to
make it still more of an irritant than it would in any case be:
especially to people raised in the liberal-democratic tradition, and
of course still more to the Jews among them. The Central and
Eastern European realities and categories of thought which constitute the essential frame of reference for this inquiry are not only
alien to their experience; they are also repellent to the basic
assumptions and postulates of the Western-Jewish and even more
so to the American-Jewish symbiosis.

Beyond that, the subject is disquieting because any discussion of
it is bound – as already hinted – to lay bare some of the most
massive contradictions and unbridgeable antinomies in the human
situation. The loftiest idealism here touches the most abysmal
criminality; total self-sacrifice dwells together with stupendous
arrogance; hope eternal alternates with tragedy irretrievable. And
over it all hovers ultimate catastrophe.

I

By revolution, I mean the process of change which has been in permanent motion first in the Western world, and now throughout the whole planet, since the French and the Industrial revolutions converged two centuries ago. It may be said that since then change – ceaseless, ever more rapid, and ever more radical – has been the only stable law of our civilisation. By now it takes an effort of imagination to visualise the infinite slowness of change in the ages in which the horse was the only means of transport and hand-made tools the only industrial implements.

The bourgeoisie – we read in *The Communist Manifesto*[1] – cannot exist without constantly revolutionising the instruments of production, and thereby the relations of production, and with them all the relations of society. Conservation of the old modes of production in unaltered form, was, on the contrary, the first condition of existence for all earlier industrial classes. Constant revolutionising of production, uninterrupted disturbance of all social conditions, everlasting uncertainty and agitation distinguish the bourgeois epoch from all earlier ones. All fixed, fast-frozen relations, with their train of ancient and venerable prejudices and opinions, are swept away, all new-formed ones become antiquated before they can ossify. All that is solid melts into air, all that is holy is profaned, and man is at last compelled to face with sober senses his real conditions of life, and his relations with his kind. . . .

The bourgeoisie, during its rule of scarcely one hundred years, has created more massive and more colossal productive forces than have all preceding generations together. Subjection of Nature's forces to man, machinery, application of chemistry to industry and agriculture, steam-navigation, railways, electric telegraphs, clearing of whole continents for cultivation, canalisation of rivers, whole populations conjured out of the ground – what earlier century had even a presentiment that such productive forces slumbered in the lap of social labour? . . . accomplished wonders far surpassing Egyptian pyramids, Roman aqueducts and Gothic cathedrals; it has conducted expeditions that put in the shade all former exoduses of nations and Crusades.

When these purple passages were written, in 1847, the Industrial Revolution had only just begun to make itself felt in a few countries outside England. The internal combustion engine had not yet been invented; cars and planes were still in the domain of fantasy. Technicians had not yet hit upon the new devices for the production of steel. It was before telephones and electricity, refrigeration and the canning of foods were introduced. Transcontinental and transoceanic transport had not yet exorcised the fear (and danger) of famine. There were as yet in Europe only two large cities, London and Paris.

The revolutionary changes in the modes of production meant equally far-reaching changes in social relationships and in the sphere of ideas. Old static society took the traditional state of things for granted as natural and God-willed, as part of the cosmic order. Order meant order of rank, of hierarchy and of class. Thus in the cosmos, thus in the Church and thus in society at large. Says Shakespeare in the famous passage in *Troilus and Cressida*,

> The heavens themselves, the planets and this centre,
> Observe degree, priority and place,
> Insisture, course, proportion, season, form,
> Office and custom, in all line of order:
> And therefore is the glorious planet Sol
> In noble eminence enthroned and sphered
> Amidst the other; whose medicinable eye
> Corrects the ill aspects of planets evil,
> And posts like the commandment of a king,
> Sans check to good and bad: but when the planets
> In evil mixture to disorder wander,
> What plagues and what portents, what mutiny,
> What raging of the sea, shaking of earth,
> Commotion in the winds, frights, changes, horrors,
> Divert and crack, rend and deracinate
> The unity and married calm of states
> Quite from their fixture! O, when degree is shaked,
> Which is the ladder to all high designs,
> The enterprise is sick! How could communities,
> Degrees in schools and brotherhoods in cities,

Peaceful commerce from dividable shores,
The primogenitive and due of birth,
Prerogative of age, crowns, sceptres, laurels,
But by degree, stand in authentic place?
Take but degree away, untune that string,
And, hark, what discord follows!

There was a time when man lived in preparation for another and more real life elsewhere. He was here on earth to atone for his sins – as the more morose teachers maintained; or to bear witness to the glory of God – as the kindlier guides taught; at all events to lead a life of service by obeying and respecting his superiors and observing loyally the duties attached to his station in life.

Almost suddenly a society based on status, on authority coming from above, on hereditary privilege, closed guilds and corporations, local autonomy and historic peculiarity, disintegrated, giving way to a society based on social mobility, *carrière ouverte aux talents*, individual initiative, popular election. Traditional communities, held together by unquestioned religious faith, burst asunder into classes and parties, faithful subjects of patriarchal rulers broke up into warring nationalities, and closely knit groups disintegrated into atomised individuals. Sir Lewis Namier speaks eloquently of a fission more violent than the splitting of the atom, all particles straining and striving.[2]

Under the impact of the revolutionary ideas man woke up to the plenitude of his rights. He became a pretender staking out claims to sovereign power. Happiness was his due. No wonder that in contrast to his long-suffering ancestors he came to experience every hardship as a mortal injury to his dignity as man. Imbued also with the tremendous newly won faith in the power of technology and social engineering, he would ascribe his suffering to an evil plot, or at least to the selfishness and the ill will of those in power. The pace and the volume of change grew too fast for the best intentioned and most alert legislator to cope with. The inevitable hiatus bteween change and remedy would confirm those seized by high expectations, and consequently only too prone to discontent, in their grim suspicion of deliberately oppressive policies practised by the established powers. If happiness was man's birthright – *idée neuve* in Europe[3] – and the provision of it the duty of government, no existing order could in the last analysis claim allegiance as incontestably legitimate and be taken for granted as natural. It was all the time threatened by a state of latent revolt. And as the law came to be looked upon as an instrument of oppression instead of the arm of even-handed justice, rebellion assumed the character of a right, indeed a duty, and direct action was seen as an effective as well as righteous deed.

> . . . the bounded waters
> Should lift their bosoms higher than the shores,
> And make a sop of all this solid globe:
> Strength should be lord of imbecility,
> And the rude son should strike his father dead:
> Force should be right; or rather, right and wrong,
> Between whose endless jar justice resides,
> Should lose their names, and so should justice too.
> Then every thing includes itself in power,
> Power into will, will into appetite:
> And appetite, an universal wolf,
> So doubly seconded with will and power,
> Must make perforce an universal prey,
> And last eat up himself.
>
> Shakespeare
> *Troilus and Cressida*

There was nothing new, writes Tocqueville, in powerful and rebellious spirits rising here and there against this or that belief of custom.'What singles out the eighteenth century . . . is that the audacious and reforming curiosity was experienced . . . by a whole generation, and was directed, at the same time . . . to all beliefs in such a way that the principles upon which the sciences, the arts, philosophy, politics rested until then, were attacked together by a sort of universal commotion.'[4]

The French Revolution and the Emperor Napoleon I – writes Guizot – have thrown a certain number of minds, including some of the most distinguished, into a feverish excitement which becomes a moral and, I would say, a mental disease. They yearn for events, immense, sudden, and strange; they busy themselves with making and unmaking governments, nations, religions, society, Europe, the world . . . they are intoxicated with the greatness of their own design, and blind to the chances of success. To hear them talk, one might think that they had the elements at their command . . . and that these were the first days of creation or the last days of the world. . . . Here they abolish the social ties, isolate the individual, deliver men to license or to the weakness of their own and only will; there they surrender them into the hands of the State charged with their fate. Some treat men like solitary animals without other resources than their personal strength . . . and fantasy; others collect them . . . like sheep into a flock under the responsibility of the shepherd . . . [all] see in democracy alone the whole of society.[5]

Here was 'a proud belief', said Tocqueville, 'that absolute truth has at last been found: these beautiful illusions about human nature, that almost boundless self-confidence, that generous élan toward the ideal'[6]

It had been change without respite and striving with no curbs, yet in a certain direction, namely towards the substitution of abstract universal patterns for local, national and racial peculiarities, of centralised anonymous forms for direct personal relationships. Again Marx and Engels:

The bourgeoisie has through its exploitation of the world market given a cosmopolitan character to production and consumption in every country. To the great chagrin of reactionists, it has drawn from under the feet of industry the national ground on which it stood. All old-established national industries have been destroyed or are daily being destroyed. They are dislodged by new industries, whose introduction becomes a life and death question for all civilised nations, by industries that no longer work up indigenous raw material, but raw material drawn from the remotest zones; industries whose products are consumed not only at home but in every quarter of the globe. In place of the old wants, satisfied by the productions of the country, we find new wants, requiring for their satisfaction the products of distant lands and climes. In place of the old local and national seclusion and self-sufficiency, we have intercourse in every direction, universal interdependence of nations. And as in material, so also in intellectual production. The intellectual creations of individual nations become common property. National one-sidedness and narrow-mindedness become more and more impossible, and from the numerous national and local literatures there arises a world literature.

The bourgeoisie, by the rapid improvement of all instruments of production, by the immensely facilitated means of communication, draws all, even the most barbarian nations into civilisation. The cheap prices of its commodities are the heavy artillery with which it batters down all Chinese walls, with which it forces the barbarians' intensely obstinate hatred of foreigners to capitulate. It compels all nations, on pain of extinction, to adopt the bourgeois mode of production; it compels them to introduce what it calls civilisation into their midst, i.e., to become bourgeois themselves. In a word, it creates a world after its own image.[7]

The vastness and rapidity of man-made change filled people with tremendous self-confidence and expectations, but being cut loose from traditional spiritual moorings also made them deeply anxious, especially as the faith in divine guidance had been greatly weakened or even entirely lost, while the changes had brought with them so much dislocation and pain. This is the background of the religion of revolution – the faith that history was moving in a preordained, predetermined way toward a great denouement, an apocalyptic consummation which would resolve the vast contradictions of social existence through the reconciliation of individual interest with the general good, individual self-expression with social cohesion, liberty with equality. It was in the power of man, indeed it was a challenge to his greatness, to lend a helping hand to history and to hasten that denouement. The main feature of this idea of revolution was again the universal nature of the vision it upheld – a vision which tended to relegate the facts of racial or national uniqueness and local or historic peculiarity into the background, if not to dismiss them as irrelevant.

The forces of relentless change and the ideology of a total transformation, both driving toward universal oneness, never ceased to encounter bitter resistance and hostility. There were those who rightly or wrongly feared extinction. There were the conservative attachments and sentimental loyalties. There were the deep convictions as well as the fierce prejudices. There was finally the recalcitrance of individual, local, national, racial or historical peculiarities. All these would stubbornly, sullenly or militantly hurl themselves in the path of the levelling hurricane of revolution.

For some hundred years the forces of reaction and counter-revolution consisted of disparate tendencies fighting a rearguard or delaying action, without much real coordination or a coherent programme, their faith in themselves and their own future having been undermined. But as the nineteenth century moved to a close, the varying sentiments of resistance to revolutionary universalism began to show signs of developing into an ideology. Gradually the forces involved coalesced into a confraternity of the counter-revolution, acquiring in the process a new dynamism and a mass following. In this encounter between revolution and counter-revolution the Jewish factor played an incalculable part. The role of Jews as agent, irritant, actor, test case and victim of that mighty clash is the subject of these reflections.

II

No other group betokened more strikingly the fact of change. With the exception of the ultra-orthodox, desperately fearful of change of any kind, Jews everywhere looked upon the French Revolution as a date comparable to the exodus from Egypt, and to the issuing of the Law from Mount Sinai, this time not to the Jews alone, but to all the nations. France of the Revolution became to them a second country, to more exalted believers in the superiority of the spirit over matter, their sole spiritual fatherland, just as the Soviet Union was to millions of Communists throughout the world just a short while ago. Indeed, as late as 1939, and only one year before the anti-Jewish laws were issued by the Vichy Government, the Chief Rabbi of France celebrated the one hundred and fiftieth anniversary of that great deliverance in precisely such dithyrambic language.

The revolution brought the Jews out of the ghetto into the forum.[8] They had never been seen there before. It was not unnatural for the casualties of the revolution to view the Jews as among its main beneficiaries, profiting from the misfortunes of the losers. In the deliberations in the French National Assembly on Jewish emancipation in 1789, some clerical right-wingers from Alsace raised the spectre of an imminent Jewish take-over of all Christian property in that most Jewish province of France: 'Within one month they will own half of the land of the province; within six years all of it.'9 In 1790 Edmund Burke called the Jews birds of prey hovering over the spoils of Church property nationalised by the revolution in France. From seeing the Jew as the beneficiary the counter-revolutionary losers soon moved to ascribe to him the authorship of the undesirable things. At the turn of the century German Romantics and reactionaries would dub the theories of natural law, human rights and popular sovereignty as a Jewish import from France. At the end of the nineteenth century Charles Maurras proclaimed the same teachings a Jewish import from Germany. In both cases the accusation was that these doctrines were part of a plot to break the natural resistance of the body politic to the Jewish invasion of the national culture and society, and of a godless resolve to destroy the Christian State.

From Burke and Bonald onward, spokesmen of the counter-revolution kept saying that they knew Englishmen, Frenchmen, Germans, for that matter a member of a class, group or locality, but had never met a man. No wonder that abstract international finance, commodity economy, mass production, standardised procedures, free trade, liberal values, not to speak of Socialist internationalism – all a-national or even anti-national – appeared in the eyes of the counter-revolution to be 'Jewish phenomena'.

For all these things involved dissolution of organic entities, destruction of rank and style, subversion of ancient stable forms, profanation of old venerable symbols, in brief insatiable restlessness.

There is no need to argue that the Industrial Revolution in England was no more made by the Jews than was the French Revolution. There were hardly any Jews among the first great inventors and the early captains of industry on the Continent. But there were the Rothschilds, spread across Europe, in Frankfurt, London, Paris, Vienna and Naples. They captured the imagination of Europe, to the point of putting all Gentile banking houses of Europe into the shade, while making the Jewish bankers everywhere appear as Rothschild agencies. And they specialised in as it were invisible, yet immensely powerful things, and no government could carry on, it was believed, without loans from them. Then there was the very great part played by Jews in covering Europe with a network of railways: the Rothschilds and Pereiras in France and Austria, at a later date the Hirschs in Turkey and the Poliakovs in Russia.[10] Railway building again meant dealings with governments, at the highest level, national decisions of the highest importance involving matters of principle, such as government intervention versus free enterprise; such operations affected the lives of countless people besides mere shareholders, and had repercussions in international politics. At a time when some of the wisest men of Europe, Thiers for instance, failed completely to grasp the revolutionary significance of railways from the economic as well as the strategic point of view, it was the Jewish Saint-Simonists who were among the most fervent apostles of railway building, as incidentally also a means of uniting Europe and in due course the world, for that peaceful industrial endeavour which was sure to exorcise the spectre of war from our planet for ever. It was no accident that Jews were the founders of the first international telegraphic news agencies and very prominent in building up the European press. In brief, they conformed beautifully to the classical image of the hinges and pegs in the European economy and polity. They became the veins through which the blood of Europe's international economy flowed – at least in the eyes of interested non-Jews, both the liberal bourgeois entrepreneurs who were leading advocates of Jewish emancipation as part of the removal of obstacles to free economic endeavour and liberal institutions, and of those who were hurt by, feared or abhorred capitalist expansion. Neurotically over-reacting to the Jewish irritant, the latter were swept into identifying the whole of the capitalist revolution with the Jews. And, as said, credence was added to this image by the conspicuousness of the Jews in the central arteries of the body politic and the most sensitive foci of the economy.

On the identification of capitalism with Jews there was the curious, and *prima facie* paradoxical agreement between counter-revolutionary writers who hated capitalism as a materialist solvent of old traditions and national peculiarity on the one hand, and Socialist revolutionaries who condemned it as a system of social oppression and human alienation on the other.

Tocqueville expresses in an elegant way the same idea which Marx was hammering out in a ponderously Hegelian and arrestingly aphoristic language: the bourgeois-liberal state had abolished all privileges and all inequalities of birth, race and creed, but failed to touch property, proclaiming economic inequality irrelevant from the legal and political points of view. It had thereby given property free rein and in fact turned it into the dominant factor. In an unrecognised, almost illegal manner, money was made into the sole and supreme privilege in a society where birth, religion, tradition had become entirely subordinated to the supremely real cash nexus. But whereas Tocqueville was not concerned with the Jews at all, partly because of his utter abhorrence of racism, as illustrated in his correspondence with Count Gobineau, Marx spells out the anti-Semitism argument fully. 'What is the secular basis of Judaism?', asks Marx. 'Practical need, self-interest. What is the wordly cult of the Jew? Bargaining. ... Money has become a world power, and the practical Jewish spirit has become the practical spirit of the Christian nations. The Jews have emancipated themselves in so far as the Christians have become Jews.' Judaism has attained 'universal dominion' by connecting 'externalised man and nature into alienable and saleable objects subservient to egoistic need, dependent on bargaining'.[11]

The very fact that the Jews had not yet gained equal rights underscored and indeed epitomised the great lie at the bottom of the liberal-bourgeois regime: the credibility gap between the official, seemingly popularly elected political rulers and the hidden holders of real power. Alluding to the Rothschilds, Bruno Bauer says: 'The Jew who is only tolerated in Vienna, for example, determines the fate of the whole Empire through his financial power. The Jew who may be without rights in the smallest German state decides the destiny of Europe. While corporations and guilds exclude the Jew or are unfavourable to him, audacity in industry mocks the obstinacy of these medieval institutions.'[12] It was a favourite argument with the early Socialists that capitalism had in fact re-established a kind of neo-feudalism, while it took great pride in having abolished its venerable predecessor. Inherited privilege and all special legal status had been abolished, but surely capitalism was bound to perpetuate the distinction between the haves and have-nots. Inherited wealth will face inherited poverty, for as the former will become more consolidated, it will become much more difficult for those plunged in the latter to come out of their penury. And so the Jews were destined to become the feudal lords of the modern world – Toussenel's 'industrial-financial feudalism'.[13]

We are thus faced with the striking paradox: to the conservatives the Jews are the symbol, beneficiary, finally the maker of the capitalist revolution which was in their eyes a kind of preparation for the Socialist revolution; to the Socialists – the embodiment and pillar of that capitalism, which the revolution was rising to destroy.

III

And yet it would be a great mistake to tar all the Socialists with the same brush and proclaim tham all anti-Semites. While Fourier, Toussenel, Proudhon, Pierre Leroux and Bakunin loathed the Jews, Saint-Simon and his disciples were emphatically philo-Semitic, whereas Marxism was in spite of Marx's spleen against his own race fundamentally not anti-Semitic. The line of demarcation in this was the approval or disapproval of change, indeed one may say of the modern world, and also the presence or absence of direct Jewish inspiration, which in most cases meant the same.

While the Saint-Simonists, and in a somewhat ambivalent

form Marx himself, saw in capitalism, notwithstanding its evils, a necessary prelude to Socialism, a station on the winding way to a Messianic denouement, a moment in the dialectic of history, the anti-Semitic Socialists regarded the emergence of industrial capitalism as an event comparable to the original Fall of Man. Whereas the former wanted to hasten the process of industrialisation, the latter would have liked to dismantle industrial society altogether. The former take a universal view of change, thrill at innovation and love bigness. The latter feel their integrity and identity threatened. It is no accident that Jews and Jewish inspiration were so prominent in Saint-Simonism and Marxism, and that the opponent of these two movements came to be motivated by such fierce hatred of the Jews.

Under the influence of his Jewish disciples, the wealthy Rodriguez brothers and their cousins, the Pereira brothers, who took care of him in his old age, and in fact played an apostolic role in his movement – that first Socialist movement in Europe – Saint-Simon quite explicitly links his vision of the future to the Messianic hopes of Judaism.

The people of God – writes St Simon – that people which received revelations before the coming of Christ, that people which is the most universally spread over the surface of the earth, has always perceived that the Christian doctrine founded by the Fathers of the Church was incomplete. It has always proclaimed that a grand epoch will come, which has been given the name of Messiah's Kingdom; an epoch in which religious doctrine shall be presented in all the generality of which it is susceptible, and shall regulate alike the action of the temporal and of the spiritual power. All the human race will then have but one religion and one organisation: the Golden Age was not behind us, it was before us![14]

In the vindication of capitalism as a necessary and beneficial phase in history, the Saint-Simonists went so far as to glorify the role of bankers as unwitting planners of the national economy through granting or withholding credit. Indeed Jewish usury, the butt of infinite contempt and moral indignation, was rehabilitated by them in a rather quaint manner. By lending money to the idle parasitic feudals, and by squeezing them dry, the Jewish usurers were instrumental in passing on unproductive money, which would otherwise have been squandered by spendthrifts, into the hands of the productive elements, bourgeois entrepreneurs, and in hastening thus the capitalist development which was the necessary prelude to Socialism.[15] And we have read Marx's hymns on the glorious achievements of capitalism on the way to Socialism.

The anti-Semitic Socialist theoreticians and prophets were united in a basic disapproval and fear of a world tossed about by incessant change and moving constantly in the direction of abstract universalism. Fourier, Proudhon, and Bakunin stand in horror before the anonymity of industrial society and the central-isation it entails. They look back, as said before, to the lost inno-cence of pre-capitalist society or to some pristine state of nature. They extol the virtues of independent craftsmen and peasants and glorify the instinctive nobility of the unsophisticated, primitive rebel. They dream of small communities, anarchistic groups held together by mutual aid. They look forward to a utopian world of 'pure justice', to the abolition of all authority and to the release of the passions. They loathe credit, exchange, the market mechan-ism, modern communications, the international press: all em-bodied for them in the Jew, the ghostly hand which holds the disparate parts together, and manipulates the figures on the chess-board. Thus Toussenel:

The Jew is by temperament an anti-producer, neither a farmer, nor an industrialist, not even a true merchant. He is an intermediary, al-ways fraudulent and parasitic, who operates in trade as in philosophy, by means of falsification, counterfeiting [and] horse-trading. He knows but the rise and fall of prices, the risks of transportation, the incerti-tudes of crops, the hazards of demand and supply. His policy in econo-mics has always been entirely negative, entirely usurious. It is the evil principle, Satan, Ahriman incarnated in the race of Shem, which has already been twice exterminated by the Greeks and by the Romans, the first time at Tyre, the second time at Carthage; the cosmopolitan Jew ... Europe is entailed to the domination of Israel. This universal domination, of which so many conquerors have dreamed, the Jews have in their hands.[16]

There surely is food for thought in the similarities between the morbidly inhibited and pedantic old bachelor Fourier and the volcanic arch-revolutionary, but sexually impotent Bakunin. Any kind of convention, restraint, authority, organisation seems to suffocate, strangle them. The one dreams of the total gratification of desire, the other of the total release of spontaneous passion, and both rail against the Jew as the principle of repression and organisation.

At another point it is Proudhon and Bakunin who meet and sharply diverge from Saint-Simonism and Marxism. The two latter philosophies shared with the former the vision of a reborn man with a new morality, but their postulate was grounded upon faith in the power of social conditions, educational influences, and reason to engender that change. The man of the future was man *per se*, neither Jew, nor Greek, nor Gentile, nor was he envisaged as being in any way helped or hampered by his ancestry, blood, race or nationality. Not so with Proudhon, who was enamoured of the peasants and artisans of France and who loathed all foreigners; not so with Bakunin, to whom the authentic revolutionary was not a man who reasoned and planned, but a creature of instinct and of an existential situation: so he successively looked for salvation to the unspoilt spontaneous Slavs, the rebellious Russian peasants of Pugatchev and Stienka Razin, the primitive bandits, finally the *déclassé* outcasts of all kinds, including criminals whose passion for destruction – the necessary condition for total reconstruction – was not hampered by any possessions or vested interests. For both Proudhon and Bakunin it was a short step from populism to racism, to the hatred of whole racial or national groups in defiance of the universality of the Socialist ideal. Bakunin could thus describe the Jews as 'an exploiting sect, a blood-sucking people, a unique, devouring parasite tightly and intimately organised ... cutting across all the differences in political opinion'.[17] But no one could have gone further in this than Proudhon:

Jews – Write an article against this race which poisons everything, by meddling everywhere without ever joining itself to another people. – Demand their expulsion from France, with the exception of individuals married to Frenchwomen. – Abolish the synagogues; don't admit them to any kind of employment, pursue finally the abolition of this cult. It is not for nothing that the Christians called them deicides. The Jew is the enemy of the human race. One must send this race back to Asia or exterminate it.

H. Heine, A. Weil and others are nothing but secret spies; Rothschild, Crémieux, Marx, Fould, malignant beings, bilious, envious, acrid etc., who hate us. By fire or fusion, or by expulsion, the Jew must disappear . . . Tolerate the aged who no longer give birth to offspring. Work to be done – what the peoples of the Middle Ages hated by instinct, I hate upon reflection, and irrevocably.[18]

This leads us to try to elicit the Jewish ingredient of the religion of revolution in contrast to the anti-Semitic strand in it, or at least as distinct from the non-Jewish elements in the revolutionary movement.

IV

Is it possible to detect significantly distinct, or at least especially accentuated characteristics in the Jewish revolutionaries in the early pre-1848 days of capitalism (and Socialism)? I believe that there is reason to speak of a certain common denominator linking the Jewish Saint-Simonists – among the first Socialists in France, Moses Hess – the first Communist (at a later date Zionist) in Germany, the two leading Socialists of Europe, Karl Marx and Ferdinand Lassalle, and many lesser Jewish figures in the camp of revolution.

To be sure, it was not the Jews who created that particular climate of Messianic revolutionary expectation and preparation which it takes today some effort of imagination to conjure up.[19] Babeuf, Buonarotti, Blanqui, Barbès, Mazzini, Harney, Mieroslavski – none of them and hardly any of their immediate followers were Jews. But it was the Jews who experienced and articulated that state of mind with peculiar intensity and their restless zeal spilled over into effective organisational activity.

No other group, not even the uprooted villagers who flocked into the rapidly growing industrial centres, underwent a more thorough break with their former mode of existence than Jews, almost suddenly cut off from their ancestral faith, unique style of life, communal cohesion and isolation, and pariah status. Nothing existing could any longer be taken for granted. Everything seemed provisional, a preparation for the real thing to come. Ready as it were to absorb all these complex feelings of malaise, expectation, hope and zeal was the ancient Messianic disposition.[20]

Having abandoned their own extremely compact tradition, but not really or fully admitted to any other living tradition, and indeed unable to respond to the myths and symbols of the surrounding nation or to share fully the life of the working classes, it was only to be expected that those alienated Jews who could not bring themselves to submit to Baptism would seek an anchor in the dream of a mankind one and undivided, in Marx's human essence, where there would be no distinction between Jews, Greek and Gentile, eventually not even between worker and intellectual, where all things were made for all men, and where only the personal qualities of mind and heart and individual merit mattered.

All life, – writes young Hess – every aspiration is bound to end in frustration, so long as the aristocratic poison flows through all the arteries of society. I do not mean only the aristocracy of blood, nor solely the aristocracy of money. I mean every type of rule which is not based upon personal merit, but derives from blind chance, privilege of birth. In brief, I mean every so-called historic right.[21]

The early Jewish revolutionaries dream of a new religion, a religion of mankind the essence of which would be a new social gospel. It is curious to see them, all the same, employing Christian imagery and ideas to express their universalist longings, and dwelling on the superiority of the universal message of Christ over the tribal exclusiveness of Judaism. Otherwise they dream of a new Christianity without dogmas. 'So long as it [Christianity]' – writes young Hess – 'has not yet become the truly universal religion . . . true entirely and solely to its Founder, striving for the salvation of man in the fullest and most human sense, will the Jew be unable to espouse it'.[22] Eugène Rodriguez, who died at the age of twenty-three, consumed by a Messianic fervour which his ailing body could not contain, translated Lessing's 'Letters on the Enlightenment of Humanity' into French, and prefaced them with a lengthy statement in which he pleaded in exalted language for a religion of mankind which would synthesize the best contained in all existing religions and turn the progressive endeavour of mankind into an act of religious self-expression. We have the striking confession from his older brother Olinde, the St Paul of Saint-Simon:

The crisis of reorganisation in politics and morality commences with me, through Saint-Simon, whose heir I am by virtue of function. . . . From the day when Saint-Simon met the man who . . . understood the sciences, was sensitive to the fine arts and practised industry, the man who carried in him by blood the tradition of Moses, by disinterestedness that of Christ; from the day when that man, who . . . had learned from contact with industrialists and scientists the secret of their force and the weakness of their morality; from the day when that man, burning to his innermost with the living flame of Saint-Simon, felt himself penetrated by a new life, and recognised in Saint-Simon . . . a new father; from that day was born the association of the universal family; from that day there became possible the reunion of Jews and Christians in the bosom of a new Christianity, a universal religion.[23]

One could quote many cases of an ardent young Jew suddenly smitten by a revelation and enabled to make the decisive leap. He feels suddenly reborn; he has discovered the real truth; he has found an anchor, a cause to live for; such was the case of Olinde Rodriguez, Marx himself, of Lassalle, and so many others; often men who had previously thought of dedicating themselves to their own suffering people, half in love for and half in contempt of them.[24]

The most distinct and most effective 'Jewish' feature of the early Messianic Jewish revolutionaries was, however, I think, their inability to comprehend, and consequently their unwillingness to accept the fundamental Christian dogma of original sin – the idea of the eternal and inescapable dichotomy between the knowledge of what was good and the impotence to do it, between what should be and what is, between theory and practice, the world of pure ideas and defective reality, private and social morality, politics and ethics, faith and works, heaven and earth, spirit and matter – as the essential human condition. No genuine revolutionary experience is in the last analysis possible as long as that fatalistic attitude persists.

The Jewish disciples of Saint-Simon, the Rodriguez brothers and the Pereira brothers, as well as the convert Gustav d'Eichthal, voice the sense of their ancestral prophetic mission to dedicate themselves to the work of bridging the gap between theory and practice. Their rational society was to be based upon the precise determinations of modern technology, and guided by technocrats filled with overflowing love and prophetic premonitions. The Gentile Saint-Simonists have visions of the Jewess from the East announcing the Messianic tidings by undoing the evil deed of Eve, and cancelling the effects of the original sin which had made man, devoured by concupiscence, impotent to secure his own salvation, and ensnared him in that terrible contradiction of 'I know the good, and cannot help doing evil', and then erected barriers of hatred between men, classes, religions and nations.[25]

'Because I not only know' – writes Hess in a letter to Herzen – 'what I want, but also want what I know – I am more of an apostle than of a philosopher' – 'the social revolution is my religion'.[26] Without a philosophy, man – says Hess in another place – often comes to doubt the supreme truth, God, virtue, morality and liberty. But knowledge alone is not enough to give one bliss. Only the identity of thought and action can give it. It was from Hess and the Pole Cieszkowski that Marx drew the inspiration for his famous device that it was not enough to understand and criticise reality, it was imperative – and possible – to change it. There was no ideal history beyond concrete history, and no transcendental meaning above the concrete logic of social development. But Marx escapes the danger of relativism – one phase as necessary as the other , one ruling class as justified in its own day as its successor next day – by the vision of the proletariat carrying the burdens, afflicted with the evils of all classes – dialectically evolving into free and pure humanity, acting as the heart of philosophy.[27]

The relentlessly universal nature of the Messianic vision and the strenuous conviction of the inevitability of its fulfilment are at the bottom of Marx's fierce condemnation of and indeed denial of any *raison d'être* to the pastoral, pig-raising and pig-headed little tribal Slav nations, and for that matter Denmark in 1848–9. Through their particularistic aspirations and alliance with feudal reaction they were impeding the march of world revolution which was carried by the great and advanced nations, like the Germans. This basic attitude will, at a later date, cause Marx to approve and extol the work of British imperialism in fighting superstition and fatalistic lethargy in India, forcing upon it industrialisation and thus bringing the great continent nearer to revolution.[28] Even Lassalle, who in stark contrast to Marx was a Hegelian believer in the state and an upholder of the Fichtean idea of *Volksgeist*, and therefore in fact strove to perpetuate the uniqueness and separate-ness of nation-states, identified the true German *Volksgeist* with the humanist universalist tradition of German philosophy, envisaged national self-fulfilment as achieved in the replacement of the old absurdities of particularistic feudal Germany by the rule of pure reason, and designated the proletariat for the role of the national-universal class.[29]

The great wave of revolutions in 1848, spreading with lightning speed from capital to capital, almost from town to town across Europe, was greeted by very many Jews as proof that all nations were about to enter into a revolutionary world association.

Not only the democratic and Socialist aspirations, but even the national liberation movements bore at least in the early phase a distinctly universalist character. So great was the enthusiasm of the Jews that they were prepared to overlook the anti-Jewish excesses or gloss them over as tokens of too great an exuberance, misguided expressions of social resentment, marginal episodes, unavoidable accidents or counter-revolutionary provocations, or 'birth pangs, which bring redemption to our world'; and even to proclaim that the victory of universal brotherhood had put 'an end to any distinct Jewish history', 'for liberty, like love, is cosmopolitan, wandering from people to people'.[30]

There was hardly a revolution – that year of revolutions – in which Jews were not prominent or at least very active.

V

In France, where there was no Jewish proletariat and where Jews, except for the Jewish Saint-Simonists, were generally no further to the Left than bourgeois republicanism, Adolphe Crémieux and Goudchaux joined the government of the Republic as mild liberal Republicans. In Germany, where the Jews were more numerous, of a lesser social status, and less a part of the general society than across the Rhine, we find a much greater proportion of Jews in the Radical Left. Karl Marx is the editor of the extreme *Neue Rheinische Zeitung*, Jacoby is the spokesman of radical democracy, who will dare to castigate Friedrich Wilhelm IV to his face for refusing to listen to the truth, Stephen Born emerges as the first organiser of trade-unionism in Germany, Gottschalk heads the Communist demonstrations in the Rhineland. Dr Fischhof is the leader of the Vienna students who raise the standard of revolt in the Danubian capital. Daniel Manin plays an immortal role in the defence of revolutionary Venice against the Austrians.

Although it would be a wild exaggeration to depict the wave of revolutions as led by Jews or as a result of a Jewish plot, it was possible for King Friedrich Wilhelm IV of Prussia to charge 'the circumcised' for having brought 'that shame upon Germany',[31] and for a Catholic journal in Vienna to speak of the 'most intense pain experienced by those who saw . . . the Jew Fischhof marching as head of the Committee of Public Safety just behind the canopy under which the Crucifix was carried, holding a candle, like formerly His Imperial Majesty the Apostolic King,' and to ask 'was it an accident or was there in it a symbol pregnant with significance?'[32] Affirmative answers to this question were given by some contemporary Jews.

We have two astonishingly similar comments on the role of the Jews in the revolution from two eminent Jews standing at opposite poles of the political spectrum. One comes from Benjamin Disraeli in his *Life of Lord George Bentinck*, published in 1852, and the other from the German-Jewish Socialist J. L. Bernays in the

New York German-Jewish journal *Israels Herold* in 1849. Disraeli had set out to prove the superiority of the Jewish race. 'The degradation of the Jewish race is alone a striking evidence of its excellence, for none but one of the great races could have survived the trials which it has endured.' There was indeed no other race 'that so much delights, and fascinates, and elevates, and ennobles Europe, as the Jewish . . . the most admirable artists of the drama . . . the most entrancing singers, graceful dancers, and exquisite musicians [including incidentally Mozart – J.L.T.] are sons and daughters of Israel', not to speak of the great bankers and advisers to great statesmen, like Friedrich Gentz, the grey eminence of Metternich. Moreover, the Jews are living proof of the nonsense of social and racial equality, of the 'inexorable law of nature which has decreed that a superior race shall never be destroyed or absorbed by an inferior'. The true Jewish values were the conservative values *par excellence*. 'They are the trustees of tradition, and the conservators of the religious element. They are a living and the most striking evidence of the fatality of that pernicious doctrine of modern times, the natural equality of man . . . of cosmopolitan fraternity . . . [calculated] . . . to deteriorate the great races and destroy all the genius of the world.'

Now if 'all the tendencies of the Jewish race are conservative . . . religion, property, and natural aristocracy, it should be the interest of statesmen that this bias of a great race should be encouraged, and their energies and creative powers enlisted in the cause of existing society'.

Instead, the Gentile world has chosen to oppress and persecute the Jews. See what has been the result.

In 1848 an insurrection takes place against tradition and aristocracy, against religion and property. Destruction of the Semitic principle, extirpation of the Jewish religion, whether in the mosaic or in the Christian form; the natural equality of man and the abrogation of property are proclaimed by the secret societies who form provisional governments, and men of Jewish race are found at the head of every one of them. The people of God cooperate with atheists; the most skilful accumulators of property ally themselves with the communists; the peculiar and chosen race touch the hand of all the scum and low

castes of Europe! Had it not been for the Jews . . . imbecile as were the
governments, the uncalled-for outbreak would not have ravaged
Europe. But the fiery energy and the teeming resources of the Children
of Israel maintained for a long time the unnecessary and useless struggle
. . . everywhere the Jewish element. . . . And all this because they wish
to destroy that ungrateful Christendom which owes to them even its
name, and whose tyranny they can no longer endure.

By contrast, 'the great transatlantic republic is intensely semitic and
has prospered accordingly'[33] – Disraeli seems to re-echo an
observation of Marx, but one made in an entirely different spirit.

Bernays gives a similar evaluation of 'the Jewish element in the
latest European movement', but in a spirit that he himself recog-
nises 'will be considered by a large part of the readers as highly
dangerous', namely that of joyous triumph, instead of the anxious
regret of Disraeli. Bernays is soaked in young Hegelian modes of
thought, and often employs the same terms as Marx, only to reach
the opposite conclusion. Both were agreed that the surest way of
destroying political and social oppression was through the destruction of the faith in and respect for God and all religious authority
– the fountain-head of all systems of oppression and alienation –
which the Gentile leftist Hegelians like Feuerbach, Fr. D. Strauss,
Rugge, and Bauer brothers actually set out to do. The Jews –
Bernays claims – have succeeded in 'galvanising the raw mob'
against Pope, bishops, kings and princes, feudal potentates
and plutocrats. They 'laid bare the human essence buried under
the thick crust of intolerance', and 'in the face of human
worth, . . . there comes an end to priest and Rabbi'. In order
to obtain their emancipation, the Jews had first to destroy
the Christian essence of the state, the 'Christian State'. 'They
criticised Christianity with great dialectical skill and with no
pity', and by becoming 'in the process atheists, radicals, they
became truly free men, with no prejudices'. And once they had
shown that the Christian religion was nothing but a myth, 'the
work was accomplished'.

More than that, the Jews 'have rescued men from the narrow
idea of an exclusive fatherland, from patriotism. . . . The Jew is not
only an atheist, but a cosmopolitan, and he has turned men into

atheists and cosmopolitans; he has made man only a free citizen of the world.' Almost consciously contradicting Marx's famous dictum on the emancipation of mankind through its emancipation from Judaism, and of the Jews from Judaism, Bernays triumphantly proclaims: 'In their struggle for emancipation the Jews have emancipated the European States from Christianity'. In other words it is not the Christians who gave emancipation to the Jews, the Jews enabled the Christians to obtain their own emancipation. 'The Jews took their revenge upon the hostile world in an entirely new manner . . . by liberating men from all religion, from all patriotic sentiment . . . from everything that reminded them of race, place of origin, dogma and faith. Men emancipated themselves that way, and the Jew emancipated them, and the Jew became free with them . . . They achieved the incredible, and historians of the people will in the future recognise their merit willingly and justly.' It was not their religion or racial qualities that enabled the Jews to accomplish all this. It was their existential situation, their fate: 'Only as the result of a general emancipatory effort could they become free themselves.' The Jews succeeded in forging for themselves some mighty levers of power to help them in their work: 'the power of mobile property represented by the Rothschilds'; the psychological, spiritually therapeutic influence of Jewish doctors whose very existence and sought-after activity defied religious taboos and differences of religion, race and tradition; and above all the press, 'which fell everywhere in Europe into Jewish hands'. And when the revolution broke out, the Jews were everywhere in the forefront. After all, Christendom had now become atheistic and cosmopolitan, the Jews might as well leave the stage as a separate people. Their mission had been fulfilled. In a Hegelian manner the highest assertion of their particularity marks their disappearance within universality.

Bernays concludes with a prophecy, which he finds himself 'unable to suppress'. There will be more waves of anti-Jewish persecution. Attacks on the Jewish religion and the Jewish nationality will be turned into an assault upon radicalism and free thought. 'Stand firm, Jews, bear that blow too, because it will be the last! He who will dare to attack the man in the Jew, will bring upon himself all mankind; and that this should not take its terrible revenge one day, of such a thing there is no example in history.'[34]

Bernays and the Jews in general, so eager in that year of universal brotherhood to renounce their corporate identity, in some cases even their religious separateness, entirely misread the real significance of the revolutionary upheaval. The victor in that revolution proved to be not universalism, but nationalism of the exclusive type; not abstract idealism, but historic continuity; not rationalism, but the powers of instinct; not the idea of concord, but the fact of force. The Jews became the test case and whipping-block, when the victory of these counter-revolutionary forces had time to work itself out.

In the meantime, some fifteen years after the *débâcle* of the revolutionary hopes in 1848–9, two Jews emerged as the acknowledged leaders of the revolution. German workers made their appeal to the Jewish *littérateur* Lassalle to become their chief and in response the young dictatorial leader launched his terrific campaign, which was cut short by his death in an absurd duel, and Karl Marx became the head of the First International.

VI

At that very time the problem of Jews and revolution began to assume truly vital significance in the Empire of the Tsars. All comprehensive bondage on the one hand and the Messianic disposition of the Russian people on the other fed here the vision of total redemption through total revolution; that yearning could not but affect most deeply young Jewish men and women, straining to enter the great stream of humanity, but hemmed in on all sides by sustained and deliberately humiliating oppression.[35]

We know of at least one Jew, actually a convert by the name of Peretz, who was involved with the gentry and officers who led the Decembrist rebellion of 1825. We then hear of a Jewish revolutionary by the name of Dr Robert Feinberg who was deported back into Russia from Prussia for his participation in the 1848 events in Berlin to be sent to Siberia and die there insane in 1860, after having been exempted from amnesty. In the fifties we hear of two doctors, Benjamin Portugalov and Lev Zelensky, who, especially the former, became popular figures as 'physicians humanists' and defenders of Jewish honour, though adversaries of traditional religion.[36] It was only in the eighteen-sixties or rather seventies that the Tsarist authorities woke up to the fact of Jewish prominence in the revolutionary underground. There occurs then a striking shift in the anti-Jewish argumentation – the charge of clannish self-centredness and superstitious backwardness gives way to the accusation of rebelliousness and nihilism. The change reflects far-reaching transformations in Jewish life in Russia. In the earlier decades the few Jews who made good by amassing vast fortunes or – less often – entering the ranks of the professions, professed deep loyalty to the state as their benefactor. Not unlike the Sephardi notables in the early French Revolution, they drew a line between themselves, enlightened and fully mature for emancipation, and their unfortunate brethren, steeped still in the dark Talmudic past. There was a kind of war between the Jewish 'progressives' and the Jewish masses which refused to be 're-educated'. The pro-Government official leadership often stooped to collaborating with the police in rounding up poor Jewish boys in their early teens for forced military service, while in their despair the orthodox elements did not shrink from acts of rebellion. The liberal reforms in the early reign of Alexander II opened the gates of secondary schools and the universities to thousands of the Jewish youth, among them sons and daughters of poor parents of the Pale, and also enabled students of the Rabbinical seminars to obtain a university education. And so, by way of polarisation there emerges a whole class of immensely rich and influential Jewish *entrepreneurs* and bankers, to whom we should perhaps also add those converts who reached the highest positions in government service and in the academic world, but retained close ties with the Jewish community, on the one side, and revolutionary extremists, especially among the Jewish students, on the other. But it would be a mistake to lump all the latter together into the one category of frustrated educated plebians. Besides the wretchedly

poor Paul Axelrod, who was later to make his living in Switzerland as a milkman, we have Michail Gotz, a member of the multi-
millionaire tea magnates family Wysotzki, besides the cobbler
Hirsch Leckert, the famous assassin of the Governor of Vilna, there
is the *grand bourgeois* Marc Natanson, and while Trotsky came from
a farmer family with not much education, Jewish or general,
Ossip Minor, the SR leader, was the son of the distinguished
Chief Rabbi of Moscow (deported for 'arrogantly' trying to build
an elegant synagogue in a posh Moscow district), and the Menshevik leader, Martov, the grandson of the leading Jewish publicist Zederbaum.

Jewish participation in the revolutionary movement in the
seventies was the excuse for both the 1881 pogroms and the new
draconian repressive legislation against the Jews, which only served
to drive many more Jews into revolutionary activity – another case
of the vicious circle, so permanent a feature of Jewish existence.

A secret police survey for the years 1873-7 speaks of 67 Jews out
of the 1054 defendants tried in courts for revolutionary activity,
which means 6 per cent, and another report of 103 Jews tried for
political offences in the Vilna district alone in the years 1875-90.
Among those sentenced for taking part in the famous demonstration on the Kazan Square in January 1877 there were 5 or 6 Jews
out of 21 detained and tried. The proportion of Jews among the
Narodnaya Volia defendants in the years 1880-90 rose to 17
per cent, and of the 54 prominent terrorists sentenced in that
period 22 were Jews. In the years 1884-90, out of 4307 serving
prison sentences for political offences 579 were Jews.[37] In his
famous interview with the Tsarist Minister Witte, Herzl was
faced with the question why the Jews who constituted only
3 per cent of the population of Russia supplied 50 per cent of its
revolutionaries.[38] In an ill-tempered note jotted down at the time
of the famous Second Congress of the Social–Democratic Party
in Brussels and London, which saw the split into Bolsheviks and
Mensheviks, Lenin refers to the fact that a third of all the delegates
were Jews.[39]

But absolute figures do not tell the whole story. The qualitative
aspects were more significant. Through their concentration in the

two capitals of Russia, in the other large cities, and in the more advanced Western provinces, like Vilna, Minsk, Kiev, Kharkov, not to speak of Warsaw and other purely Polish cities, the Jews were able to play a role out of all proportion to their numbers. And if for reasons to be soon adduced there were no Jews among the leading theoreticians and terrorists in the Narodnaya Volia phase of the Russian revolutionary movement, they were extremely important and fulfilled the role of pioneering leadership as far as organisation is concerned; in setting up organised groups, in obtaining the finances, in the creation of printing shops and the distribution of illegal literature, in smuggling men, arms and literature through the borders, in initiating periodic publications, and above all in maintaining contacts between the centre and the periphery within and outside Russia.

Mark Natanson was the real founder and Semion Klatchko, Tchudnovski and Axelrod were the leaders in Moscow, Odessa and Kiev of the Czaikovski circle. Four of the twenty-five members of the Grand Council of 'Zemlya i Volia' were Jews and upon the famous 'Ispolinitelin' Committee of the Narodnaya Volia in 1879 there were three Jews out of twenty-eight: the famous Aron Zundelewich, Grigori Goldenberg, Saveli Zlotopolsky. The first two took part in the consultation (of six) which authorised the famous (abortive) attempt of Soloviev on Alexander II, and Goldenberg had a month earlier shot the Governor-General of Kharkov. Jews were prominent among the leading Bakuninists in Russia itself, notwithstanding the leader's bitter anti-Semitism; it is enough to mention the first Jewish woman revolutionary, Anna Rosenstein-Makarewitch, Moisei Rabinowitch and Lev Deich, who was destined to become a legendary figure, the elusive and ubiquitous Flying Dutchman of the Russian revolutionary underground.[40]

The first Jew to be hanged for terrorist activity was the shoemaker, later railway worker, finally mechanic, Aharon Gobet, the son of a poor artisan, who at the age of eleven was forcibly drafted into the Tsarist Army and served in it for thirteen years, coming out of it a non-commissioned officer, hard as steel, with intimate knowledge of Russian life, looking also a typical Russian, and wholly dedicated to the cause. All these qualities made him into a most effective conspirator and propagandist. He was the soul of the first mass strike of industrial workers in Russia (in 1878) to have been inspired by a political organisation, and his shoemaker workshop served as the headquarters of the strike. He was sentenced and executed under a different name, Fiodorov, after having been arrested in Kiev in 1879 for holding dynamite, false papers and revolutionary literature and plotting the assassination of the Tsar.[41]

The second Jew to be hanged for acts of terror was Meyer Mlodetzky, son of a petty tradesman in Slutsk and former Yeshiva student who failed at the Gymnasium and the Technical Institute and then made the unsuccessful attempt on the life of the virtual dictator of Russia of the day – 1880 – Loris-Melikov. But he was virtually disowned by the Narodnaya Volia for having acted on his own, without formal authorisation. Shortly before his attempt, he embraced 'the truth of Christianity', in order to escape 'the nonsense of the Jewish teaching and the Jewish teachers'. This did not prevent the unchaining of so violent an anti-Jewish agitation around his case that the foreign press, notably the London *Times* itself, was moved to protest.[42]

There were some formidable obstacles to Jewish participation in the Narodnaya Volia. It was a populist movement operating with ideas and employing methods which were highly uncongenial to Jews. Its peasant Socialism derived its inspiration from the Russian village commune, the *Mir*, and the peasant *jacqueries* of bygone days. It glorified the pristine purity of the Russian popular masses, and preached against Western materialistic individualism, urban capitalism, ultimately the modern world. The young conscience-stricken sons of gentry who went 'to the people' intended not so much to impart modern Western ideas to the village as to re-awaken the slumbering revolutionary urges and to enable the true soul of the peasant to reassert itself. Natural spontaneity was considered sacrosanct, and every form of self-expression, especially of the rebellious kind, noble, which in some cases meant condoning, if not abetting, anti-Jewish pogroms, as part of the revolutionary upsurge.

Not only were these ideas wholly indigestible to Jews, it was not easy for young men and women of Semitic features, often speaking Russian with an accent, or even ungrammatically, completely unfamiliar with peasant life, to 'go to the people', who were deeply steeped in religious superstition and anti-Jewish folklore. Suspicion and hostility often vented themselves in the unanswerable and final argument 'but you are a Jew', thus cutting short the mission of the young man or woman.

Although the association with the Narodnaya Volia was an uneasy partnership for them, the Jewish members absorbed much of the heroic and romantic mysticism of their Russian comrades.

It is no accident that such a high proportion of them became converted to Christianity. It was to them a way to both a total espousal of the Russian popular tradition, and yet also to Messianic universalism. Thus for instance the ardent Narodnik Aptekman, who as we shall see was acutely aware of the incongruousness of his position as a Jew in the ranks of peasant populism, writes about his 'complicated and deeply disturbed state of mind, when the concrete universal aspiration of Socialism fused with an evangelical-Christian mood . . . and I decided to adopt the Greek Orthodox religion before setting out for the village'. After the baptism, which raised many eyebrows, 'I felt as if newly born. I go to the people, I thought, no more a Jew, but a Christian, I have joined the people'. Aptekman is described by Deich as 'a physically weak little Jew, a born revivalist preacher', with the Gospel always in his hands.[43] Tscherikover calls the 'most Christian document of the revolutionary literature' the astonishing testament of Wittenberg, the son of a poor pious Jewish craftsman, written in the death cell on the eve of his execution for taking part in several plots to kill the Tsar Alexander II. Of course – writes Wittenberg – he does not wish to die, but this should not throw a shadow upon his deep faith:

Remember, the greatest example of love of man and of devotion was surely given by the Saviour; and yet He prayed, 'turn away this cup from my lips'. . . . And I say to you as He said . . . if it is not possible otherwise, if it is necessary for the victory of Socialism that my blood be shed, and if the passage from the present social order to a better one is impossible without the road being strewn with our corpses – let our blood be shed, let us serve as sacrifice for mankind. And that our blood will purify the soil, out of which the seeds of Socialism will sprout forth, and that Socialism will triumph and indeed soon – of that I have no doubt! And I remember again the words of the Saviour: 'I tell you in truth many of those here will not feel that taste of death, and the Kingdom of God will arise.' I am as convinced of that as I am sure that the earth is turning round. And when I mount the scaffold and the cord is around my neck, my last thought will be: 'And yet it moves, and no one in the world is able to stop it . . . and if you have any consideration for my last wish . . . then give up any idea of revenge . . . forgive them, for they do not know what they are doing.' For this too is a sign of time. Their reason is deranged: they see that different times are coming, and know not how to turn them back. I beg you once more: renounce any thought of revenge.

As if this were not enough, there is a record of the last conversation of the doomed young man with his parents, an exchange worthy of the pen of a Corneille or Schiller. The father was just able to stammer out the suggestion that perhaps the son might send a prayer for clemency to the Governor-General. To which the young terrorist replied: 'It is said that if the condemned accepts baptism, the punishment is diminished still more.' Now the mother broke in: 'die what you are, your son will grow up and revenge your death. . . .'[44]

Besides cases of unsurpassed heroic steadfastness and romantic chivalry, the history of the Jewish revolutionaries in Russia does not lack typical Dostoyevskean instances of the most morbid confusion. Following Tscherikover we shall cite the famous case of Grigori Goldenberg. This *exalté* was the son of middle-class Jewish parents in Berdichev. He was unsuccessful in his attempt to enter the Petersburg Technological Institute, and became an ardent professional revolutionary (like incidentally his brother and sister), in due course member of the innermost circle of the terrorist organisation, participating most actively in several terrorist plots against the Tsar, and, as said before, killing with his own hand Prince Kropotkin, the Governor-General of Kharkov. After five months of prison, during which in the words of the Chief of the Odessa *gendarmeré* 'the methods used to influence him were not always moral', the recklessly brave young man broke down. 'The cries of mothers and sisters, which reach my ears from the corridors, the spies, the triumphant *gendarmerie*, the military judges . . . the arrests, house searches, exile, gallows and forced labour . . . have shattered my nerves to such an extent that I see no way out.' He reached the conclusion that the terror was senseless, the sacrifices vain, because the régime was too strong and Russian society 'a herd of sheep'. He decided to reveal all the secrets to the police in the hope that his act would put an end to terror on one side and government persecution and death sentences on the other. He feels elated at having had such 'a stroke of genius', although he fully realises the 'horror of revealing secrets', and is aware of the fact that people may treat his plan as fanciful and irresponsible and stupid. But still more terrible, he thought, was the fact of their existence and the amount of misfortune and pain they caused. He is at all events sure of his own sincerity and noble intentions. He offers himself as a sacrifice for 'the holy cause'. At the same time he writes:

> I consider it a piece of good fortune and an honour to die on the gallows: may Socialism be sown by my blood, just as once the blood of the early Christian martyrs made the Christian Church sprout forth . . . I personally look upon Socialism as a new revelation which will in time replace religion, and the victory of the new religion will usher in a new era. . . . A new Christ will soon make His appearance and will with His Socialist and ecstatically religious message sweep the whole world.

Since the greatest potentates of Russia, Loris-Melikov and Plehve themselves, came to his cell to negotiate with him, Goldenberg deluded himself into believing that his confession had gained him far-reaching concessions from the Government – an amnesty, an end to the death penalty, freedom of speech, of political activity, trial by jury for political offences, finally a constitution ('long live the constitution!'), all of which made him feel that he had become saviour of the fatherland.

Still, at moments of doubt he implores the gaolers to execute him first so that he does not witness the death of his beloved comrades: 'Lately I am being visited by certain doubts and fears about the fate of my comrades.' The story reaches its terrible climax with the visit to Goldenberg's cell of one of the most heroic and soberest figures among the Jewish revolutionaries, Zundelewich. The tormented and demented prisoner is suddenly made to realise the enormity of his failure. Goldenberg hastens to add a codicil to his confession: 'Now I understand that it was all ciminal lightheartedness and phantasy. The *gendarmes* have taken advantage of my shattered nerves, brain-washed me and led my imagination to this state of hallucination,' and he sends frantic messages to his friends imploring them to forgive him, and not to brand him as traitor. He writes to his parents: 'My nervous system is now so shattered that I have indeed lost my human face; ... I had committed many stupidities when I was free, and more now in prison ... I have punished myself ... Know, dear mother, that nature takes its pitiless revenge upon those who ignore its laws ... nervous people mostly end by taking their own lives ... oh, mother, if you only knew what evil comes from one's own (too vivid) imagination.' He implores her to educate his younger brother and sister to sober thinking. 'I despise myself.'

On July 15 1880 Goldenberg was found dead. He had hanged himself on his towel.[45]

Although he was not the first Jewish revolutionary to commit treason, having been preceded by the Bakuninist Moisei Rabinowitch, who broke down under interrogation, gave away his accomplices but recanted during the trial, was exiled to Siberia and there went insane, the consequences of Goldenberg's failure were momentous.

The Jewishness of Goldenberg could not fail to evoke the image of Judas, in the same way as did a quarter of a century later the admittedly infinitely worse case of Asef, who in his double capacity as head of the military organisation of the SR Party and police agent initiated the assassination of the highest dignitaries in the

Government and at the same time handed over twice the whole terrorist personnel to the Okhrana. Goldenberg left the impression if not of a deliberate Judas, at least of a Jew, too weak, too vulnerable to torture and too easily influenced to be trusted. At the time when the attempt was planned, and Goldenberg insisted on being accorded the honour of executing it (and at the trial he indeed took the chief blame upon himself), there were strong voices that the assassin should be a Russian, neither a Jew nor a Pole. Zundelewich spoke out strongly against Goldenberg's candidature 'because of the tendency of the Christian world to make the whole Jewish people responsible for the crimes committed by an individual Jew'.[46]

But if the Gentile Narodniks were awakened by Goldenberg's act to a suspicious Jew consciousness, many of the Jewish members had their secret misgivings about their association with the populist movement strengthened by the crisis. This leads us to the question of their motivation in general.

The Jews, as said earlier, could neither share the veneration for the Russian peasant nor the feelings of guilt and of need to atone experienced by the young Gentile students, who went to the people. Thus the utterly devoted Aptekman to whose conversion to Christianity we have referred earlier, writes in his Memoirs: 'I had no trace of feelings of contrition. And whence should such a bad conscience have come to me? Rather should I, a son of an oppressed people, have presented a bill, than feel obligated to pay some imaginary debt!' As a townsman he had had no contacts with peasants and the countryside, and was aware of 'having foreign blood'. Russian history he hardly knew and what he knew he disliked. He kept asking himself how would the Russian peasants respond to the propaganda of a Jew.[47]

The less well known Abraham Magat from Vilna writes to his sister in 1879: 'Jews realise that they lack freedom, rights. How has this come about, they ask: we are the oldest, the most intelligent, best educated and most energetic people and we are deprived of all the rights possessed by the other subjects of Russia. ... No!

We have to fight for our rights and our equality, no matter what the cost.' If others are indignant because discrimination prevents them from engaging in profitable business, the author 'looks differently upon the problem. I see before me two and a half million people in bondage and say: one has to take the side of the oppressed and the defenceless, to fight for their liberation. Would the people as a whole rise against its oppressors, with sword and revolver! . . .' Since this was impossible, some leading Jews decided to resort to the written word. But not words, only deeds, a revolution, could wrest from the rulers of Russia a constitution 'which would grant also the Jews equal rights'.[48]

The saintly Paul Axelrod confesses that like so many other Jewish Socialists he deserted the Jewish masses, although he had at first considered it – like at a somewhat later date Martov – his mission to devote himself to their 'social and spiritual renewal'. It was Russian literature and Western Socialism, in the first instance Lassalle, that soon made him ashamed of his interest in Jewish affairs.

What significance can the interests of a handful of Jews have, I thought, compared with the interests and the 'idea of a working class', with which Socialism was imbued? For there is actually no Jewish problem, but only the general question of liberating the working classes of all nations, including also the Jewish masses. With the victory of Socialism, this so-called Jewish question will be solved. How senseless then and indeed how criminal to devote oneself to the Jews are who only a small part of the vast Russian Empire.[49]

No wonder the Jewish Narodniks were deeply shaken by the famous proclamation to the Ukrainian people issued by the executive committee of Narodnaya Volia on August 30 1881, in the wake of the pogroms, which were unleashed by the Tsarist authorities as a reply to the terrorist activities, culminating in the assassination of Tsar Alexander II by that very organisation.

Good people, honest Ukrainian people! . . . the damned police beat you, the landowners devour you, the Yids, the dirty Judases rob you. People in the Ukraine suffer most of all from the Yids. Who has seized the land, woodlands, the taverns? The Yids. Whom does the peasant beg with tears in his eyes to let him near his land? The Yids. Wherever you look, whatever you touch, everywhere the Yids. The Yid curses the peasant, cheats him, drinks his blood. The Yids make life unbearable.[50]

This moved Axelrod to draft a pamphlet, in which with many quotations from letters by Jewish revolutionaries and students, he describes the shock experienced by the Jewish comrades.

Most shocked of all were the Jewish Socialists. The pogroms and public opinion, especially among the Russian intelligentsia, after the pogroms, were a revelation. Little by little after a bitter struggle, they acknowledged the full meaning of these events. Long accustomed to the idea that there was really no such thing as a Jewish people, that Jews were merely a group of Russian subjects who would later become a group of Russian citizens, that Jews could not be segregated socially or culturally from the 'native' population, the Jewish Socialist intelligentsia suddenly realised that the majority of this Russian society did, as a matter of fact, regard the Jews as a separate nation, and that they considered all Jews – a pious Jewish worker, a *petit bourgeois*, a money-lender, an assimilated lawyer, a Socialist prepared for prison or deportation – as Yids harmful to Russia, whom Russia should get rid of by any and all means.

The Jewish student youth suffered their greatest disappointment when they realised that the Socialist-minded Russian students sympathised with the crusade against the Jewish masses and, worse yet, exhibited their anti-Semitic feelings toward their Jewish fellow-revolutionaries.

Thus, the pogroms made the Jewish Socialist intelligentsia realise that the Jews as a people were in a unique situation in Russia, hated by the most diverse segments of the Christian population; and that they, the Jewish Socialists, had committed an error in overlooking the actual condition of the Jews as a people different from the rest of the population. The Jewish social revolutionaries understood now that they were wrong in forsaking the Jewish masses in the name of cosmo-politanism. The 'native masses' not only lacked cosmopolitan feelings and ideas, but were wanting even in the idea of class solidarity among the poorer classes of Russia's nationalities. These were the conclusions to which a sizeable part – perhaps even most – of Jewish youth had come.[51]

Axelrod was prevailed upon by the Party authorities not to publish the pamphlet, and he yielded. But soon after he took the road to cosmopolitan Marxist Social-Democracy. It would be an exaggeration to say that it was under the impact of his Jewish disillusionment with the populist movement that he made the passage, since he had even before been the most Western of his comrades. This was also true of a great many other Jewish Narodniks. But the disappointment helped them in shedding any illusions about the innate goodness of the Russian peasant, or the Russian masses. Thus Zundelewich had all along been quite contemptuous of work among the peasants, since 'they did not have the slightest inclination to Socialism and revolution'. He was therefore considered to be at heart a German type of Social-Democrat by Lev Deich as well as by Alexander Michailov. In a letter written from prison in October 1880, Zundelewich says as much as that: had he been free he would not stay another day in Russia. 'In the Russian prison I got to love America.' He had stayed on in Russia, which he never liked, for so long, because of his loyalty towards his suffering comrades, 'But now I am myself a sufferer', and so his debt has been paid.[52]

Yet even after savage repression had broken the back of the Narodnaya Volia, on the morrow of the assassination of Alexander II in 1881, Jews continued to be active in the movement, constituting now an even higher proportion of the declining membership. The bitter resentment against the notorious anti-Jewish Manifesto was stilled by the rage against the Government-sponsored pogroms and new anti-Jewish legislation. The Social-Revolutionary party which came into being at the turn of the century as the heir of the Narodnaya Volia, counted many Jews among its most prominent members. Its leader Victor Czernov, Minister in the ill-fated Government of Kerensky in 1917, has devoted a whole book to his Jewish comrades in the party.[53] And what a gallery of splendid men they were: the indefatigable organiser Marc Natanson, a man of compelling moral authority in his dual capacity of high government official and the conscience of the revolution; the

'Foreign Secretary' of the party, Ilya Rubanowich, technically a French subject, who represented his party abroad with singular dignity in the face of the interminable and often squalid quarrels among the various groups of Russian revolutionary exiles; the saintly martyr of the revolution, Michail Gotz, born amidst fabulous wealth, but taking upon himself all the sorrows and pains of all the persecuted and dying a terrible death at the age of forty; last but not least Grigori Gershuni, the unbelievably daring and resourceful head of the terrorist section of the party which sowed death and fear among the highest dignitaries of the Tsarist régime; finally, the utterly baffling Asef, chief-terrorist and chief-traitor at the same time.

The Social-Revolutionary party had inherited much that was noble in its predecessor, the Narodnaya Volia, and moreover developed a genuine respect for the peculiarities of each of the Russian nationalities to the point of recognising the right of every ethnic group to self-determination. A prominent member of the party fell dead defending Jews in the Zhitonir pogrom. The SR had also veered away from an exclusive preoccupation with the peasant problem towards the somewhat vague but generous conception of the 'toiling masses'. Still, it was in the final analysis a party of Russian populism. By then most Jewish Leftists were already looking in other directions: to the universalist Marxism of the Social-Democratic party, soon to split into Bolsheviks and Mensheviks, or to separatist Jewish Socialism – the Bund and Poalei Zion. Together the latter groups out-numbered the Russian Socialist parties. They certainly represented a greater intellectual potential. A propaganda manual written by the Bundist Arcady Kremer became the almost official *vade-mecum* of all the Russian Socialist activists. Unwittingly the Bund decided, as is well known, the issue in the momentous dispute at the Second Brussels-London Congress of the Social-Democratic party that resulted in the fateful split. Lenin had been voted down and Martov had won on the question of the definition of the party and conditions of membership in it – mass party versus an elitist vanguard of professional revolutionaries – and the Congress passed on to discuss the demand of the Bund to be recognised as the sole representative of all Jewish workers, whatever the language spoken by them. The Gentiles took the back seats to watch the Jews Trotsky, the former Bundist Martov, and other Jewish internationalists fight tooth and nail the nationalist Jewish deviation. Defeated, the Bundists left the Congress, thereby securing to Lenin and his followers a majority.[54]

It is customary to regard Nicolai Utin, the son of a very wealthy Jewish banking family and brother of high dignitaries and eminent academic lawyers, as the first Russian Marxist. As a young brilliant student he became head of 'Utin's Party' at St Petersburg University, being active in the student riots of 1861. He then joins the Zemlya i Volia and obtains a seat upon the Central Committee, taking the place of the arrested leader, the well known Serno-Solovievich. He plunges very deeply into conspiratorial work, organising what was virtually the first illegal revolutionary printing press in Russia, and more so – entering into close collaboration with the leaders of the Polish rebellion of 1863. He is then forced to flee abroad and is some months later sentenced to death by a Tsarist court. In the meantime Utin joins Bakunin in Geneva and becomes his close collaborator. Soon however Utin abandons anarchism for a vague and half-populist Marxism, places the Bakuninist journal 'Narodnoie Dielo' at Marx's disposal, forms a Russian section of the International, obtaining Marx's consent to represent it on the General Council of the International. Those were the days of the titanic struggle between Marx and Bakunin, which broke the First International. In his violent attacks upon his Marxist opponents, Bakunin lumps together the two converts Marx and Utin as the embodiment of all that is evil in Judaism and German State worship. Utin plays a decisive part in unmasking Nechaiev, the evil spirit and in due course destroyer of Bakunin, whose tortuous crimes in the cause of revolution gave Dostoyevsky the theme for his famous novel *The Possessed*. Utin's revelations, obtained by very doubtful methods, were the immediate cause of the split in the International. Some years after Utin forsakes revolutionary activity for patriotic work for the Tsar and the Russian fatherland as associate of the Jewish millionaire Poliakov in building a strategic railway line to facilitate the movement of the Russian troops against Turkey in the war of 1878. He writes a repulsive begging letter of humble contrition to the Tsar, and, thanks to his patriotic work and the great connections of his father and brother obtains a pardon.[55]

In spite of his pioneering role Utin was only an episodic figure in Russian Marxism. His Jewishness was very marginal to him, although much noticed by his enemies. It was perhaps his Jewishness that caused his revulsion – as was also the case with some other Jewish anarchists – from the deep irrationality of Bakunin, and still more so the criminality of Nechaiev.

About a quarter of a century elapsed before Marxism entered upon its momentous career in Russia, and in its ranks the Jews.

On the original editorial Board of *Iskra*, the journal which in fact fathered and led the movement, we find three Jews, Martov, Axelrod and Trotsky, besides the Gentiles Plekhanov, Lenin, Petrosev and Vera Zasulich.[56] Although most leading Jews went into the Menshevik camps – in addition to Martov himself Dan, Lieber, Abramovich and others – and Trotsky remained a lone wolf, quite a few Jews followed Lenin, gaining a name for themselves well before 1917, to mention only Kamenev and Zinoviev.

VII

Immensely significant as the participation of the Jewish Social-Revolutionaries and Social-Democrats of both wings in the pre-1917 revolutionary movement in Russia proved to be not only from the Russian, but also from the universal point of view, a no less vital and lasting contribution of Jews to the cause of revolution is to be found in the role played by Jewish revolutionaries from the Russian Empire in the International Socialist Movement in the West, above all Germany, in the two decades before 1914; more precisely in their strenuous efforts to revive in the European Labour Movement, grown flabby and smugly complacent, the ideal of the total 'World Revolution', and to restore to it the enthusiasm and the will of a church militant poised for world conquest.

Curiously enough the growing tendency of the Western Socialist parties to develop into part and parcel of the national body politic as its parliamentary left wing also had much to do with Jews. The Dreyfus affair prompted the French Socialists to hasten to succour the Republic and to defend republican legality against the plots of nationalists and clericals, in spite of their initial reluctance to take sides in an internal bourgeois quarrel. Jaurès was thus led to define Socialism not as the antithesis of bourgeois liberal democracy and all its works, but as the distilled, purified substance of all that was good in the common European and humanist heritage, more precisely – the French tradition.[57] It was then the Jew Eduard Bernstein in Germany, who by rejecting Marx's prophecy of gradual pauperisation on the one side and monopolist concentration on the other, and of the inevitability of a revolutionary break-through – in favour of parliamentary democracy, trial and error procedures, gradualism based on adaptation to circumstances, national spirit and tradition – cut the very nerve of revolutionary universalism. Some of his disciples, like Schippel, Hildebrand and others, went so far as to adopt frankly nationalist attitudes on such matters as colonialism and naval rivalry.[58] The radical anti-revisionists, in the first place Rosa Luxemburg and Alexander Israel Parvus-Helphand, grasped at once that not merely questions of economics or philosophical doctrine were at stake, but the fundamental issue of the Socialist International Revolution.

The question was put even more sharply by the growing demand of the Socialists of the various nationalities in the Austro-Hungarian and Russian Empires for the right to constitute separate parties, instead of forming part of one single national party. The claim to a right of secession and the espousal of policies aiming at establishing an independent nation-state were bound to be understood as granting higher significance to nationhood than to international Socialist unity.[59]

The appearance of Rosa Luxemburg, Israel Helphand-Parvus,

Leo Jogiches and Karl Radek on the Socialist-Democratic scene in Germany in their fight against revisionism and nationalist deviation marks the first leap of East-European Jewry into the arena of world politics. Endowed with exceptional natural gifts of brain, pen, wit and eloquence, at home in several languages and cultures, fantastically broad in their interests, of volcanic energy and immense power of endurance, seething with passionate Messianic conviction, these Jews give the impression of a suppressed coil suddenly released. They had only yesterday broken away from the Jewish tradition, rejecting centuries of fatalistic resignation and ritualistic constraint with furious gusto, only to have their great powers confronted by the fact of their external bondage. They gave themselves passionately and lovingly to the fatherland of universal revolution which knew no boundaries. They were, in the language of Martin Buber, Atopians,[60] men of no particular place, citizens of an ideal spaceless country. They were probably incapable of seeing that their enemies might regard them in a quite different light, as alien intruders, foreign adventurers without a country and tradition, arrogant cosmopolitan sophists, fomentors of trouble, without a sense of or understanding for the ancient and complex ways and attachments of the deeply rooted natives.

Rosa and Parvus were the classical gad-flies and disturbers of peace.

I recognise no compromise – wrote Helphand-Parvus – in the sphere of thought. I submit everything to criticism, the Revolution and Socialism, the concepts of good and evil, including those of justice and morality. . . . Because I am what you, who are revolutionaries by sentiment, by programme, by hearsay, by tradition, by chance of circumstances, are least able to understand: I am a Revolutionary of thought.

And to such a one there were no differences of race or nationality, boundaries meant nothing – Parvus goes on to say.[61]

Neither he nor Rosa Luxemburg could have known that Bebel was writing to Kautsky about them: 'You cannot imagine the intense animosity among the rank and file against Rosa and Parvus. I do not say that that should influence us, but it would be difficult to ignore it altogether.' There was widespread and vehement condemnation of the behaviour and style of the 'male and female imports from the East', and a delegate at the Lubeck Party Congress went so far as to charge Parvus with responsibility for the growth of anti-Semitism in Germany.[62]

No student of Rosa Luxemburg,[63] whatever his own ideological commitment, can fail to fall under the spell of this frail, short, slightly deformed and limping young Jewish girl from Zamosc (the town of J. L. Peretz), jumping up on a stool to make herself visible at Socialist congresses where in a marked foreign accent she would flail veterans who had grown white in the service of the party, trade-union bosses commanding millions of workers – whom she herself hardly knew – for their lack of revolutionary zeal, their ignorance of Marx, their indifference to doctrine. She carries in her head a wealth of statistics. Few can rival her knowledge of economics. No one can match her skill as a dialectician. She has mordant wit, and her natural fluency and felicity of expression are heightened by irresistible passion. Her opponents and enemies dismiss her as a soulless fundamentalist, a doctrinaire and a pedant. Yet what passion and tenderness stand revealed in her private correspondence, ringing with echoes of Polish, German, Russian and world poetry. How feminine she appears in her love letters to the intellectually much inferior Leo Jogiches, pining away, counting the days and hours until their next meeting, full of trepidation and uncertainty as to whether he really loves her.

Jogiches himself comes straight out of a novel, a mystery man, an inveterate plotter with a passion for anonymity, a revolutionary moving from country to country with many aliases and addresses. Born in Vilna to rich parents, he goes West and places his whole fortune at the disposal of the revolution. Fanatical and arrogant, he even tries to make the great Plekhanov his subordinate on the editorial committee of a journal he undertakes to finance. There comes a day when he and Rosa cease to be lovers, and although she at least is one gaping wound, they continue their joint work for the cause in the same way as before. Fully dedicated to the Social-Democratic Movement in Germany, Rosa nevertheless dislikes the German Socialists. When they betray the cause of proletarian internationalism by supporting Germany in World War One, she sinks into a state of utter anguish. Her flaming yet closely reasoned Junius letters against the war make up one of the most effective pieces of pamphleteering in world literature. She lands in prison. From there she writes some of her most moving letters; in one of them she replies to a Jewish correspondent, 'Why do you worry me about the Jewish sorrows?' She has no room in her heart for the special sufferings of the ghetto; her soul goes out to all human beings in pain.[64] When she is released from prison in 1918, she is in the grip of an unbearable exaltation. She feels the hour of destiny has been opened by the Bolshevik revolution, although she has her qualms about the way the revolution is going in Russia, and indeed voices them. She realises that the Social-Democrats are determined to stop the revolution in Germany. She knows that her own small party, the Spartakists, stands no chance. She disapproves of a revolutionary demonstration her party stages but she goes along and there meets with her death.

Rosa heads the long list of Jewish women revolutionaries who in their own right or as wives of revolutionary leaders (mostly non-Jews) played an incalculable role in the movement. The list starts with the pioneer-women in Russia in the seventies, like the two girls who were sentenced to death, Hessia Helfman and Henrietta Dobruskin; the other two young women, Betty Kaminsky and Sophia Ginsberg, who took their own lives; the four Kaminer sisters, daughters of the Hebrew poet; the Ratner sisters; it includes the exceptionally talented and versatile Anna Rosenstein, who manifested her decision to become a professional revolutionary by tearing up her university diploma, marrying the revolutionary populist Makarewich, then exchanging him for the Italian anarchist Costa, finally abandoning him to become the morganatic wife of the Reformist Socialist leader Turati, and under the name of Anna Kulichev, to lead in all but name the Italian Labour Movement; and Rosalia Bograd, who married Plekhanov. The latter wrote a letter of heart-rending contrition upon learning of the outbreak of a new wave of pogroms: 'Deep down in the soul of each one of us, revolutionaries of Jewish birth, there was a sense of hurt pride and infinite pity for our own, and many of us were strongly tempted to devote ourselves to serving our injured, humiliated and persecuted people.'[65] Closing that very selective list is Angelica Balabanova, friend of the young revolutionary Socialist Benito Mussolini as well as of Lenin, the soul of the international Zimmerwald-Kiental anti-War Conferences during World War One; and finally the Rumanian Communist leader and Foreign Secretary Anna Pauker.

No novelist could have imagined a more astounding and more colourful figure than Dr Israel Helphand (Parvus), and no anti-Semite could have invented a more effective model for the Jew of the Nazi demonology. Born in White Russia in the heart of the Jewish Pale to a poverty-stricken artisan family, as a child he experiences hunger, witnesses pogroms, and sees ghettoes set on fire. He wanders with his family over the vast expanses of Russia. He rejects Judaism very early, and like Rosa and the other internationalist Jewish revolutionaries, feels nothing but contempt for the civilisation from which he springs. In 1892 – years before the first Zionist Congress – he warns Jewish workers against Jewish nationalists, enjoining them not to lend an ear to seducers who speak of Jewish settlement in the Argentine or Palestine.[66]

Like so many Russians, Jews and non-Jews, Parvus makes his way to a Swiss University and joins the *émigré* revolutionary circle there. He then establishes himself in Germany, if the life of a homeless vagabond without a home or permanent address, without a family, a fixed job or an income, may be so described. Starving, unwashed, dressed in rags, ungainly, fat, with jerking movements, rapid nervous speech, wild gestures, full of sarcasm, alien, repulsive, sinister, he is nevertheless regarded as the best mind of the Second International, the great expert on international economics, and the great connoisseur of modern literature and modern art. He is the mentor of Trotsky, who gets the idea of Permanent Revolution from him.[67] His contributions to the organs of German Social Democracy are read with intense interest and indeed fear. His polemical style is savage, his disregard of the usual courtesies is absolutely revolting. People loathe and avoid him, which bothers him not a whit. He is also utterly unreliable. With a disarming smile, Parvus can tell Maxim Gorky, in answer to an inquiry about the royalties of a novel by Gorky brought out by Parvus's short-lived publishing house, that he has spent them on a recent journey to Italy. No one can find out from him whether he is married or single, although he seems to have been a bigamist several times over.

With the outbreak of the Balkan Wars, the curtain raiser to World War One, Parvus gets himself sent over as a war correspondent. Soon he is doing business with all the warring parties and in no time amasses a fortune. Yet he remains the radical revolutionary. He entertains hungry Russian comrades in luxury hotels, he smokes Havana cigars, dresses in fine clothes, and surrounds himself with women, somehow still uncouth and repulsive as ever. Then the Great War breaks out. Parvus assumes several roles at the same time. He becomes a war profiteer on a grand scale, almost monopolising German trade with the Scandinavian countries, especially in coal and iron. He becomes a confidential adviser to the German Foreign Office on Russian affairs. He is the editor of a shamelessly nationalistic German journal. And he is most active – in collusion with the German Foreign Office and the German High Command – in fomenting and financing the revolution in Russia. But when Lenin's revolution does break out, the former radical revolutionary develops an implacable hatred for it – it is not the revolution he wanted. He becomes the grey eminence of the reformist Social-Democrat Government of the Weimar Republic. To cap it all, the sumptuous villa in the wealthy suburb in which he spends the last years of his life becomes some ten years after his death the private residence of Dr Joseph Goebbels.

Rosa, Parvus, Trotsky and their friends unfurled anew the banner of revolutionary universalism by proclaiming the nation-state an anachronism. With their consummate knowledge of economics they were able to show the absolute interdependence of the economies of the most remote countries and thus to confound the preachers of economic autarchy and of national sovereignty of small countries in an age of industrial giants and vast armaments. Economics were thus revindicated by them as more decisive than national uniqueness or national sentiment, and materialism than any form of idealism. Bernstein had tried to show that the modern parliamentary system enabled the representatives of democracy, in the first place the Socialist party in it, to curb the selfish interests of the capitalists through the use of political means, and to build the road to Socialism through legislative enactments by stages. Well versed in the problems of imperialism, the radicals would counter this argument by pointing to the rapacious capitalist monopolists in search of quick profits and slave labour, dragging their governments to defend or promote their selfish interests and predatory ventures in disturbed remote corners of the earth. Not only were they thus the cause of militarism, the armaments race and navalism, they were in fact – openly or in a camouflaged way – dictating their will to governments and parliaments, who were 'in it' – in the imperialist business, whether they wanted or did not want it. Instead of democracy controlling the capitalists, the capitalists were pulling the wires of the democratic parliamentary institutions: a monopolist class versus the nation. In the West capitalism had become more circumspect and more 'liberal' thus giving rise to a Labour aristocracy which by degrees became the beneficiary and ally of imperialism. The capitalists were enabled to make good their lower profits at home by the totally unrestrained and shameless exploitation of the colonial proletariat. In brief, the grand vision of the early Marx of a capitalism which had spread to the confines of the earth and united the planet into one economic unit, facing a united world proletariat, had come true, and the hour of the universal revolution was near. The world's most wretched proletarians – those in the colonial countries – maddened by social exploitation and national oppression were about to rise and to stretch out their hand to the European proletarian revolutionaries. The hour would be sounded – again in accordance with the expectations of the early Marx and the early nineteenth-century revolutionaries – by an international war. The imperialist rivalries were making such a war inevitable. Horrible as the test was bound to be for all the peoples, and above all for the masses, war was the midwife of revolution. The weakest link in the capitalist chain would snap first. The backward, internally undermined Empire of the Tsars could not stand the strain of defeat, domestic unrest, strikes, armed clashes. Admittedly, as the least advanced country in Europe, Russia could not by herself make the leap from decaying feudalism and absolutism into Socialism, without going through a bourgeois phase. But once the dams of the system were breached she could be held in the throes of a permanent revolution and enabled to take soon the step from the bourgeois–democratic revolution to the Socialist revolution, if she could throw the burning torch of her own revolution into the West, and thus set the Socialist revolution aflame there.[68]

It would hardly be possible to exaggerate the importance of this seemingly only doctrinal clash between Socialist reformism and revolutionary universalism. Although Bernstein himself developed an anti-war attitude fairly early in the War, and such a rabid preacher of anti-patriotism in France like Hervé turned overnight into a militant chauvinist – and more such examples of inconsistency could be cited – it remains by and large a fact that the pre-1914 cleavages prefigure the later splits.

If the idea of national or racial uniqueness can be considered the main plank of the crystallised counter-revolution, and if the orientation towards national parliamentary systems can be seen as the decisive feature of Reformist Socialism, the idea of proletarian internationalism was the linchpin of the theories upheld by the radical revolutionaries with whom we are here concerned. Out of the counter-revolution came Fascism and Nazism; out of the revisionism came Social Democracy; and out of the revolutionary radicalism came Communism. The Social-Democrats, the liberal democrats, and above all the Jews were destined to be crushed some decades later in the apocalyptic struggle between those who saw in World War One the prelude to the world revolution, and those to whom the War vindicated the idea that the supreme reality of history was the nation or the race fighting for survival and power.

As late as 1913 an international Social-Democratic Conference in Basle called upon the workers to do all in their power to prevent a world conflagration. When in less than a year the trumpets were sounded, all Socialist leaders, with a few exceptions, especially in England, were swept off their feet by patriotic fervour. Defending himself for having betrayed the early vows, a French Socialist leader exclaimed: 'But we would have been torn to pieces by the rank and file, had we tried to oppose the national war effort.' And a German Socialist leader confessed to the relief he felt in being able to intone *Deutschland, Deutschland uber Alles* with a full throat. There were, of course, strong consolations for both sides: the French Socialists were fighting *Junker* militarism, the Germans the unspeakable Tsar, and a victory over either was a pre-condition of the revolution.[69]

VIII

Georges Sorel says somewhere that the eighteenth century came to an end only in 1848. The first half of the nineteenth century continued to believe in the goodness of man, indulged in spinning utopias to secure the happiness of mankind. *'On est à la fois rationaliste et sensible.'* The revolutions of that memorable year shattered the belief in the power of rational argument, appeal to conscience and the wish for peace based on reciprocity. In France a feast of universal reconciliation and love comes to an end in a frightful massacre of have-nots by the haves, to be followed by Bonapartist dictatorship. In Germany the finest spirits of the nation fail to reach agreement, or rather to make their hope of national unity based upon universal popular consent prevail, and they collapse in face of the compact ranks of the armed forces commanded by the old powers. The hopes for harmony between liberated nations are given the lie by the bitter conflict between the historical and ahistorical nations, the former refusing their own minorities the rights they claimed for themselves. Force appears as the only arbiter between classes, parties and above all nations. Many German liberals became 'sick of principles and doctrines, literary existence and theoretical greatness. What it [the German nation] wants is Power, Power, Power! And whoever gives it power, to him will it give honour, more honour than he can imagine!'[70] If the old dream of achieving both *Einheit* and *Freiheit* at the same time had proved an illusion, let it be Einheit without Freiheit: the pagan superiority of the strong instead of the Jewish harmony between equals.

The man who epitomised this change more than any other person was Richard Wagner, who was destined to exert such colossal influence upon the minds of some of the most decisive figures in world affairs as well as upon millions of educated or semi-educated ordinary people. As is well known, Wagner fought in 1848 on the barricades of Dresden alongside the knight errant of world revolution, Michael Bakunin. At that time he still believed that mankind could not be considered free as long as a single individual was abandoned to oppression and art remained a merchandise to the rich in search of amusement or snobbish prestige. The failure of the universal revolution on behalf of universal liberation – of man and artist – led him to the conclusion that universalist abstract idealism was infinitely weaker than the vital forces of race, instinct and the past. Proof of that was the Gentile attitude towards the Jews. Rational principle tells the Gentile to consider and treat the Jew as equal, instinct just refuses to listen to the voice of reason, and empirical observation confirms the utter 'otherness' of the Jew: the German-speaking Oriental. Authentic and real were therefore the primary, instinctive reflexes. Ratiocination was derivative, a contrivance, a pretence, a piece of hypocrisy, if not a deliberately imposed mystification. In this quest for the authentic, the genuinely German, Wagner would not stop till he reached Odin and Wotan and the other Teutonic deities in the dark forests of pre-Christian Germany. It was not just eighteenth-century rationalism and materialist capitalism, but Judaic Christianity that came to be branded by Wagner as the root of the great lie, the cause of the fateful distortion of the Germanic, Nordic, indeed European spirit.[71] In the language of Nietzsche, to whom Wagner was at first the acme of all perfection, and then the embodiment of all evil,

The Jews ... that priestly people ... succeeded in avenging themselves on their enemies and oppressors by radically inverting all their values, that is, by an act of the most spiritual vengeance ... with frightening consistency, dared to invert the aristocratic value equations good/noble/powerful, beautiful, happy/favoured-of-the-gods, and maintain, with the furious hatred of the underprivileged and impotent, that only the poor, the powerless, are good; only the suffering, sick and ugly, truly blessed. But you noble and mighty ones of the earth will be, to all eternity, the evil, the cruel, the avaricious, the godless, and thus the cursed and damned! We know who has fallen heir to this Jewish inversion of values . . . The Jews have launched . . . this most radical of all declarations of war . . . started the slave revolt in morals, a revolt which has two millennia of history behind it, which we have lost sight of today simply because it has triumphed so completely.[72]

Not a revolution to enthrone the abstract ideas of human equality was called for, preached Wagner, but a revolution to release the forces of racial authenticity from the inhibiting and distorting influences of Judaic-Christian-rationalist universalism and materialism: a counter-revolution of the most fundamental kind. It was not to be a counter-revolution to restore a social or political order, but an effort to affect a spiritual cleansing and rebirth. And this was to be accomplished – not with the help of *ukase* or changes in the distribution of property or machinery of government, and not with the aid of arguments and elections, but through the power and influence of art or rather the combination of all the arts in a type of religious worship – the Wagnerian opera. The intention was not to call back the powers of bygone days, princes, potentates, bishops and feudal lords, but to tap and release the deep forces slumbering in the popular soul, the *Volk*. The counter-revolution was to liberate the *Volk* from the spiritual bondage to the Semitic race, from the corroding influence of the sterile contrivances of Jewish intellectuals and artists, with their congenital lack of originality, style and taste, but abundance of impotent sarcasm, as well as from the degrading patronage of plutocratic Jewish buyers of art, finally from the shackles of Jewish enterprise centred upon maximum exploitation of fleeting opportunities.

Wagner's *Juden un der Musik* of 1850 is the first message of the philosophy of counter-revolution which will become crystallised and begin to be effective around 1880, and then achieve such a frightful triumph between the two World Wars.[73] Before analysing that *Weltanschauung* of which Jews and revolution were the real focus, we should ask ourselves what were the concrete conditions and circumstances which not only gave rise to these ideas, but – more importantly – made so many people receptive to them.

In the first half of the nineteenth century nationalism was or appeared to be a revolutionary force. Although the Herderian and Burkean ingredients of the nationalist creed, which stressed the unfathomable uniqueness of the natural and historic personality of the nation, were calculated to offer leverage to conservatism and traditionalism, post-1815 realities threw nationalism into the camp of revolution. Europe was sharply polarised into the camp of legitimacy, law and order, and hierarchical authority, on the one hand, and the forces of revolutionary change proclaiming the rights of man, the rights of workers, and the rights of nations, on the other. Mazzini profoundly believed in the alliance of peoples pitted against the alliance of despots, and in Italy's mission to head the brotherhood of liberated nations conceived as confraternities of the regenerated. Marx and Lassalle as we know saw in the proletariat the 'national' class. In the event, the unification of Germany was carried out not by a proletariat with universalist visions, but by those forces which in the earlier part of the nineteenth-century had feared the revolutionary and democratic potentialities of nationalism. Italy and the Balkan countries owed their liberation to great power intrigues and rivalries. The cause of internationalism suffered a crushing blow in the Franco-German War of 1870. An abyss opened up between the two most important and most advanced nations, with the strongest revolutionary movements on the European continent. In the aftermath of the war, an anguished, humiliated, resentful France was possessed by the craving for revenge, and a Germany drunk with triumph and pride was both impatient to make good the centuries of disunity and weakness by catching up with the old colonial empires, and worried over being surrounded by envious neighbours lying in wait for an opportunity to strike. Few Socialists or revolutionaries in either country were quite immune to these feelings, or able in the prevailing climate to resist the general trend. It was the lower middle class, the *petite bourgeoisie*, formerly associated with revolutionary Jacobinism, that now took possession of the nationalist banner. Nationalism, which had earlier been so closely associated with the revolution, now became the battlecry of the counter-revolution.

For decades the *petite bourgeoisie* had been told that its demise was near. In comparison with the proletariat, which had developed a sense of purpose, indeed a buoyant conviction that the earth belonged to it, as well as strong organisational cohesion, the lower middle class lacked a sense of mission. Despised both by the upper and educated classes and by the workers, it responded with its own version of nationalism – the claim that *it* was the real nation as against the selfishly privileged upper classes and the Socialist workers with their internationalist ideals.[74]

In this assertion by the lower middle class of its identity, anti-Semitism played an indispensable part. Identity is always brought into relief by contrast, cohesion requires enmity, solidarity implies strangers. In countries like France and Germany the position of the Jews as a well-to-do and educated minority which was at the same time a pariah community, made them a perfect target for those who were neither rich nor educated, and had nothing to recommend them except their blood, 'the most precious thing in the world', in Hitler's words. The nationalism of the lower middle class quite early acquired a social slant. But it was a Socialism of a distinctly authoritarian temper, and above all an anti-Semitic rationale.

The nationalist paroxysm in Germany and France coincided with the introduction of universal suffrage, but also with feverish capitalist speculation to be followed by the inevitable economic crisis, which was accompanied, especially in France, by financial scandals involving statesmen, parliamentarians, journalists and politicians. The magic spell of the vote as a panacea for all evils was broken. Not only had the national parliament proved itself unable to protect the welfare of the people and prevent crisis – its most important task after all; it revealed itself as a corrupt agency of sinister selfish interests. This immediately gave rise to a very strong anti-parliamentary agitation among the lower income groups, who were especially hit by the crisis and to whom the workings of high finance were always a kind of black magic. Parliament was depicted as a façade, and its members as marionettes in the hands of wire-pullers and conspirational plotters in dark conclaves outside parliament.

A nationalist ingredient was soon added to this anti-parliamentary sentiment by such revanchists as Déroulède, the leader oi the League of Patriots, and Maurice Barrès, the erstwhile narcissistic worshipper of the 'culte de moi' turned poet of 'energie nationale'. A corrupt assembly could not be trusted to act as guardian of the national interests. If not downright traitorous, it was too supine, too flabby and too preoccupied with other interests to defend the honour of the nation and take care of its defence. And so the social and nationalist elements combined to raise the cry for a general who, as the embodiment of all military virtues and pure patriotism, could place himself at the head of the uncorrupt and the brave, clean the stables of parliamentary corruption and lead the nation to victory. This was the background of that strange curtain-raiser of Fascism, the Boulanger episode.[75]

Early enough the economic crisis and parliamentary corruption were laid at the doorstep of the Jews. Some French historians claim that modern anti-Semitism as a mass movement emerged upon the collapse of the Union Générale banking concern, which was a Catholic enterprise catering for the lower-middle-class interests, as a result allegedly of the machinations of the rival House of Rothschild.[76] It was in those days that the distinction between productive industrial capitalism, practised by high class Gentiles, often noble or ennobled, or married into nobility, and parasitic predatory speculative finance capitalism, entirely Jewish by definition, won much currency. It is also only too true that among the master minds and the go-betweens in the Panama scandal, the chief hero of which was the venerable Ferdinand Lesseps of Suez Canal fame, were many Jews, indeed foreign Jews, the German baron Reinach, the American Jew Cornelius Hertz, and Artom from Italy. The image of Judas Iscariot and

Shylock fitted them beautifully. No wonder the wire-pullers and corrupters were immediately identified as an international Jewish conspiracy. It did not escape the notice of contemporaries that in the financial negotiations following the 1870–71 War, Rothschild represented France and Bleichröder, Bismarck's private banker and financial adviser, Germany. The Jews were thus made into the shock-absorbers of the most potent and most explosive forces of modern times – social resentment, nationalist wrath and the authoritarian temper.

In the late seventies two very important groups in Germany ran into a grave crisis, threatening their very existence. The opening of the American prairies and of the vast wheat and cattle growing areas in the Argentine, Australia and New Zealand, coupled with technological advance in agriculture and the expansion of the railway system and steamship navigation, administered a shattering blow to the agricultural interest in Germany, above all of the big landowners and peasants, endangering thus the very foundations of the social-political regime of the Second Reich, and its military might. The clamour for protection tariff policies abounded with strong anti-Semitic overtones, and these were aggravated by the passionate defence of free trade by leading Jewish liberals. The Right protectionists hinted that their Jewish opponents neither spun nor wove, but throve on speculation, and therefore had no interest in protecting the honest tiller of the soil and the national patrimony. As was to be demonstrated at a later date, a threatened and demoralised aristocracy, which has lost its leading position and self-assurance, easily forgets its standards of *noblesse oblige* and chivalry, and finds little difficulty in making common cause with plebeian rabble-rousers, and in rediscovering affinity between its own deep-rootedness and the authenticity of the unspoilt lower orders, both being close to the ancestral soil and perennial traditions.[77]

In the same decade the Catholic Centrum was engaged in a bitter struggle against Bismarck's *Kulturkampf*, in which the Iron Chancellor was abetted and supported by the liberals. The German Catholics vented their wrath on the Jews as standard-bearers of that type of anti-traditional individualism which leads straight to materialist atheism, moral nihilism and unrestrained selfishness.[78] The main impulse behind the European counter-revolution in all its various facets was anxiety. Change was feared because it was disturbing. It created uncertainty, and above all forced man to make choices and take decisions, of which necessity he was spared in a static traditional society. Ceaseless change deprived man of his self-assurance. He no longer was sure what he wanted, and who he was.

In this respect the Jew appeared as especially threatening. There were, to be sure, always Gentiles who admired the analytical acumen displayed by so many Jews, their agility in roaming through the vast expanse of culture, their freedom from the weight of conservative tradition, routine, and inertia, their ability to see through cant and humbug parading as eternal truths or sacred values, their almost compulsive quest for underlying primary universal elements and structures. D. H. Lawrence, for example, credited 'the Jewish intelligence' with driving people from 'false, automatic fixities',[79] while Thorstein Veblen spoke of the 'intellectual pre-eminence' of the Jew, attributing it to his alienation from tradition and convention: 'Among the vanguards, the pointers, the uneasy guild of pathfinders and iconoclasts', who liberate us 'from the dead hand of conventional finality ... disturbers of the intellectual peace ... wanderers in the intellectual no man's land. ... They are neither a complaisant nor a contented lot those aliens of the uneasy feet.'[80] To the fearful traditionalists, however, the alienated Jew appeared as the solvent of established orders and organic cohesion; a nihilist rejoicing at the sight of disintegration and confusion; the rootless, botched and resentful outsider, who could never feel at home and at ease, and who therefore turned his impotent and envious rage against ancient loyalties, sacred myths and hallowed symbols: the Jew, in brief, was cosmopolitan radicalism incarnate. His tremendous curiosity and receptiveness betokened the lack of inner core. His mental agility was nothing but glibness or the sterile erudition of Alexandrian grammarians. His *penchant* for abstract generalised thinking was the sign of an inability to come to grips with the concrete realities, the deep facts of life. His worldly successes were gained by trickery and unscrupulousness.

French integral nationalism, German racism, Russian Slavo-philism and the Teutonic myth in the Anglo-Saxon countries at the turn of this century – all these tendencies were in fact a direct function of that crisis of identity and of the fear of freedom in a changing world. Racial theory came forward to bestow upon the particular, as contrasted to the abstract and universal, the dignity of a fundamental and all-determining datum of nature, not at all something to be overcome. More than that, the early mysticism of the German romantics could now claim the dignity of science, and the poetic quest for mysterious qualities, hidden in myth and legend, in the slumbering depths of the collective unconsciousness, could now aspire to certainty. Blood, unconscious reflexes, law, the social order, the sciences and the arts appeared linked indis-solubly in a predetermined organic pattern.[81] Barrès would no longer be embarrassed to define truth as the perspective of French interests.[82] Charles Maurras, a pagan at heart, becomes an up-holder of Catholicism not because of the truth it professes but for the principle of order and discipline it embodies.

The result of this belief in the unerring instinct of the race was a terrible anxiety to secure its integrity, and consequently to defend it from being diluted, debilitated, distorted and undermined by poisonous alien influences. Conversely all its failures and frustrations could be blamed on alien solvents. Here again the Jew emerged as the gravest danger. He was an outsider and insider at the same time. He was or was seen as ubiquitous and most dynamically active at the well-springs of the national culture. In Europe 'Aryan' would have been meaningless, without 'the Jew' as its concrete negation. The very juxtaposition was a function of the horror-stricken obsession of all the prophets of race with the decay of cultures, doom of civilisations, disintegration of societies. That was the point of departure of Gobineau, that was at the bottom of Houston Stewart Chamberlain's preoccupation with the mongrelisation of races. Drumont starts his work with gloomy meditations on these topics. Hitler is driven by visions of our planet, emptied of life – as a result of Jewish domination – and circling around among the other silent planets. Anxiety and aggressiveness are so often inseparable. The anxiety about one's identity engenders an aggressive urge to assert it and ascertain it.[83]

The people with whom we are here concerned were quick to seize upon Darwin's theory as proof not only of the unalterable natural inequality of races, but of the fact that the struggle for Life was waged not just or solely by individuals, but by the species, with the individual reduced to the role of the chip of the great rock, the function of the whole. There was nothing new in the idea of war and struggle for power as the natural state of mankind. Machiavelli taught that, and Hobbes improved upon him. But the former spoke of princes, and the latter of individuals and states. Neither of them had any conception of nation or race as a unique compound of blood, soil, history, peculiar modes of reacting to stimuli, of instincts evolved through centuries of struggle; religion, law, philosophy, the sciences and the arts being the product of that process of self-adaptation, in a certain sense weapons in the struggle.[84]

The apotheosis of struggle and the emphasis upon fighting prowess were bound to devaluate the reasoning faculty. The paramount reality was the struggle for a share of Life, and not the cooperative effort to increase knowledge, establish objective truth, or enthrone equal justice. Once this was granted, discursive, analytical ratiocination, critical weighing of alternatives, comparing of cases, began to be looked upon as signs of indecision, irresolution, inability to act, feebleness of will, as proof of the decline of the vital instincts, of a lack of cohesion and dynamic strength. 'They were forced' – says Nietzsche – 'to think, deduce, calculate, weigh cause and effect – unhappy people reduced to their weakest, most fallible organ, their consciousness!'[85] The Jewish intellectual with his *penchant* for doubt and analysis again appeared a menace. Self-assertion, self-realisation by the strong, the vital, was hailed and contrasted by Nietzsche with the hypocrisy of the weak, the botched and the resentful, who cunningly conspired to catch the eagles in spiderwebs of the so-called virtues of humility, tolerance, reciprocity, consideration for others, majority vote, compromise and concord. They themselves loved and aspired to power, but lacking the qualities of true leadership,

had to resort to ruse, guile, manipulation. They would inveigh
against violence, the rule of the strong, but in fact their whole rule
was nothing but hypocritically camouflaged force. Nietzsche,
Sorel and Pareto compare this sinister conspiracy of bourgeois
mediocrity and pusillanimity working in the dark, with open
violence, and find the latter so much nobler and finer as a token of
absolute determination, unflinching and total commitment,
readiness for undisguised and total confrontation. Sorel and
Pareto call for physical violence against corrupt politicians and
perverse intellectuals.[86] The Jews were singled out as the representatives *par excellence* of the reign of cunning and manipulation.
Weak and few, their success could not be due to qualities of
natural leadership. Reasoners who recoil from and fear physical
violence, their only strength was in persevering, wire-pulling and
manipulating; their weapons were only the abstract intellect and
abstract money, neither of them a function of natural superiority,
genuine direct experience, or authentic effort. The *vérité idéelle* of
the Jews was ranged against the *vérité charnelle* of the French,
against French blood – proclaimed Georges Valois, the French
Nietzschean and disciple of both Georges Sorel and Charles
Maurras; who as early as around 1910 spun visions of the forth-
coming 'most beautiful massacre of Jews in history', but who was
to end his life in 1944 at . . . Bergen-Belsen.[87]

The extreme practical conclusions were drawn by Hitler and
applied to a concrete political situation long before he started his
career on German soil. He tells us himself in *Mein Kampf* that
when he reached Germany on the eve of World War One, his for-
mation had been completed by the impact of Austro-Hungarian
realities and the teachings of Leuger and Schönerer.[88] For
centuries the Danubian Monarchy was ruled by a German
minority, who lorded over the Slav masses of hewers of wood and
drawers of water. With the growth of the democratic ideas of one
man one vote, and the rule of majorities, the Germans found
themselves threatened by the despised Slav masses, whom they
considered irredeemably inferior. Brought up on the crudest kind
of biological Darwinism, Hitler viewed the German-Slav conflict
as a war of races, by definition a war to death. It was also to him

a clash between quality and quantity, race excellence and numbers, the rule of elite and the vote by feet. Parliamentary democracy had to be rejected so that the Germans could live and fulfil their destiny. All those ideologies and groups which preached democracy or put common Austro-Hungarian citizenship above racial uniqueness, proletarian solidarity above national-German cohesion or humanitarianism above race loyalty, emerged in his eyes as enemies, traitors and poisoners. The Jews as an ethnic group were deeply anxious to maintain the supra-national Habsburg Empire, and Jews were also prominent in the leadership of the Liberal as well as Socialist parties, and they were the spearhead of universalist culture. They became therefore the enemy *par excellence*, the most alien, the most odious of all. All Jews were assimilated in Hitler's mind to that strange apparition on the streets of Vienna, which Hitler describes as having been the trauma of his life: an old Jew with a beard and sidelocks, in a strange attire, looking so indescribably alien and sinister. Could such a one be a German, or even a human being? Hitler asked himself.[89] All non-Jewish enemies were in turn assimilated by him to the Jew. After 1918 Hitler transposed Austro-Hungarian realities on to Germany. The defeated German nation was in a state of siege, and in danger of extinction from the hands of the external enemies, in alliance with the Jews, their accomplices inside Germany and international Jewry everywhere.

The Jews appeared to their racist enemies in two forms, as a universal solvent and a ghostly anti-race on the one hand, and as a most cohesive and tenacious racial group determined to establish its rule over the whole world on the other. The Jews preached brotherhood of men, the superiority of universal values, the irrelevance of blood, race, nationality, history. Jewish capitalism destroyed national cohesion through materialist individualism, Jewish socialism with the help of class war. But the Jews themselves, in spite of their dispersion, retained their clannishness, remaining a nation apart, held together by unbreakable ties. The preaching of the Jew was subtly intended to drug and weaken the nations of Europe, while Judah, congregated in metropolitan centres, master of the mass media, close to the most sensitive arteries of power, bent upon experiment and adventure in every new field, spread his dominion over them all.

Erikson suggests that the anti-Semites were filled not only with fear, but also envy of what to them seemed the Jew's supreme instinctive self-assurance and single-minded purposefulness, the very things they lacked and craved for.[90] Hence the fear of being submerged and swamped by Jewish world mastery. Well before the Protocols of Zion had started upon their career, with their lurid descriptions of secret conclaves of the sinister sages formulating precise blueprints for debauching and dominating the Gentile world, of the worship of Satan and anti-Christ upon deserted cemeteries and under a pale moon, culminating in a dance around the golden calf, men of exceptional erudition and acumen were writing seriously about the danger of Jewish world domination.

The fastidious defender of the beauty and the integrity of the classical heritage, Jacob Burckhardt, who would date his letters '1872 = the 83rd year of the Revolution', and who in his desperate anxiety to stem the flood of plebeian barbarism fought against schools for the poor and health service for the needy and dreamt of secular monasteries as a refuge for the chosen few from the *hoi poloi*, gave vent to his hatred of Jewish obtrusiveness in such vulgar and blood-curdling abuse as this (admittedly in the secrecy of private correspondence):

The Semites I would advise now to exercise great wisdom and circumspection, without believing myself any longer that the present agitation will subside. Liberalism, which had up to now defended the Semites, will soon be unable to resist the temptation to shake off that odium. It will not be able for long to let the Conservatives and Catholics keep and use the most popular trump card that there is, and play it against them (. . . the complete emancipation of the Semites must be removed in due course from its luggage, even if its heart breaks, which I do not believe it will . . .) and then there will come a change in the law, and I would not guarantee to the (Herren) Semitic lawyers their careers for long . . . the Semites will have to give up their entirely unjustified interference in everything possible, and the newspapers will have to dismiss their Semitic editors and correspondents, if they want to continue their existence. Such a thing may take place suddenly and overnight and (spread) contagiously. . . . Nine-tenths of the German press is produced by Jews . . . a referendum of the continued existence of Jews in the German Reich would, I guarantee, give a still larger vote for the expulsion of the Jews than our (Swiss) referendum of 26 November (1882) [on some local non-Jewish issue in which progressives were ranged against conservatives].[91]

Burckhardt's younger friend and colleague and in some ways disciple at the venerable University of Basle, Friedrich Nietzsche, had a much more ambivalent attitude toward Jews. Nothing could be more startling and in retrospect appear more ominous than the following passage, actually written in the praise of Jews:

The People of Israel – One of the spectacles which the next century will invite us to witness is the decision regarding the fate of the European Jews. It is quite obvious now that they have cast their die and crossed their Rubicon: the only thing that remains for them is either to become masters of Europe or to lose Europe, as they once centuries ago lost Egypt, where they were confronted with similar alternatives. In Europe, however, they have gone through a schooling of eighteen centuries such as no other nation has ever undergone, and the experiences of this dreadful time of probation have benefited not only the Jewish community but, even to a greater extent, the individual. Now, however, that they unavoidably intermarry more and more year after year with the noblest blood of Europe, they will soon have a considerable heritage of good intellectual and physical manners, so that in another hundred years they will have a sufficiently noble aspect not to render themselves, as masters, ridiculous to those whom they will have subdued. And this is important! and therefore a settlement of the question is still premature. They themselves know very well that the conquest of Europe or any act of violence is not to be thought of; but they also know that some day or other Europe may, like a ripe fruit, fall into their hands, if they do not clutch at it too eagerly. In the meantime, it is necessary for them to distinguish themselves in all departments of European distinction and to stand in the front rank: until they shall have advanced so far as to determine themselves what distinction shall mean. Then they will be called the pioneers and guides of the European whose modesty they will no longer offend. And then where shall an outlet be found for this abundant wealth of great impressions accumulated during such an extended period and representing Jewish history for every Jewish family, this wealth of passions, virtues, resolutions, resignations, struggles, and conquests of all kinds – where can it find an outlet but in great intellectual men and works! On the day when the Jews will be able to exhibit to us as their own work such jewels and golden vessels as no European nation, with its shorter and less profound experience, can or could produce, when Israel shall have changed its eternal vengeance into an eternal benediction for Europe: then that seventh day will once more appear when old Jehovah may rejoice in Himself, in His creation, in His chosen people – and all, all of us, will rejoice with Him!⁹²

One would give much to know whether Hitler ever read this prose poem, and what impression it made on him.⁹³

The first anti-Semitic parties in the sense of having not merely an anti-Jewish bias, but of putting anti-Semitism at the centre of their programmes, and of writing the word into their titles, make their appearance more or less simultaneously, and independently, in a number of countries around 1880. Drumont's book *La France Juive* runs into dozens of editions, and his paper reaches a mass circulation which no respectable French journal could dream of rivalling; in Germany, the Protestant pastor and court preacher Adolf Stoecker organises his lower-middle-class following into the anti-Semitic Christian Social party; in Austro-Hungary his counterpart Dr Leuger goes from strength to strength on his way to the Mayoralty of the great capital city of Vienna, with its large and vital Jewish community, while his rival, the racist Freiherr von Schönerer, rallies the Austro-German intelligentsia against the Jews, the Habsburgs, the Slavs, and for a pan-German empire. Russia is swept by a wave of pogroms in 1881 after the assassination of Alexander II by revolutionary terrorists. Mass petitions are circulated in Germany demanding the abrogation of Jewish emancipation, and the right-wing debaters in the *Reich-*

stag use the occasion for issuing hardly veiled warnings to the Jews to learn how to behave.

All these groups – clericals and Teutonic pagans, feudals and artisans, racists and mystics, nationalists and Christian Socialists – claim to be defending the national spirit and the old decencies against cosmopolitan Jewish solvents. Paradoxically, however, the Jewish issue turns them into an international confraternity themselves; this will happen again under Hitler's New Order. Meanwhile, the first series of international anti-Semitic congresses are held in the 1880s, with the aim of giving expression to 'the protest of the European peoples against the modes of thought and behaviour of an Asiatic race'.[94]

The new movements are all consciously and strenuously counter-revolutionary. But unlike the old feudal-clerical groups, which swore by legitimacy and law and order, feared the mob and abhorred mass violence, the temper and methods of these new counter-revolutionaries have all the qualities of violent mass phenomena. Charismatic demagogues send huge audiences into deliriums of spiteful hatred or rowdy enthusiasm, or indeed into the streets to engage in direct action. It is not only a different clientele. An ideological shift takes place: chauvinist passion is fused with anti-capitalist slogans. From now on, however, the capitalist is the Jewish capitalist. It is no exaggeration to say – and this indeed was the view of contemporaries, of anti-Semites and Marxists alike – that anti-Semitism becomes elevated into an alternative and rival creed to Socialism. It was incidentally Stoecker and the anti-Dreyfusards who cured Marxist Socialists in Germany and France from their occasional addiction to anti-Jewish rhetoric, such as the slogan 'The social question is a Jewish question, and will not be solved till a Rothschild is put before a firing squad'.[95]

By the end of the century Charles Maurras, the founder and prophet of the *Action Française*, the philosophically richest and most vigorous of all the counter-revolutionary anti-Semitic movements, could say in answer to the objections of a young follower that anti-Semitism was no programme: 'One of these days it will be shown that on the contrary, it is as a function of the

anti-Semitic programme that all the rest of nationalist and mon-
archist programmes will be able to pass from conception to
execution.' Similarly, Schönerer called anti-Semitism 'the
mainstay of our national ideology', and the Russian anti-Semite
Rozanov proclaimed that 'there is no problem in Russian life in
which like a comma there is not also the question – how to cope
with the Jew'.[96] Not only was anti-Semitism turned into 'the
Socialism of the fools', in the language of Bebel – or the Socialism
of the *petite bourgeoisie*, as Engels would have it – it emerged as the
nucleus of race theory,[97] which in turn assumed the dimensions of
a *Weltanschauung*, not to say the religion of the counter-revolution: an alternative to and a refutation of the *Weltanschauung* of
liberal, rationalist, universalist Enlightenment. Thus, Mussolini
would proclaim in 1926: 'We represent a new principle in the
world: we represent the exact categorical, definitive antithesis of
the whole world of democracy, plutocracy, freemasonry, in
short the whole world of the "immortal principles" of 1789,'
while his German counterparts would speak of the race theory as
'another Copernican revolution'.[98]

Houston Stewart Chamberlain supplied a philosophy of history
to this *Weltanschauung*. It depicted the whole of history as the
struggle between the Jewish and Teutonic races. The darkness of
the dark centuries was due to the mongrelisation of the European
races by the strong admixture of Jewish blood and the sway of
priestly Jewish ideas. The turning-point came around 1200 when
the Germans seized the lead in Europe. All that is valuable and
positive in the European heritage ever since can be traced to the
German ingredient and its opposite to the Jewish element. The
nineteenth century had become another 'Jewish' century in that it
had let loose the Jews and Jewish influence upon the world. The
twentieth century was called upon to reverse this dangerous trend
in a revolutionary and radical manner.[99] Here was an alternative
to the Marxist conception of history as a struggle between
oppressing and oppressed classes, with blood taking the place of
modes of production, and the victory of the Nordic race serving
as a substitute for the vision of classless society, universal consent
and the end of human alienation. Chamberlain was Richard

Wagner's son-in-law and the direct inspirer of Adolf Hitler and Alfred Rosenberg.

A few decades later Ernest Krieck, the Heidelberg philosopher of Nazism, defined the Nazi 'heroisch-völkische Realismus' of the Nazi revolution as the uprising of the 'blood against formal ratiocination, race against rationalist utilitarianism, honour against profit, allegiance against individualistic dissolution, combativeness against bourgeois security, politics against the primacy of economics, state against society, Volk against the individual and the mass'.[100]

IX

The theory of the counter-revolution was elaborated in the West, above all in Germany. The gigantic confrontation between revolution and counter-revolution was destined to be unrolled upon the Jewish bodies on the plains of Poland and Russia.

Upon examining the Russian-Jewish relations on the eve and in the early days of World War One, the historian is smitten by the realisation that he is faced with a kind of prefiguration of the Nazi catastrophe of nearly twenty years later.

Tsar Nicholas II was immensely impressed by the Protocols of Zion, when he was shown them for the first time in 1905, and he gave vent to his impressions in such exclamations as 'What depth of thought!' – 'What foresight!' – 'What precision in the realisation of the programme!' – 'Our year 1905 has gone as though managed by the Elders' – 'There can be no doubt as to their authenticity' – 'Everywhere one sees the directing and destroying hand of Judaism.' It is true that when persuaded of the forgery, the Tsar instructed his aides to drop the Protocols. 'One cannot defend a pure cause by dirty means.'[101] This however did not prevent him from giving in 1906 his full support to a plan of his Foreign Minister Count Lamsdorf for concerted action by Russia, Germany and the Vatican against the Alliance Israelite Universelle as the front organisation of the Elders of Zion: 'Negotiations must be started at once. I entirely share the opinions expressed here.'[102] The steps adopted by the Russian High Command in the face of its calamitous defeats in the early days of World War One bear striking resemblance to the Nazi policies of a quarter of a century later, short of the overall 'final solution' plan and gas chambers. The Tsarist Minister A. M. Yakhontov tells us:

At the GHQ they have formed the opinion that the Jewish population in the war theatre is a hotbed of espionage and assistance to the enemy. Thus the idea was put forward that it was necessary to evacuate the Jews from the areas adjoining the front. This measure was first applied in Galicia. Authorities at the rear of the army began to deport thousands upon thousands of Jews into the interior of Russia. This of course was done on a compulsory, not a voluntary basis. Jews were expelled wholesale regardless of age or sex. The deportees included the sick, the invalid and even pregnant women. Rumours concerning this measure and the accompanying violence have spread both inside Russia and abroad. Influential Jewry has sounded the alarm. Allied governments have begun to protest against this kind of policy and have pointed out its dangerous consequences. The Ministry of Finance has experienced various difficulties in carrying out its financial operations. The Council of Ministers has repeatedly drawn the attention of the Supreme Commander and of General Yanushkevich, both in writing and in personal representations by the Premier and individual ministers, to the necessity of dropping the persecution of Jews and the wholesale accusations of treason against them, explaining that this was required by considerations of both internal and foreign policy. Yet GHQ has remained deaf to all arguments and persuasion. On the contrary, when in the course of our retreat the evacuation of Russian provinces began, compulsory migration of Jews on a large scale was carried out by specially assigned military detachments, first in Courland and then elsewhere. What went on in the execution of these operations defies description. Even inveterate anti-Semites came to members of the Government with protests and complaints concerning the revolting treatment of Jews at the front. As a result, life in those provinces of the Pale of settlement to which the involuntary refugees have been driven by the military authorities has become intolerable not only for the motley crowd of destitute newcomers but also for the indigenous population. All sorts of crises – of food supplies, housing and so on – have become even more acute. Epidemics have broken out. The mood on the spot has assumed an increasingly alarming character: the Jews have a grudge against all and sundry, and the local people resent both the uninvited guests, who in any case are branded as traitors and spies, and also the intolerable deterioration in their own living conditions.[103]

In this threatening atmosphere the Minister of the Interior, Prince Shcherbatov, urged the Council of Ministers to take immediate steps to remedy the situation:

> Our efforts to talk reason to GHQ [he said] have all been in vain. We have tried all possible means of combating their prejudiced attitude. All of us, both together and individually, have spoken, written, begged, complained. But the almighty Yanushkevich does not feel bound to consider the interest of the state as a whole. Part of his plan is to nurture the army's bias against all Jews indiscriminately and to make them responsible for the setbacks at the front. This policy has already borne fruit, and a pogrom mood is ripening in the army. However unpleasant it is to mention it, I will not conceal my suspicion from you in this private meeting that Yanushkevich is using the Jews as a scapegoat [for his own failures].[104]

Three years later the Tsar and his family were helpless prisoners guarded by a Jew and a few Latvian assistants.

'There was grim although probably quite accidental retribution' – says W. H. Chamberlain in his monumental *Russian Revolution* – 'in the fact that the chief executioner of Tsar Nicholas II and his family in the Ekaterinburg cellar was a Jew', Jacob Yurovsky, a photographer born in Siberia, who lived for some time in Berlin, becoming converted to Lutheranism, and then returned to Russia as one of the obscure activists in the beehive of revolution. 'The family of the Tsar died very much as many a Jewish family had perished during the pogroms of 1905 . . . very symbolic of the Bolshevik revolution . . . a plain, unadorned, unsentimental, utilitarian massacre . . . no parade of a public trial, no chance for dramatic exhange of speeches between prosecutor and accused';[105] to the great chagrin incidentally of Trotsky, who had dreamt of acting as prosecutor in the intended trial of the Tsar, and of flamboyantly re-enacting another drama on the stage of history. As if to heighten still the symbolism of that dreadful end of one of the most powerful Royal dynasties in history at the hands of an obscure Jew, soldiers of the counter-revolutionary army seized Ekaterinburg a short time after, and found in the murdered Tsarina's room a copy of the Protocols of Zion with drawings of the Swastika. There is little doubt that the latter had no political significance and was only a superstitious emblem to the poor, hysterical and half-crazy woman. Still, here was an Aryan royal martyr at hand for future use.[106]

The role of the Jews in the Bolshevik revolution and in the establishment of the Soviet system is a daunting subject which still awaits its historian. We can presume here no more than some general marginal comments.

In a recently published collection of autobiographies and authorised biographies of the makers of the October revolution, followed by commentaries and rectifications, *Les Bolshevistes par eux-mêmes*, the authors, G. Haupt and J. J. Marie, divide their heroes into (1) the great protagonists, (2) the *Pléiade* of October, (3) former dissidents and (4) '*Les rallies*' of 1917, new recruits, foreigners. We find in the first category, out of eight, four Jews, in the second, three out of thirty, in the third, two out of seven, and in the fourth, four, or if one counts the intensely pro-Trotsky Karaite Adolf Yoffé as a Jew, five out of ten.[107]

In the early days of the USSR it was natural to couple Trotsky with Lenin as the two makers of the revolution. As far as will and authority are concerned there was only one Maker, and that was Lenin, without whose early and monumentally unflagging resolve to the point of coercing his hesitant comrades with the threat of resignation to instant action, there would have been no October. In execution, in effective decisive break-throughs, in raising an event to the level of high drama, no one's role could compare with Trotsky's furious deeds, and no one was more aware of that than Lenin himself, in spite of rankling memories of the past and a fundamental dislike of Trotsky's theatrical personality, mitigated though it was by deep respect for the younger man's enormous intellect and brilliant artistry as a writer. To mention only a few significant points: re-enacting his role of 1905 as Chairman of the Petrograd Soviet, but now lording over a Bolshevik majority in it, Trotsky in fact creates and heads the instrument of the October coup – the Military Commission – and fixes its modes of operation; he makes the leap into the lion's den, the decisive Petro-Pavlovsk garrison, and his flaming oratory brings the hesitant or unfriendly soldiers over to the Bolsheviks; he hurls the supreme insult at the Mensheviks and Social-Revolutionaries filing out of the Congress of the Soviets, throwing them upon the 'rubbish heap of history where they belong';[108] he holds the world enthralled with his titanic debating match with the German ministers and generals and their allies at Brest Litovsk on the real meaning of free self-determination; in the name of the General Will of the revolution he adopts an extreme centralist attitude towards the trade unions, which are aspiring to direct workers' control; he has his way not only in organising the Red Army, but in stiffening it with old Tsarist officers and technicians.

Ruthless, unscrupulous, opportunistically pragmatic as Trotsky could be, arbitrarily cruel as the early Chekist Uritsky was, *exalté* an agitator as Volodarsky was (both of them perished by assassination), a closer look will reveal that on the whole even the Bolshevik Jews, not to speak of course of the Menshevik or most of the SR Jews, displayed a greater respect for legality, or at least deeper inhibitions in breaking or ignoring it, than most of their Gentile comrades, above all Lenin. One is familiar with the stubborn rearguard actions – condemned by Lenin as sabotage and treason – of Kamenev and Zinoviev, otherwise so very different from each other in mentality and temperament, to preserve a semblance of legality, to secure some form of legal authorisation, above all not to act without or in the teeth of opposition from the other Socialist parties. While Lenin cared nothing for any formal legality, considering the party, if not indeed himself, the *Urim ve'thummim* of history, of revolutionary legality, it was Trotsky who stumbled upon the idea of attaching formal responsibility for the October coup to the St Petersburg Soviet, and its arm – the Military Commission.[109]

It is by far not enough to limit the consideration of the part of Jews in the Bolshevik revolution to the role of Jews in the top layer of leadership. Not less vital was the role of Jews in the cadres, in the machine, the bureaucracy, administration, party organisation, the economy, technical services, in a situation in which the civil servants of the former regime as well as the professional intelligentsia refused to collaborate or could not be trusted. In all this the contribution of the Jews to keeping the system going in a country shattered by external and civil war, afflicted by famine, was of the utmost importance. Many Jews gave their services not because of any Bolshevik conviction, but because they were left with no choice; the counter-revolutionary forces in the Civil War had embarked upon a campaign of pogroms.

The most distinct feature of the Jewish revolutionaries in 1917 and after was certainly their internationalism. Lenin himself professed more than once that he would hardly have embarked upon his course, had he not believed that a revolution in the West, above all Germany, was imminent. If the Gentile Bolsheviks thought the revolution in the West a guarantee of success of the revolution in Russia, the Jews, like Trotsky, Radek, Zinoviev and others, felt most intensely that the Russian revolution was only a local version of the world revolution. It is no accident, and not only a matter of linguistic proficiency, that Jews, and such non-Russian Jews as Radek and Larissa Reisner, were so active in the Comintern and at international Communist Congresses such as the famous Baku Congress of the Asiatic and African Communist parties.[110] Radek kept shuttling backwards and forwards between Russia and Germany, and while in a German prison negotiating with the leaders of the German *Reichswehr* and political leaders, Borodin went East – to China.

The fact that apart from the inevitable and largely decorative woman-worker and bearded peasant practically all the Soviet negotiators at Brest Litovsk were Jews, was sure not to escape the notice of the opposite side, for instance, General Hoffman, who was to crush the Jewish-led Communist regime in Bavaria less than two years later.

One may say that once the momentous struggle between Trotsky and Lenin was decided in favour of socialism in one country,

Russia had taken the first step towards that development, which was to lead to a revival of Jew consciousness in the masses and a renewal of the special status of the Jews.

But before these things had time to work themselves out, the world, or at least that part of it which was disposed that way, had imprinted upon its consciousness the image of a sinister Judeo-Bolshevik world conspiracy.

X

The Bolshevik revolution posed a tremendous question to Russia's neighbours, both the countries reeling from defeat as well as those which had just won their independence – to join the revolution under the aegis of Russia or to struggle to assert their historic uniqueness. When the representative of the old ruling classes, Prince Max von Baden, the last Prime Minister of Imperial Germany, handed over the seals of office to the former saddler and innkeeper Ebert, with the words, 'I entrust you with the destiny of the German nation', he implicitly asked the most meaningful question: Did the German Social-Democrats see themselves as executors on German soil of the world revolution which was begun a year earlier by the Bolsheviks, or did they regard themselves as the trustees of German national history, responsible for the national heritage and the reconstruction of the defeated and shattered fatherland? Ebert's reply to Prince Max that he would know how to guard the trust, having lost two sons in his country's war, was a clear option for the latter course. Once this decision was taken – and there could never have been any doubt that it would be – everything else followed.[111]

Nothing could have played more into the hands of the anti-Semitic, racist counter-revolution and serve better as a corroboration of the Jewish stab-in-the-back legend than Kurt Eisner's revolutionary seizure of power at that time in conservative, royalist and Catholic Bavaria, and then the prominence of Jews like Jogiches, Levine, Levinas, Georg Landauer and Joffe in the short-lived Communist government after Eisner's assassination and in the Spartakist and Marxist parties in general. To a Germany exasperated by defeat, inflation, unemployment and hunger, moreover, the central role of Jews in the Weimar Republic lent further credence to the legend. The Jew Hugo Preuss was the author of the Weimar Constitution; Walter Rathenau was the first German Foreign Secretary to make an agreement with Bolshevik Russia; and Kurt Eisner published classified Foreign Office documents to show German guilt for the outbreak of the war, in the hope of showing to the West Germany's repentance and thereby obtaining better terms.[112] The somewhat too zealous and aggressive interrogation of Field-Marshal Hindenburg by Cohn, the Counsel of the *Reichstag* Committee set up to investigate the military conduct of the war gave rise to a most effective slogan, 'Cohn versus Hindenburg'.[113] It was no use arguing that in the war the Jews had been as overwhelmingly patriotic as everyone else. They were 'anti-national', and by the time Hitler came along hardly a German could be found to speak out in their defence.[114]

The struggle between nationalism and revolutionary universalism achieved still greater poignancy in Eastern Europe. The most important and most striking example was Poland, but the same drama was to be played out in the other countries as well. It had been a cardinal point with the European camp of revolution, and very much so with Marx and Engels, that Poland must be resurrected. The Poles were the oldest freedom fighters on all the barricades and battlefields of Europe, and the restoration of Poland was sure to deal a mortal blow to the Tsarist regime. Rosa Luxemburg, however, as leader of the internationalist Polish Socialist party, never tired of reiterating the conviction that with the emergence of a vast revolutionary movement in Russia, it was the sacred duty of the Polish workers to join hands with their Russian comrades and not squander their energies on a nationalist deviation which was sure to help to bring about a bourgeois capitalist Poland. In brief, there was no such thing as a Polish national interest, there were only class interests, and Poland as a political entity was altogether an abstraction. It is easy to imagine the fury and the rage this caused among the majority of Polish Socialists – among them incidentally, many Jews – to whom the resurrection of Poland was a supreme goal, a glorious vision.[115]

The group headed by Rosa, and containing a very high proportion of Jews in its leadership as well as in the rank and file, became the nucleus of the Polish Communist party after 1918, while some of the leaders made their way to Moscow. Soviet Russia disclaimed any imperialist designs. She proclaimed herself at the same time duty bound to help to make the revolution victorious everywhere. To the small and weak nation states which had just regained, or indeed for the first time won their independance from Russia and her former allies, a revolutionary Russia was in a sense a greater danger and a more insidious menace to their national uniqueness and integrity than Tsarist Russia. After World War One, the Jews overnight found themselves no longer citizens of vast multi-racial empires and participants in great cultures like the German and the Russian, but minorities subject to Poles, Lithuanians, Latvians, Slovaks, Rumanians and Hungarians, whose social and cultural development had been arrested centuries before, whose languages they often did not know and did not care to learn, and whose anxious, jealous nationalism was as intense as their resources were scarce. Treated as aliens, undesirables, an obstacle to national self-expression, many of the best of the Jewish youth responded with a thrill to the message of universal revolution. When the test came, twenty years later, the Rumanians, Slovaks and Hungarians let their differences sink, and became the willing allies of the great standard-bearer of anti-Semitism and anti-Bolshevism; Latvian, Lithuanian, Ukrainian and White Russian thugs were employed by the Nazis for the dirtiest jobs in the liquidation of the Jewish ghettoes in Poland and the despatch of their inmates to the death camps.

The Bolshevik revolution was seized upon by Hitler as final proof of the revolutionary role of the Jewish ingredient in the drama of history from the beginning to the end of time. Ernst Nolte has recently drawn our attention to a forgotten pamphlet published in

1924, containing a series of conversations held between Hitler and his 'fatherly friend' and mentor, Dietrich Eckart, a 'metaphysical' poet, to whom the future Führer looked up as to the North Star, and whose 'pupil' he solemnly acknowledged himself to be on assuming power in 1933. The dialogue is called *'Der Bolschewismus von Moses bis Lenin: Zwiegespräch zwischen Adolf Hitler und mir'.*[116] If the 'natural order' was envisaged by the believers of the revolution to be disturbed by avaricious exploiters, the two counter-revolutionaries see their 'natural order' – that of pure and sharply contoured races, – the world of 'what is and what remains' – disturbed by 'the Jew', the germ of dissolution. Already the Jewish exodus from Egypt, in fact an expulsion, was nothing but the result of a revolutionary Jewish assault on the ruling elite of Egypt. The Jews tried – 'just as among us' – to incite the 'rabble' against the superior elements. The slaying of the first-born was to be a signal to a general revolution. But the 'nationalist' Egyptians stood their ground and threw the Jews out, with Moses, the first leader of Bolshevism, at their head. Christianity was another chapter in the story of Jewish Bolshevism. St Paul 'goes to the Greeks, to the Romans, and he takes to them *his* "Christianity": something which can unhinge the Roman Empire. All men are equal! Fraternity! Pacifism! No more dignity! And the Jew triumphed.' The Reformation was another manifestation of Jewish Bolshevism, except for Luther, whose anti-Semitism saves him from condemnation: 'Puritans, Anabaptists, Jehovah's Witnesses, those are the juiciest ones. In each of them sits the Jewish maggot.' Eckart had earlier called the Bolshevik revolution 'the ritual slaughtering of Christians by the dictatorship of the Jewish world salvation of Lenin and his Elijah, Trotsky-Bronstein'.[117]

This last revelation of the true spirit of Judah, coming at the end of the greatest of wars, whose real instigator and author was again the Jew, was to enable the nations to see through him and his role in history and to rise against that 'parasitic growth over the whole earth, sometimes creeping, sometimes leaping . . . sucking . . . at first the bursting abundance, finally the withered sap'. 'No people in the world,' not even Attila's race of murderers, would allow him [the Jew] to remain alive if it could suddenly see through what he is, what he desires; shrieking with horror it would strangle him the very next instant.' Eckart suggests to Hitler Luther's recipe – burning of synagogues. 'Hopeless' – answers Hitler – 'burning down would do us precious little good. That's the trouble! Even if there had never been a synagogue, or a Jewish school, or the Old Testament, the Jewish spirit would still exist and exert its influence. It has been there from the beginning, and there is no Jew, not a single one, who does not personify it.' There is just no other way but to destroy the 'substance of flesh and blood'.[118]

Now begins the last great revolution – writes Hitler in *Mein Kampf*. By wresting political power for himself, the Jew casts off the few remaining shreds of disguise he still wears. The democratic plebeian Jew turns into the blood-Jew and the tyrant of peoples. In a few years he will try to exterminate the national pillars of intelligence and, by robbing the peoples of their natural spiritual leadership, will make them ripe for the slavish lot of a permanent subjugation. The most terrible example of this is Russia.... But the end is not merely the liberty of the peoples suppressed by the Jew: it is also the end of this parasite people itself. After the death of the victim, sooner or later the vampire dies too.[119]

The counter-revolution assumes thus the dimension of a universal revolution of the 'elite races of the world' against that Manichean incarnation of all evil, to whom 'each and every social injustice of significance, as well as every upheaval', could be traced: again a replica of the Marxist world revolution against social exploitation.

The last and only claim to the gratitude of posterity that Hitler staked before dying by his own hand in the squalid Berlin bunker was for having accomplished the liquidation of the six million Jews. 'National Socialism deserves eternal gratitude for having eliminated the Jews from Germany and Central Europe ... who wanted war and engineered it ... international politicians of Jewish extraction ... on behalf of Jewish interests.'[120]

XI

At the end of World War Two the Jewish survivors in Central and Eastern Europe everywhere greeted the Soviet armies as liberators and redeemers. Forgotten was the Nazi-Soviet pact of 1939 which unleashed the horrible war, and forgotten was the fact that after all Soviet Russia had taken up arms when invaded and not in defence of the Jews or other persecuted peoples. The world had come to such a pass that not killing Jews and allowing them to breathe the fresh air freely was considered a tremendous altruistic deed. But there were still deeper reasons for the pro-Soviet sentiments, besides gratitude and admiration for their valour. World War Two had revealed the atrocious character of racist nationalism gone mad, just as the Great Depression had earlier confirmed to so many non-Marxists the bankruptcy of capitalism. The ruling groups of all the Eastern European countries – with the possible exception of Czechoslovakia – had played themselves out by then, by having dismally failed to defend their countries against Hitler or by having treacherously made common cause with him. In such semi-feudal countries as Poland and Hungary a social revolution was long overdue. No wonder that the surviving Jews hastened to give a hand to a new beginning, to the building of Socialism in countries which had for centuries seen nothing but injustice and oppression. On the objective plane, the death of the millions of Jews in Poland, Rumania, Hungary and the Baltic countries meant the disappearance of a whole middle class of shopkeepers, artisans, middlemen, and in this respect considerable easing of the way to social ownership and Communist planning. Old Jewish Communists, who had spent half a lifetime in prison and had suffered martyrdom for their convictions, saw in Soviet-imposed Communism – notwithstanding its less attractive 'transitory' aspects – the fruition of their most cherished dreams, while many non-Communist Jews flocked into the party as a haven calculated to offer them a sense of belonging and purpose, after they had lost all their next of kin as well as the spiritual home of a closely knit Jewish community.

The surviving Jews were picked up by the Russians as the most reliable instrument of their policies in the lands on the Soviet perimeter. The native intelligentsia could not overcome its nationalist loathing of Russia; but the Jews had every incentive to cooperate with the Soviets, and in some cases, little choice. Anna Pauker in Rumania, Rakoszy in Hungary, Jacob Berman and Hilary Minc in Poland, Slansky in Czechoslovakia became associated in all minds with Stalinism. The revulsion against the latter, not a little hastened by non-conformist Jewish intellectuals like the Polish-Jewish poet Wazyk, author of the poem which became the marching song of the 1956 October uprising in Poland, forced out many Jews from positions of influence. But when the men of the Polish October uprising themselves became an establishment, fearful of criticism and the winds of change, the Jewish non-conformist intellectuals were proclaimed, as earlier in Stalinist Russia itself, rootless cosmopolitans, spineless sophists, perverse revisionists, finally part of the international Imperialist-Zionist-American conspiracy against the Socialist and peace-loving countries; a pernicious influence upon the simple, law-abiding and faithful masses, with their sound instincts and implicit trust.

As at the end of a Shakespearian tragedy, the stage is strewn with corpses. Leon Trotsky has his skull split by the axe of a Stalinist agent; Rosa Luxemburg's battered body is dragged out of the river; Kurt Eisner and George Landauer fall victims to assassins' bullets; Zinoviev, Kamenev and so many others are hanged in the small hours in some cellar; Slansky perishes as a traitor; the Paukers, the Bermans, are dying in oblivion and obloquy. The survivors live not only to be dismissed from their posts and abused, but to be told in the words of one Polish official spokesman, that no self-respecting movement could allow a disproportionate number of the members of an alien race to have an undue influence on its national policies[121] – this from the mouth of a representative of a regime which claims to derive its inspiration from the cosmopolitan German Jew, Karl Marx, and guidance from the teachings of the son of a hereditary enemy nation, Lenin.

The story seems to have come full circle. Preachers of revolutionary universalism and of the subordination of national sovereignty
to the interests of the whole Socialist community, place racial
uniqueness above revolutionary universalism – where the Jews are
concerned. It is they, and not the nationalist-racists of old, who are
putting an irreversible and irrevocable end to a thousand years of
Jewish history. One is reminded of another momentous development many centuries earlier. No sooner had the pagan nations
joined the Jewish sect than they turned in fury against the be-
getters of their religion.

A little while ago it seemed as if the book 'Jews and Revolution'
had been closed. But it appears now that new pages are to be
added to it, in the turbulent universities of America and Europe
and in the tumultuous conclaves of riotous demonstrators. This
time it is not oppression or humiliation that egg on the young Jews,
children of comfortable homes and young men to whom the
whole world seems to be open, to rebel and often to lead the
rioters: the Pavel Litvinovs and Ginsburgs in Russia, the Gins-
bergs and Rudds in the US, the Cohn-Bendits in Europe, not to
speak of such veterans, loaded with memories of some three
scores of years of turmoil and disaster, as Herbert Marcuse.
They seem to be driven by the kind of guilty conscience that
plagued the Russian intelligentsia in the nineteenth century. The
descendants of countless generations of victims of injustice, and the
heirs to a most ancient tradition of revolt against it, they feel
uncomfortable, unhappy and guilty for being comfortable, while
there is so much evil and falsehood around; 'a little more so' than
their Gentile comrades, because of the great intensity peculiar to
their race, and the unquenchable spirit of non-conformism and
restless quest which partly at least stems from the lack of a
firm Jewish commitment and an anchorage in a vital collective
experience. The latter makes the Jewish rebels turn with obvious
self-hatred against their own race. Having absorbed the criteria of
the detractors of Judaism and never having quite come to terms
with their Jewishness – in a positive or negative way – they are

unable to take Judaism as it is for granted. They are defying it with standards which can never be met, and attack Israel with ferocious glee for its 'crimes'. Ultra-internationalists, they become racists where Jews are concerned. They are incidentally taking in that way their revenge upon parents who themselves preached 'revolutionary' values, but then settled down very comfortably to enjoy all the good things provided by our rotten society.

All the same, the European observer, with the European experience in his mind, cannot but wonder in a *déjà vu* mood, whither things are moving. There is to him something ominously familiar in such terms as the 'system' as something all embracing and indivisible and more real than individual men with their conscious ideas and free choices. Similarly sinister sounds the apotheosis of the existential situation, which makes those within it appear right and innocent whatever they do, and altogether dooms those outside. The devil is lying in wait for protagonists of such views, and behind him the mass murderer.

NOTES

1. Karl Marx and Friedrich Engels, *Selected Works*, Vol. I (Moscow: 1958), pp. 37–8 ('The Communist Manifesto').
2. Sir Lewis Namier, *Vanished Supremacies: Essays on European History 1812–1918* (London: 1958), pp. 21 ff.
3. Charles Vellay, *Oeuvres Complètes de St. Just*, Vol. II (Paris: 1908), p. 248.
4. Alexis de Tocqueville, *Oeuvres Complètes*, 9 vols., Vol. IX (Paris: 1864–6), pp. 2, 3.
5. François Guizot, *Memoires Pour Servir à l'histoire de Mon Temps*, 8 vols., Vol. II (Paris: 1858–67), pp. 257–8.
6. Tocqueville, *loc. cit.*
7. K. Marx and F. Engels, *loc. cit.*
8. Simon Dubnow, *Weltgeschichte des Jüdischen Volkes*, Vols. VIII–IX (Berlin: 1929); Jacob Katz, *Tradition and Crisis* (in Hebrew), Part III (Jerusalem: 1958); Maurice Liber, 'La Revolution, les Juifs et le Judaisme', in *Univers Israélite*, 25 août–1 sept., 1939; Hannah Arendt, *Rahel Varnhagen: Lebensgeschichte einer deutschen Jüdin aus der Romantik* (München: 1959); Eliahu Tscherikover, *Jews in Periods of Revolution* (in Hebrew) (Tel Aviv: 1957), Ch. I, pp. 23–103; Isaac Deutscher, *The Non-Jewish Jew* (London 1968), Chs. I–III.
9. Jacob Touri, *Turmoil and Confusion in the Revolution of 1848* (in Hebrew) (Tel Aviv: 1968); Achille E. Halphen, *Recueil des Lois concernant les Israélites en France* (Paris: 1851), p. 187.
10. K. Grunwald, *Europe's Railways and Jewish Enterprise*, Leo Baeck Institute Yearbook XII, 1967; D. Landes, *Bankers and Pashas* (London: 1958).
11. Karl Marx, *Early Writings*, Translated and edited by T. B. Bottomore (London: 1964), p. 34.
12. Bruno Bauer, *Die Judenfrage* (Braunschweig: 1843), p. 14; Jacob Touri, *op. cit.*, p. 198; Nathan Rotenstreich, *For and Against Emancipation: The Bruno Bauer Controversy*, Leo Baeck Institute, Yearbook IV (London: 1959).
13. E. Silberner, *Anti-Semitic Tradition in Modern Socialism* (Jerusalem: 1953), p. 2; A. Toussenel, *Les Juifs, vers de l'époque histoire de la féodalité financière* (Paris: 1845–7), pp. 73–4; George Lichtheim, 'Socialism and the Jews', *Dissent*, July–August 1968, pp. 314–42.
14. Saint-Simon, *Oeuvres Choisis*, Vol. II, pp. 328 ff.
15. J. L. Talmon, *Political Messianism – the Romantic phase* (London: 1960), p. 96.
16. Quoted in Lichtheim, *op. cit.*, p. 321.
17. Mikhail Bakunin, *Gesammelte Werke*, ed. Nettlau, 3 vols., Vol. III (Berlin: 1921–4), pp. 204–16; E. Silberner, *Western Socialism and the Jewish Question* (in Hebrew) (Jerusalem: 1955), p. 354; Lichtheim, *op. cit.*, pp. 323, 338.
18. P. J. Proudhon, *Carnets: Texte inédit et integral*, ed. P. Haubtmann, Vol. II (Paris: 1960–61), pp. 337–8; Lichtheim, *op. cit.*, p. 322.

19. J. L. Talmon, *The Origins of Totalitarian Democracy*, Part III (London: 1952); *Idem., Political Messianism*; Ph. Buonarotti, *Conspiration pour l'egalité* (Bruxelles: 1828); A. B. Spitzer, *The Revolutionary Theories of Louis August Blanqui* (New York: 1958); E. H. Carr. *Bakunin* (London: 1937); *Idem., Studies in Revolution* (London: 1950).

20. G. Scholem, *Messianic Idea in Judaism and Other Essays in Jewish Spirituality* (New York: 1970).

21. Edmund Silberner, *Moses Hess* (Leiden: 1966), p. 29: Hess Tagebuch. 13 July 1835.

22. *ibid.*, p. 27.

23. Saint-Simon, *Oeuvres de St-Simon et d'Enfantin*, Vol. VI (Paris: 1865–78) pp. 43–4.

24. Shlomo Na'aman, *Ferdinand Lassalle: Deutscher und Jude* (Hannover: 1968).

25. See below in: 'Types of Jewish Self-Awareness'.

26. Edmund Silberner, *Moses Hess*, p. 1.

27. J. L. Talmon, *Political Messianism*, pp. 210 ff.; Shlomo Avineri, *The Social and Political Thought of Karl Marx* (Cambridge: 1968).

28. Karl Marx, *Colonialism and Modernisation*, ed. S. Avineri (New York: 1968).

29. Ferdinand Lassalle, *Gesammelte Reden und Schriften*, ed. Eduard Bernstein, Vol. VI (Berlin: 1919): (1) 'Fichte's Politische Vermächtins und die neueste Gegenwort', (2) 'Die Philosophie Fichtes und die Bydeutung des Deutschen Volksgeistes'.

30. Jacob Touri, *op. cit.*, pp. 68, 72.

31. V. Valentin, *Geschichte der Deutschen Revolution 1848-9*, 2 vols. (Berlin: 1930–1); R. Stadelmann, *Soziale und Politische Geschichte der Revolution von 1848* (Müvehen: 1948); Jacques Droz, *Les Revolution Allemandes de 1848* (Paris: 1957); F. Fejto, ed., *The Opening of an Era: 1848*, An Historical Symposium (New York: 1966).

32. J. Touri, *op. cit.*, pp. 118–19.

33. Benjamin Disraeli, *Life of George Bentinck* (London: 1905) Ch. XXIV: 'The Jewish Question'; Cecil Roth, *Benjamin Disraeli* (New York: 1952); Robert Blake, *Disraeli* (London: 1966).

34. I wish to thank Dr J. Touri for placing at my disposal the relevant issues of *Israel's Herold*.

35. Eliahu Tscherikover. *op. cit.*; E. Litwak, *Selected Writings* (in Yiddish). (New York: 1945); *idem., Things Past* (in Yiddish) (Ohio: 1925); M. W. Rosenbaum, *Memoires of a Revolutionary Socialist* (in Yiddish) (New York–Warsaw: 1924); Xenia, *With my Generation* (in Hebrew) (Haifa: 1956); J. Maor, *The Jewish Question in the Liberal and Socialist Movements in Russia 1890-1914* (in Hebrew) (Jerusalem: 1963); Victor Tchernov, *Jewish Leaders in the Socialist-Revolutionary Movement* (in Yiddish) (New York: 1948); Lev Deich, *Jews in the Russian Revolution* (in Yiddish) (Berlin: 1923); Israel Getzler, *Martov* (Cambridge: 1967); Leonard Schapiro, 'The Role of the Jews in the Russian Revolutionary Movement', *Slavonic and East European Review*, Vol. XL, 1961–2; F. Venturi, *Roots of Revolution* (New York: 1960); A. Yarmolinsky, *Road to Revolution* (New York: 1962).

36. E. Tscherikover. *Jewish Revolutionaries in Russia in the 1860s and 1870s*, Historical Studies of Yivo, Vol. III (Paris: 1939) (in Yiddish). For the whole present chapter I have been leaning very heavily on this most important and

detailed study which also forms a part of E. Tscherikover's above-cited more comprehensive book. The following references are from the Yiddish original.

37. A. Tscherikover, *op. cit.*, pp. 124 ff.; Thomas Masaryk, *The Spirit of Russia*, 3 vols., Vol. II (London and New York: 1955), Ch. XIV, XV, XVIII, XIX.

38. Th. Herzl, *The Diaries of Theodor Herzl*, ed. M. Lowenthal (London: 1958) p. 395; Quoted in L. Schapiro, *op. cit.*, p. 148.

39. L. Haimson, *The Russian Marxists and the Origins of Bolshevism* (Cambridge Mass: 1955), p. 60.

40. A. Tscherikover, *op. cit.*, pp. 126 ff.

41. *ibid.*, pp. 140–41.

42. *ibid.*, pp. 142–3; A. Yarmolinsky, *Road to Revolution* (New York: 1962).

43. A. Tscherikover, *op. cit.*, p. 132.

44. *ibid.*, pp. 138–40.

45. *ibid.*, pp. 145 ff.

46. *ibid.*, p. 150.

47. *ibid.*, p. 158A.

48. *ibid.*, pp. 136–7.

49. Lucy Dawidouriz, ed., *The Golden Treasury* (New York: 1967), pp. 406–7.

50. *ibid.*, p. 406.

51. *ibid.*, p. 410; A. Tscherikover, 'Revolutionary and Nationalist Ideologies among the Jewish Intelligentsia in Russia in the 1870s and 1880s' (in Hebrew), in *Jews in Periods of Revolution*, pp. 366–420.

52. A. Tscherikover, *Jewish Revolutionaries*, p. 160.

53. Victor Tchernov, *op. cit.*

54. J. L. H. Keep, *The Rise of Social Democracy in Russia* (Oxford: 1963), pp. 107 ff., 131 ff.; L. Schapiro, 'The Role of the Jews in the Russian Revolutionary Movement' in *Slavonic and East European Review*, Vol. XL, 1961–2. L. Schapiro, *The Communist Party of the Soviet Union* (London: 1960); Haimson, *op. cit.*, pp. 167 ff.; Dan, *The Origins of Bolshevism* (London: 1964), pp. 243 ff.; I. Getzler, *Martov*, pp. 75 ff.

55. Tscherikover, *Jewish Revolutionaries*, pp. 82 ff.

56. E. H. Carr, *The Bolshevik Revolution*, Vol. I (London: 1954), pp. 5–6; Keep, *op. cit.*, p. 116.

57. J. L. Talmon, *The Unique and the Universal* (New York: 1965), pp. 180 ff.; George Lefranc, *Le Mouvement Socialiste sous la troisième Republique, 1875–1940* (Paris: 1963), pp. 102 ff.

58. Peter Gay, *The Dilemma of Democratic Socialism* (New York: 1952); Koppel S. Pinson, *Modern Germany* (London: 1966) Ch. X, 'The Socialist Tradition'; J. Labedz, *Revisionism* (London: 1962).

59. R. A. Kann, *The Multinational Empire*, Vol. I–II (New York: 1964); Otto Bauer, *Die Nationalitätenfrage und die Sozialdemokratie* (Wien: 1907).

60. Z. A. B. Zeman and W. B. Scharlau, *The Merchant of Revolution: The Life of Alexander Israel Helphand (Parvus) 1867–1924* (London: 1965).

61. Winfried Scharlau, *Helphand Parvus der Theoretiker* (Düsseldorf: 1964), p. 290.

62. *ibid.*, pp. 111–12.

63. J. Nettl, *Rosa Luxemburg*, 2 vols. (London: 1966). Paul Frölich, *Rosa Luxemburg, Her Life and Work* (London: 1940).

64. Rosa Luxemburg, *Briefe ans der Gefänguis*, (Basel: 1945).

65. Yarmolinsky, *op. cit.*, p. 310; A. Tscherikover, *Jewish Revolutionaries*, pp. 129 ff.

66. I. Ignatieff (pseudonym), *Russisch-jüdische Arbeiter über die Judenfrage* (Neve Zeit: 1892), pp. 175–9.

67. Isaac Deutscher, *Trotsky: The Prophet Armed*, Vol. I (Oxford: 1954), pp. 101 ff., 149–162; Keep, *op. cit.*, pp. 191 ff., 198, 240 ff.

68. W. Scharlau, *op. cit.*, p. 95 ff.; Deutscher, *op. cit.*, pp. 103 ff, 119; Keep, *op. cit.*, pp. 191 ff.; Bertram D. Wolfe, *Three Who Made a Revolution* (Boston: 1948), pp. 284 ff; L. Trotsky, *The Permanent Revolution* and *Results and Prospects* (New York: 1965); Helphand Parvus, *Der Arbeitersozialismus und die Weltrevolution* (Berlin: 1919); Iden, *Die Gewerkschaften und die Sozialdemokratie*, Dresden, 'Sächsische Arbeiterzeitung', 1896; idem., *Der Iddenkampf gegen den Sozialismus* (Berlin: 1910); idem., *In Kampf un die Wahrheit* (Berlin: 1918); idem., *Der Klassenkampf des Proletariats* (Berlin: 1911); idem., *Die Kolonialpolitik und der Zusammenbruch* (Leipzig: 1907); idem., *Der Staat, die Industrie und der Sozialismus* (Dresden: n.d.); idem., *Wohin führt die politische Massregelung der Sozialdemokratie;* 'Sachsische Arbeiter-Zeitung' (Dresden: 1897); Rosa Luxemburg, *Gesammelte Werke*, edited by Clara Zetkin and Adolf Warski, Vols. 3, 4, 5; idem., *Briefe an Freunde* (Hamburg: c. 1950); idem., *Die Krise der Sozialdemokratie von Junius* (Berlin: 1916); idem., *The Russian Revolution* and *Leninism or Marxism* (Ann Arbor: 1961–2).

69. Carl Shorske, *German Social Democracy 1905–17* (Cambridge Mass: 1953) p. 290; Hermann Heidegger, *Die Deutsche Sozial-Demokratie und der Nationale Staat, 1870–1920* (Göttingen: 1956); Merle Fainsod, *International Socialism and the World War* (Cambridge Mass: 1935); M. Drachkovitch, *Les Socialismes et Allemand et le Problème de la Guerre, 1870–1914* (Genève: 1953).

70. Heinrich, Ritter von Srbik, *Deutsche Einheit* (Munich: 1935); Sir Lewis Namier, *1848: The Revolution of the Intellectuals* (London: 1946).

71. George Mosse, *The Crisis of German Ideology* (New York: 1966); Hans Kohn, *The Mind of Germany* (New York: 1960).

72. Dietrich Eckart, *Der Bolshevismus von Moses zum Lenin*, quoted in Ernst Nolte, *Three Fasces of Facism* (New York: 1965), pp. 329 ff., 406.

73. G. Mosse, *op. cit.*; Hannah Arendt, *The Origins of Totalitarianism* (New York: 1958); Fritz Stern, *The Politics of Cultural Despair* (New York: 1965).

74. Eugen Weber, *Action Francaise* (Stanford: 1962); P. G. Pulzer, *The Rise of Political Anti-Semitism in Germany and Austria* (New York: 1946).

75. Adrien Dansette, *Le Boulangisme* (Paris: 1946); Walter Frank, *Demokratie und Nationalismus in Frankreich der Dritten Republik* (Hamburg: 1933) pp. 135–252; René Rémond, *La Droite en France; de la Première Restauration à la Ve République*, 3rd edition (1966); Edouard Drumont, *La France Juive*, 2 vols., (Paris: 4th edition).

76. Jacques Chastenet, *Histoire de la Troisième République*, Vol. II (Paris: 1952–62), p. 110.

77. Erich Eyck, *Bismarck*, 3 vols., Vol. III (Erlenbach-Zurich: 1941–44), pp. 278 ff., esp. pp. 286–7.

78. Koppel S. Pinson, *op. cit.*, Ch. IX, 'The Catholic Tradition'; Paul W. Massing, *Rehearsal for Destruction. A Study of Political Anti-Semitism in Imperial Germany* (New York: 1946), pp. 14 ff.

79. D. H. Lawrence, *Fantasia of the Unconscious: The Lower Self*, p. 209.

80. Joseph Dorfman, *Thorsten Veblen and His America* (New York: 1947), pp. 424-6, 242, 323.

81. J. A. Gobineau, *Essai sur l'Inégalité des Races Humaines*, 2 vol. (Paris: 1933); Houston Stewart Chamberlain, *Die Grundlagen des XIX Jahrhunderten*, 9th edition, 2 vol. (München: 1909) Ch. V; Heinrich von Treitschke, *Deutsche Geschichte in Neunzehuten Jahrhundert*, Vol. III (Leipzig: 1927) Ch. 9: 'Radikalismus und Judentum', pp. 701–14; idem., *Ein Wort über Unser Judentum* (Berlin: 1881); Massing, *op. cit.*, Part II, Ch. VI, VII; R. Fr. Byrnes, *Antisemitism in Modern France* (New Brunswick: 1950), P. G. Pulzer., *op. cit.*; H. Arendt, *The Origins of Totalitarianism;* Ernst Nolte, *op. cit.*

82. Phil. Barrès, *Scènes et Doctrines du Nationalisme* (Paris: 1902).

83. Erik H. Erikson, *Childhood and Society* (London: 1951), pp. 311 ff., pp. 359 ff.

84. G. Himmelfarb, *Darwin and the Darwinian Revolution* (New York: 1968), Ch. VI; William Langer, *The Diplomacy of Imperialism* (New York: 1956), Ch. III.

85. Fr. Nietzsche, *The Genealogy of Morals* (Anchor Book: 1956), Ch. XVI.

86. J. L. Talmon, 'The Legacy of George Sorel', *Encounter* (Feb. 1970); J. H. Meisels, ed., *Pareto and Moseca* (New York: 1965).

87. J. L. Talmon, *loc. cit.*

88. A. Hitler, *Mein Kampf* (English translation) (New York: 1943), Chs. II, III; Alan Bullock, *Hitler: A Study in Tyranny* (New York: 1962), pp. 36 ff.

89. Hitler, *op. cit.*, p. 56.

90. Erikson, *loc. cit.*

91. Jacob Burckhardt, *Briefe an Fr. von Preen 1864–1893* (Stuttgart: 1922), pp. 144, 188.

92. Fr. Nietzsche, *The Dawn of Day*, p. 205.

93. R. Hollingdale, *Nietzsche, the Man and His Work* (London: 1965).

94. Massing, *op. cit.*, p. 107.

95. Drumont, *op. cit.*, Vol. I, p. 136: 'ils ont créé une question sociale, on la résoudra sur leur dos'; E. Silberner, 'French Socialism and the Jewish Question, 1865–1914,' in *Historia Judaica*, Vol. XVI (April: 1954); idem., 'Anti-Jewish Trends in French Revolutionary Syndicalism', in *Jewish Social Studies*, Vol. XV (1953).

96. E. Weber, *The Nationalist Revival in France, 1905–1914* (Berkeley: 1959); H. Arendt, *The Origins of Totalitarianism*, pp. 228–9.

97. Fr. Engels, in a letter of 9 May 1890, published in the *Arbeiter-Zeitung* of Vienna. See Massing, *op. cit.*, Document No. IX, pp. 311–12.

98. Alfred Bäumler, *Bildung und Gemeinschaft* (Berlin 1942), p. 81; *The Third Reich: A Collection of Essays on the National-Socialist Movement* (London: 1955); (published by Weidenfeld and Nicolson, under the auspices of the International Council for Philosophy and Humanistic Studies and UNESCO), III-V, XX, XXIII, XXVI-XXVII.

99. H. St. Chamberlain, *op. cit.*, Vol. I, Abschmitt II.

100. Herbert Marcuse, Otto Bauer, Arthur Rosenberg, et al., *Der Kampf gegen*

den Liberalismus in der Totalitären Staatsanffassung, in Faschismus und Kapitalismus (Frankfurt: 1967).

101. Norman Cohn, *Warrant for Genocide* (London: 1967), pp. 114–15.
102. *ibid.*, p. 113.
103. George Katkov, *Russia 1917: The February Revolution* (London: 1967), pp. 58–9.
104. *ibid.*, p. 60.
105. William Henry Chamberlin, *The Russian Revolution*, Vol. II (New York: 1965), pp. 91–2.
106. Norman Cohn, *op. cit.*, p. 128.
107. G. Haupt et J. Marie, *Les Bolsheviques par-eux-mêmes* (Paris: 1968).
108. Trotsky, *The History of the Russian Revolution;* 3 vols. (London: 1932–3); idem., *My Life*, (New York: 1960); *Deutscher, Trotsky*, Vol. I. (New York: 1965), p. 314; W. H. Chamberlin, *op. cit.*, Vol. I, p. 321.
109. Deutscher, *op. cit.*, pp. 298 ff.
110. W. H. Chamberlin, *op. cit.*, Vol. II, pp. 392 ff.
111. Erich Eyck, *History of the Weimar Republic* 12 vols., Vol. I (Cambridge, Mass: 1962–3), p. 45.
112. *ibid.*, p. 58.
113. *ibid.*, pp. 135 ff.
114. Rosa Luxemburg, *Wybor Pism (1908–1919)*, Vol. II, 1959, pp. 114 ff., Kwestja Narodowosciowa, Autonomja.
115. *ibid.*, pp. 56 ff. Socjalpatryotyzm w Polsce; Nettl, *op. cit.*, Vol. II, pp. 842–62; Appendix 2, 'The National Question'.
116. E. Nolte, *op. cit.*, p. 329.
117. *ibid.*, p. 328.
118. *ibid.*, p. 332.
119. *ibid.*, p. 406.
120. H. R. Trevor-Roper, *The Last Days of Hitler* (New York: 1966), p. 237.
121. Deutscher, *The Non-Jewish Jew*, Ch. III, 'The Russian Revolution and the Jewish Problem'; Andrzej Werblan, Przyczynek do Genezy Konfliktu, Miesiecznik Literacki, July 1968.

2

Types of Jewish Self-Awareness:
Herzl's 'Jewish State' after Seventy Years
(1896-1966)

The history of the Jewish people in the last two hundred years
could to a very large extent be treated as the history of Jewish
self-awareness. In the general ways of life there was, after all,
increasingly less to differentiate Jews from non-Jews. The ceaseless
effort of self-identification has been conducted not so much in the
form of soliloquy as in the form of dialogue. Under the impact
of every new ism – like rationalism, liberalism, democracy,
nationalism, dialectical materialism, socialism, indeed even
psychoanalysis – Jews would set about re-interpreting the
meaning of their existence and the mystery of their fate. Every
change in the socio-economic and political-cultural constellation
– to mention only the era of German liberalism, British tradition,
the American way of life – would give rise to another version of
Jewishness.

In perspective, Zionism may no longer appear as *the* response,
as was thought only a little while ago, but as the most significant
of the reactions of Jewry to the challenges of the modern world;
not the ultimate goal for which all Jewish history had served as a
kind of preparation, the total solution to all the riddles and the
final answer to all the evils which had beset our existence, but the
Jewish reaction to the most potent force in the modern world –
nationalism, and indeed the Jewish variety thereof. The wide range

of trends and orientations in Zionism itself, transposed as it has been on to the party structure of Israel, helps to bring into relief the image of Jewish history as a prism which absorbs and breaks the rays coming from outside, the inner, eternal kernel remaining all the time an intractable Kantian *Ding an sich* (thing in itself).

We propose treating Herzl's 'Jewish State'[1] rather as a station in the history of Jewish self-identification in modern times – conceived in terms of a dialogue – than as the ripe fruit of some entirely immanent development. On revisiting Herzl's 'Jewish State' on its seventieth anniversary – some fifty years after his ardent wish, the Charter, was realised in the form of the Balfour Declaration; at the end of nearly twenty years of Jewish state-hood; and a generation after the attempted 'final solution' to the Jewish question in Europe, which problem was uppermost in Herzl's mind to the point of having become an obsession – it is not only legitimate, but imperative to re-examine the vision of the 'Jewish State' from the vantage point of the Jewish world and the world in general at the end of the second third of this terrible century or ours, and to take a look at ourselves in the light of 1896–7.

An act in the dialogue: we have chosen to juxtapose Herzl's Jewish self-questioning, and the resolve which sprang from it in the late 1890's, with the ways in which two earlier and highly significant Jewish figures in the nineteenth century grappled with their Jewishness, the young Ferdinand Lassalle in the early 1840s, and Moses Hess some twenty years later in the early 1860s, in his *Rome and Jerusalem*, in order to see whether one would be entitled to assume a line of evolution.

I

In the *Nachgelassene Briefe und Schriften* of Ferdinand Lassalle, superbly edited by the famous historian of Socialism and author of the massive biography of Friedrich Engels, Gustav Mayer,[2] we find in Vol. I. pp. 72 ff. a most interesting letter of the eighteen-year-old dreamer, dated 1843, and addressed to Dr

Theodor Creizenach, poet and literary critic, and one of the leading protagonists of reform in German Jewry, who, however, in 1854 took the road to Christianity.

Ferdinand Lassalle starts the letter by expressing his joy at the news that Dr Creizenach has founded in Frankfurt a society with the aim 'of breaking the rusty chains of Orthodoxy and restoring the anatomy of the human spirit, the inalienable eternal rights of which had been suppressed in Judaism for over fifteen hundred years'. To remain aloof from such an undertaking, whose goal must be 'to mediate between Judaism and the lights of the age' (*Zeitbildung*), would mean, again in the words of young Lassalle, 'indifference to human interests verging on irreligiosity, a sin'.

Lassalle interprets Dr Creizenach's intentions as comparable to the endeavours of the prophets of the Protestant Reformation over three hundred years earlier. Like the latter in the sixteenth century, the Jewish reformers in the nineteenth wished to return to the authentic source and kernel of the faith – the Bible – by jettisoning the deformities which had grown up in the intervening centuries, in Christianity the Catholic-Papal tradition, in Judaism the Talmud. But Lassalle perceives grave difficulties. Steeped in Hegelian modes of thought and expression, the young author takes it for granted that 'Mosaism' was the 'highest abstraction of the *Urzeit*', as well as a 'historic substance' which could not but develop and evolve. Well, that it did, giving rise to Rabbinic-Talmudic Judaism. No one could deny the provenance of the Talmud from Scripture. But how can one close one's eyes to the fact that although 'an organic development' of Mosaism, the Talmud stood in contradiction to 'the idea and theorems of the present'? And so although theoretically vindicated as a natural development, the Talmud was in practice to be set aside, in favour of pure Mosaism. But then could one say that authentic Biblical Judaism really accorded with the ideas and exigencies of the present stage in human progress?

Surely, even Protestantism had in spite of its avowed aspirations, not been able to reconcile an antiquated and 'surmounted phase of the Spirit' with the ideas of the time. While consciously and sincerely appealing to the apostolic example, it did in fact lead to rationalism and modern philosophy. What in 1517 was a world-historic event of a most revolutionary and progressive significance, would in 1843 be a totally retrograde step. Why should the Jews in 1843 look back, beyond the three hundred years since Luther, and not forward from the heights of the achievements of the intervening ages? It was no use ordering the 'dialectical stream of history' to retreat, and trying to turn a 'putrefied' substance into 'the foundation of a lifegiving present'.

Lassalle therefore defines the dilemma: The Talmud is to be negated, the restoration of Mosaism is inconceivable, what are you going to erect as a positive foundation of faith? Then there are the tactical difficulties. One must guard oneself against complete *Parrhesie* (sic) in these matters, Lassalle goes on to say. For to come out with the whole radical truth at once, would not only encounter the most passionate resistance on the part of Talmudic Judaism, but estrange even the most enlightened Jews who could not bear to have their till now most deeply cherished articles of creed submitted to 'the fire of criticism'. But we dare not remain behind the 'achievements of German scholarship and science', and isolate ourselves from the currents of the age.

Thus we see the sensitive and aspiring youth, who a few years earlier had had dreams of becoming a second Judah Maccabeus, painfully grappling with the question of Jewish identity and future.

In a letter a year later, May 13 1844, to his father, Ferdinand Lassalle writes jubilantly: 'The philosophy [of Hegel] has got hold of me, and I have been reborn, and [endowed] with a new spirit. That rebirth has given me everything: clarity, self-awareness ... the absolute powers of the human spirit, the objective substance(s) of ethics, reason, etc.; in brief, it has made me into Reason conscious of Himself.'[3] A little later came Lassalle's transition from young-Hegelianism to Communism, and this is reported in a letter to his father just a month later, June 12 1844, written under the impression of the famous uprising of the Silesian weavers. 'No, no, let there be no mistake about it. This is the beginning of that war of the poor against the rich, which is frightfully near. These are the first stirrings ... of Communism, which penetrates into and fills all our veins theoretically and practically.' And the march of Communism was irresistible. It could no more be halted, no more than the birth of a child out of the womb of the mother in travail could be stopped. Communism was emerging 'from the womb of all the ages of the past'. The mother had reached her zenith and fulfilled her destiny in that she became the source of a new life – concludes the young Hegelian.[4]

Against the background of these intense inner developments there comes in a letter to his mother, some six weeks afterwards July 30 1844[5] the following pronouncement on Judaism: 'The world of the Hebrew nation presents the image of accomplished ugliness of the extreme suppression (*Gedrücktheit*) of man by God, of the innermost fragmentation (*Zerissenheit*) and absurdity (*Haltlosigkeit*), in brief of the absolute self-alienation of the spirit.' The Jewish world was, as Hegel pertinently expressed it, 'the world of the wretched and pitiful (*erbärmliche*) personality'. 'The Jewish spirit had lost all foothold (*Halt*) and it was twisting and winding, like a worm in the sand, before the abstract Deity.' If emptiness (*Wesenlosigkeit*), worthlessness, disintegration 'are the characteristic marks of all the ideas of Jewry in the natural and human spheres', misfortune (*Unglück*) was the distinct characteristic of all Jewish history – its fate. The Jewish religion was the religion of utter bondage to the abstract spirit, God; the Jewish fate was that of irretrievable slavery. No other people has been so persecuted in history. Why? Judaism had been a phase in the spiritual evolution of mankind, but one which mankind was destined to overcome

What did that 'Jewish' station in the Spirit's march represent? Not necessarily something entirely squalid. Also a certain grandeur: the grandeur of the doom-laden. Judaism was animated by the conscious will to break 'with nature and creatureness' (*Kreatürlichkeit*), a close relationship common to all the older religions. Nature and the finite appeared to Jews as unsubstantial. The absolute substance was the abstract God. But the Jews remained in fact stuck in that unsubstantial empty world of the bodily creatures. Hence the misery of the Jew who hated his own inadequacy – that subjection to matter which to him signified nothingness. Hence the split personality of the Jew, and also incidentally his panic-stricken hostility towards the plastic arts and all beauty, the essence of which were 'harmony . . . the unity of man within himself', whereas the Jew suffered from an incurable split: 'the most cruel self-alienation that history has brought about'.

One should not overlook in all this – says Lassalle – the *'punctum saliens'*: 'The spirit conceived itself as absolute reality and truth not in its possession of the natural, [but] saw its essence in the liberty of the abstraction as opposed to the natural (*Natürlichkeit*), which earlier constituted its substance . . . If one likes, the very ugliness of Judaism was its beauty.' The painful break and split in the history of the spirit was unavoidable. The earlier unity had to be lost so that the spirit could become conscious of itself. – 'The period of that anguish that was Jewry.' The Jews had to bear the cross till Christianity was ready to heal the rift by making the spirit identical with 'the total principle of love'.[6]

We do not know how Lassalle's mother, the Breslau Jewess, hardly out of the ghetto, brought up on a kind of *Deitschmerisch*, spending most of her time if not in kitchen and nursery, then haggling with peasant customers behind the counter, reacted to such a highly philosophical belabouring of her people, or whether she even understood what it was all about. She was probably overawed by the flights of her young eagle. The blind adoration bestowed on gifted children by Jewish parents who had divested themselves of the fear of God and had not yet developed any deep impersonal loyalties, and therefore concentrated all their sentiments on the worship of their offspring, has contributed not a little to fostering that type of extremely egocentric Jew, who expects all men to burn incense at his feet, and treats the world as a stage to perform and astonish upon.

We do know that Lassalle turned away from his people and developed a thoroughly contemptuous hatred for them. He became possessed by that restless striving which – there can be little doubt – was due not merely to his volcanic energy and phenomenal ability, but to a gnawing uncertainty about his own identity, the very *Wesenslosigkeit* he was so quick to detect in

Judaism. There was the craving to ascend to the German world (pure spirit), and the inability to rise from the Jewish one (that of nature). He became therefore frantically anxious not to miss any single occasion of asserting his name and worth, as if in desperate need to test himself again and again, in a terrible hurry to succeed and achieve, for who knows, life may not be long enough. He throws himself into the fray on behalf of a wronged lady of aristocratic birth; he embarks upon a most ambitious scholarly undertaking designed to elaborate a new philosophy of law; he dons the mantle of Fichte as the national prophet of Germany; he gets himself acclaimed the dictatorial *Führer* of the German workers; he dreams of a Lassalle empire to replace the Hohenzollern dynasty; he believes he can outsmart Bismarck himself; with hidden though noble designs he tries to manipulate whole classes and nations; he is in the end killed in an absurd duel on behalf of a little damsel, again of high birth.[7]

II

Just about the time, in the early 1860's, when Lassalle, as if sensing his approaching death, was developing a phenomenal activity as Socialist and national German leader, Moses Hess was making his way back to Judaism. It was the same event that released their energies: the liberation of Italy. But how different was their reading of the meaning of the event, and consequently their aims. While to Lassalle the outbreak of the Italian war seemed to be the heaven-sent hour for the German movement of national liberation to take off in the form of a popular uprising and revolutionary war, the liberation of Rome inspired Hess with the vision of a liberated Jerusalem.

Although colleagues and political collaborators in the Socialist fold, no two men could have been more different than Lassalle and Moses Hess. Sir Isaiah Berlin in a brilliant aside rightly says that if ever there was a person of pure saintliness, the 'positively good man' of Dostoyevsky in *The Brothers Karamazov* and *The Idiot*, it was Moses Hess. And 'a Jewish Communist is the last human type in which Dostoyevsky would have looked for any semblance to his ideal.'[8]

If religiosity means the sense of utter dependence, the vibrant awareness of awful purport, the need to worship and serve, then Moses Hess was one of the most religious persons the world has ever seen. He went through life a true pilgrim, poor, utterly selfless, living only for others; eternally excited and thrilled, because of his unbelievable responsiveness; sensing everywhere tokens and signs of hidden meanings, vast happenings, cosmic designs coming to fruition; always discovering great men to worship, always searching for occasions to be of help – to the point of marrying a prostitute in order to redeem her; exploited, ill-used, mocked, insulted, rejected, but again and again with a smile of incomprehension and a shrug of the shoulders picking up his bundle and the pilgrim's staff to seek another cause to live for, and another good man to admire. He was like that holy man in the beautiful hassidic story: seeing a Jew breaking the Sabbath, the Rabbi went up to him and gently asked him whether he had forgotten that it was a Sabbath. When rebuffed by the sinner that he knew it was Sabbath, the holy man lifted his eyes to heaven: 'What a wonderful people you have, God! Break the Sabbath he will, but he won't tell a lie!'

The 'Communist Rabbi', and Nestor of German Socialism, had an uncanny gift of divination, and although anything but a thinker of rigorous coherence, he was capable of astounding intuitive flashes, and his powers of association were truly marvellous – all perhaps qualities of the seeker and seer. He could describe Karl Marx, then only twenty-three years old: 'My idol ... who will administer the last blow to medieval religion and politics; he combines the deepest philosophical seriousness with the most cutting wit; think of Rousseau, Voltaire, Holbach, Lessing, Heine and Hegel in one person, I say united, not thrown together (*zusammengeschmissen*) – and you have Dr Marx.'[9] In Lassalle Hess saw 'the man with the head of Goethe on Jewish shoulders'. He forged that little link in the chain which became the bridge from young-Hegelianism into Marx, and then threw out a complete theory of Jewish nationalism.[10]

Although Hess speaks of the re-awakening of his Jewishness, his theory of Jewish nationalism was by no means the ripe fruit of Jewish thought or the articulation of truly personal Jewish experience which had reached self-awareness. Anyone with the slightest acquaintance with Western thought in the nineteenth century will find no difficulty in deciphering Herder, Saint-Simon, Hegel, Mazzini, Michelet, to some extent even Marx and Proudhon. These are applied by Hess to the Jewish phenomenon, or, if one prefers, Judaism is re-interpreted by Hess in their light.

After an estrangement of twenty years, I am back with my people. I have come to be one of them again, to participate in the celebration of the holy days, to share the memories and hopes of the nation, to take part in the spiritual and intellectual warfare going on within the House of Israel, on the one hand, and between our people and the surrounding civilised nations, on the other, for though the Jews have lived among the nations for almost two thousand years, they cannot, after all, become a mere part of the organic whole. A thought which I believed to be forever burned in my heart, has been revived in me anew. It is the thought of my nationality, which is inseparably connected with the ancestral heritage and memories of the Holy Land, the Eternal City, the birthplace of the belief in the divine unity of life, as well as the hope in the future brotherhood of men.[11]

It is important to note that even in his return to the tents of Israel, he is no more than Lassalle, both true children of the Hegelian and Messianic philosophy of the age, able to treat the case of Israel as *sui generis*, and an end in itself, but feels compelled to link it with the vision of universal unity and brotherhood of men. Only for Lassalle the Jewish 'moment' in world history had to be overcome, whereas for Hess it was the guarantee of some final universal fruition.

About that time, 1860, Lassalle wrote about the Jews: 'I do not like the Jews at all, indeed in general I abhor them. I see in them only degenerate sons of a great, but long past, age. In the course of centuries of bondage those people acquired the characteristics of slaves, and this is why I am extremely unfavourable (*ungünstig*) to them.'[12]

While seemingly employing Jewish terms of reference, Hess in fact re-echoes general modes of thought which were current at the time and with which he was intimately familiar. Thus he tells us that his reconversion to Judaism was due to the inspiration he had received from an anonymous Jewish lady in sorrow, and the letters which compose *Rome and Jerusalem* are addressed to her. 'Every Jewess . . . a Mater Dolorosa', a redemptress. In spite of what Hess says about the merits of the pious Jewish women in bringing about deliverance from Egypt and their destiny to bring about the future Messianic redemption, this is the pure romanticism of the Saint-Simonist school, with its vision of a Jewess as Mother-Messiah. The curious hint that whenever he found himself in a state of anguish at the parting of the ways, he always sought and found succour in a woman reads as if almost verbatim taken from a letter by Mazzini.[13] Hess's glorification of the Jewish family too owed no doubt something to Proudhon's cult of the family. In his monumental biography of Hess, Professor E. Silberner traces another inspiration of *Rome and Jerusalem*, namely Armand Levy, to whom Hess makes a number of references. Levy was a scion of a baptised French-Jewish family who became an ardent Jewish-Zionist nationalist under the influence of the great Polish poet Adam Mickiewicz. The two joined hands in 1853–4 in an attempt to raise a Polish and Jewish legion to fight against the Tsar in the Crimean war, with the hope of regaining Poland and Palestine.[14]

Hess claims to have experienced his first Jewish awakening at the time of the famous Damascus blood libel in 1840. But his service in the cause of the world proletariat made him soon forget his Jewish sorrow. An awakening or a re-awakening, his Jewish experience of twenty years after was stimulated not so much by anti-Semitism as by the quest for a salvationist truth, and the promise of its coming victory implicit, as he believed, in the liberation of Italy.

Hess does not really argue against anti-Semitism, of which Hess was not of course unaware, and with which he was not unconcerned. He directs all his critical acumen against Jewish religious reformers and assimilationists. And he does that entirely in the spirit of Herder and Mazzini.[15] Desirous of appearing as enlightened

humanitarians, the Jewish reformers were emasculating and falsi-
fying a concrete, historical, living and authentic substance in
favour of a pale lifeless abstraction: universalist deism and humanitarian benevolence. But the historic, genuine personality of the
Jews had found its articulation in historic memories, beliefs,
customs, rites. In this respect it was impossible to dissect and sever
an organic whole into a pretended rational essence and supposedly
historic accidents, external excrescences. The life and antecedents
of the individual were rooted in a social-historical texture, for no
one was able to live alone and by himself, and we received more
than we gave, inherited more than we created. In other words,
the most real thing in history was the life of the nation, the race, in
comparison with which the individual was a mere abstraction, in
isolation a shrivelled leaf. But abstract universalism could not of
course exist without isolationist individualism. In brief, all that
frantic anxiety of Jewish reformers to divest the Jewish religion of
all that was specific to it, historical memories, national pride, re-
miniscences of and hopes for Zion, not to speak of those who were
trying to run amok away from the Jewish fold, showed only pitiful characterlessness, indeed lack of self-respect and even honesty,
and not a striving for light. Far from a way to equality and happiness, it betokened irretrievable inner misery. Hess states emphatically that if he had the choice before him of either equality at the
price of assimilation or the maintenance of Jewish identity in a
ghetto existence, he would unhesitatingly choose the latter. If he
were convinced that sacrificial offerings were an essential part
of the Jewish religion, he would insist on their restoration in the
future Temple.

Hess almost justifies anti-Semitism if it takes the form of a de-
fensive reaction of Gentiles rooted in their nation and past to
Jewish over-eager and gate-crashing attempts to prove themselves as good and even better Germans or Frenchmen than themselves. Hess recalls the wounding incident of twenty years earlier.
At the time of the Franco-German tension around 1840, the patriotic German poet Nicolas Becker wrote the famous poem *They
will not have it, the German Rhine*. Hess got so excited by that
Marseillaise that he sent the author a musical composition for his

hymn. Becker wrote back a frigid letter of acknowledgement and then scribbled on the cover as if from a foreign hand 'You are a Jew'. Remembering the incident Hess feels less disgusted or hurt by the rudeness of the poet, than ashamed of himself.[16]

Following in the footsteps of Herder and the other philosophers, Hess seems to deny reality to any abstract dogmatic religious doctrine. There are ultimately no universal religions, there are national cults. It was not the Jewish religion that shaped the Jewish nation: the Jewish genius engendered that type of religion (future Ahad Ha'am?), just as medieval Christianity was more an expression of the Germanic spirit than the pure Christian message. Hess is too much of a Hegelian and indeed too much of a Marxist to admit the distinction between pure spirituality and concrete external phenomena, spirit and matter, theory and practice. This enables him to elevate the Jewish phenomenon into a decisive force in the history of mankind.

The two most remarkable religions of antiquity were national religions, the Greek and the Jewish. The Greek was that of nature, the Jewish of history, that is to say grounded upon historic events, Abraham, the exodus etc., but also upon a messianic vision of the purposeful unity of history in the hands of Providence. It was a national religion also in the sense that its concern was not the individual, but the nation and its fate, not his personal salvation or immortality, but social justice. The Jewish religion made in that respect no distinction between private ethics and the general interest, individual conscience and the laws of the land. Stern and exacting, it left the individual no easy escape into a private realm of human frailty and self-indulgence.

It was the decay of national sentiment at the end of the ancient era that turned Christianity into an abstract universal religion, and at the same time into the faith of the individual. Owing to that gap between its Judaic provenance and the concrete personalities of the barbarian races in Europe, Christianity was forced to become that exclusively spiritual religion which severs theory from practice, the individual from the collectives, by making original sin the basis for the perpetuation of this dualism. Weak, sinful men will never be able to realise perfect justice, to live by the light of the pure truth. They will never be able to redeem themselves by their own exertions. Only grace from above embodied in a church of superior priests, could save them. This led to self-contempt, resignation. It encouraged the self-willed to oppress the lowly, and deprived the exploited of any pride and strength necessary to resist and fight for their rights.

When the Reformation and Descartes brought the Christian dualism to culmination, the Jewish spirit, working through Spinoza, came astir, as it had fifteen hundred years earlier, to reassert the divine unity of life, nature and history. And then came the French Revolution and gave a most powerful impulse to the Judaisation of the modern world.

It broke the trauma of original sin-ridden society. Men felt free to shape their own lives, and confident that a just and perfect society would in every case be a national society, based upon the national characteristics, the history, the unique destiny of each nation, free and able to realise at last that positive freedom which comes from free self-expression. In this respect every nation will like the Jews evolve a national religion. As a society of free and equal men the nation of the future will be a true confraternity. The life of the nation will be a true partnership of all in all, things unlike the aggregate of classes hostile to one another, which the nations had been in the past. There will then be no distinction between the private and the general good. And since there will be no room for different standards, clash of interests, for that discrepancy between different imperatives, between theory and practice, every nation will become a real nation of priests, a holy nation, like the Jews. To Marx the expression of utter selfishness, Judaism is to Hess the very embodiment of the spirit of solidarity.[17]

The final defeat of the Papacy at the hand of Italian nationalism marked the ultimate victory of that uprising against the forces of old, of which the French Revolution was the first act. The rise of the Italian nation precisely upon the ruins of Papal Rome betokened the triumph of the principle of nationalities, the national cults. To this authentically Mazzinian prophecy Hess adds his gloss: the liberation of Rome presages the imminent liberation of Jerusalem to crown the process.

For the final revindication of universal justice and the reassertion of meaning in history, it was absolutely imperative, nay inevitable, that the people, whose earliest destiny was to foreshadow this late Messianic fruition, should be restored as of old. And all the nations will come to bow before the Lord, on Mount Moriah, and the Great Sabbath, the pre-ordained goal of all history, will come about.

There were other signs of that Second Coming. The idea of the restoration of the Jews to Palestine was steadily gaining momentum among Jews and Gentiles. France, the leader of nations, the standard-bearer of their liberation, was now directing her efforts towards the Middle East. The Suez canal had been dug. The Orient was awakening from its centuries-long slumbers. A French official close to Napoleon III, Laharanne, was crusading for a return of the Jews to Palestine as a spearhead in the effort of reviving the East with the help of Western dynamism. The nations of the West were ostensibly looking for a road to India. One such quest, centuries earlier, led to the discovery of America. Man proposes, God disposes. The present search was destined to engender another unexpected and momentous result: the restoration of Israel in his Land.

The revival of the Jewish national consciousness through Jewish learning, above all the national conception of Jewish history represented by Graetz, the vitality of hassidism – the religion of the heart – the multiplication of Zionist programmes in various parts of the world, were all tokens of the ripening of the Jewish national resolve.[18]

Hess reveals an ambiguity of the most far-reaching significance. The dilemma and the solution proposed by Hess remind one irresistibly of the French prophet-historian Michelet, whom the author of *Rome and Jerusalem* of course knew. Largely influenced by his interest in the sciences on the one hand, and by Ernest Renan on the other, Hess came to regard race as a primary datum, and a present-day reader is made to feel somewhat uncomfortable by his hymns to the purity and tenacity of the Jewish race. Without, of course, the latter-day implications, Hess accepts the fundamental division into Semitic and Aryan races. The unique and

integral character of the Jewish heritage was to him, as already
hinted, the result of race.[19]

At the same time Hess's fondest dream, in fact the sole way of
vindicating meaning and purpose in history, was the future
universal harmony of free nations. With the aid of quite fanciful
and abstruse speculations, Hess tries to prove that the cosmic
evolutionary process was about to be accomplished in the 'historic
Sabbath': social harmony within each national society and international concord, both represented by Judaism and post-rev-
olutionary France, were about to be enthroned, bringing thus to
final consummation the evolutionary cosmic process which had
already resulted in the wonderful harmony in nature. This
consummation demonstrates to Hess as to Michelet the victory
of the spirit over matter, of free reason over blood and soil de-
terminism, of history over geography, of willed unity over
irrational multiplicity.[20]

The gravamen of Hess's argument against the Germans is that,
unlike the French and the Western nations, the Germans had
remained steeped in exclusive, instinctive racialism, and of course
anti-Semitism, so that even their pretended philosophical universalism was in fact a rationalisation of racial pride, and their
irrational aversion to men of other races, especially Jews, was
never far below the surface. It is difficult to make out whether
Hess expected that German disposition to change. At all events, no
true unification of Germany seemed to Hess possible so long as
that racial exclusiveness remained a force, because it was indis-
solubly connected with the deep class divisions in German society
– the consequence of the fateful fact that the German social
revolution had been arrested in the sixteenth century with the
bloody suppression of the peasant revolt. And Hess could not
envisage a national rebirth which was not at the same time a
social-democratic transformation.[21]

Little did Hess, Mazzini, Mickiewicz and their like know that in
endowing nationalism with the dimension of a salvationist
religion, and in transferring to it so much of the Socialist appeal,
they were unwittingly offering a rationale to that type of racial,
exclusive nationalism, which Hess so abhorred among the

Germans, and indeed to anti-Semitism, in both its racial and social versions. 'Nationalism that is Socialism reduced to one country' – were the Fascists to say in the next century.

Terrible are the adventures or misadventures of ideas, and they mock the consoling prophecies of well-meaning humanitarian rationalists and their neat schemata and patterns of harmony.

But all this was in 1862 still in the womb of the future.

Actually the 1860's were the heyday of European liberalism, and of Jewish emancipation. The vindictive post-1848 reaction was everywhere giving way to more liberal tendencies on the morrow of the defeat of the Tsar Nicholas I, the implacable guardian of 'order', at the hands of the Western Powers in the Crimean War. In Russia itself Alexander II embarked upon a series of momentous reforms, of which the most important was, of course, the emancipation of the peasants. In Prussia the 'new course', started in 1859, gave the liberals and progressives strong majorities in the legislative assemblies. In 1867 Austria made a thorough house-cleaning and emerged a liberal multi-national Empire. The Tory Government under Disraeli accorded in 1867 the franchise to the urban proletariat. As the decade proceeded, the Imperial regime in France grew increasingly more liberal. The commercial treaty between England and France was a landmark, perhaps the greatest triumph of free trade in Europe. Across the ocean President Abraham Lincoln was winning his triumph in the cause of human freedom.

From the Jewish point of view this was the decade that saw Disraeli effectively in power, Lassalle creating the German labour movement, Fould administering the finances of France, the Rothschilds and Pereiras building up her credit system and carrying out her industrial revolution, a galaxy of able and influential Jewish parliamentarians playing a very considerable part in the Prussian *Landtag*, and Karl Marx presiding over the First International. Soon after 1870 clouds began to gather over a fair sky, and by 1890 the sky looked dark and menacing to Jews.

III

In 1896 Herzl speaks a different language from Lassalle in the
1840's, and Hess in the 1860's. This difference is accounted for not
only by personal differences, but by a change of historical
context.

On reading Herzl's *Judenstaat* with a detached mind and against
the background we have been trying to trace, the historian cannot
but be struck by the fact that whereas Lassalle seems not to give a
thought to anti-Semitism, and Hess only refers to it almost cas-
ually when speaking of the Germans, it is to Herzl a reality which
is overshadowing everything else. The same is true of Pinsker,
some fifteen years earlier. That flaming manifesto by a man who,
unlike Herzl, lived within the rich texture of the Eastern European
Jewish civilisation, was also born from a sense of injured pride,
and not from a positive consciousness of a distinct national
identity.

The mood of Herzl and Pinsker seems so remote from the
conquering, brash self-confidence of the young Lassalle with his
unquenchable faith in the imminent world revolution, an arrogance, incidentally, still alien to a Jew of an earlier generation,
with his feet still in the ghetto. It is worth quoting a description
of young Lassalle by Heine in 1846:

... a young man of the most distinguished mental gifts, the widest
learning, the most thorough scholarship and the greatest penetration I
have ever met. He combines the most extraordinary power of penetration with a vitality in knowledge and a skill in action which amaze me
... Lassalle is emphatically a son of the new age and will have nothing
to do with that renunciation and humility with which we in our time
more or less hypocritically bungled our way and drivelled our way
through life. This new generation is determined to enjoy itself and make
itself felt in the visible world; we older ones, bowing down humbly
before the invisible world, chased after shadow kisses and the scent of
blue flowers, renouncing and snivelling, and yet perhaps we were
happier than those tough gladiators who go forth so proudly to death
in battle.[22]

In the case of both Pinsker and Herzl it is not the pressure of some inner light seeking expression, as with Hess, but the fact of rejection by others that throws the authors, and the Jews, back upon themselves. They do not want us, so we shall be ourselves, for indeed we are different and we have a past and dignity, a character and values of our own.

Are we worse or less significant than the Serbs, the Rumanians and Bulgarians, who have just obtained or been granted national freedom? Who had ever heard of them in the West?

Earlier as well as later national movements have shown the same dialectic in their historical development: we are not they – the majority or ruling nation; we are different; we have to show what our distinctness consists of – the Czechs, Rumanians, Pakistanis, etc.

The other difference between Herzl and the earlier Jews is in the fact that Herzl completely eschews any attempt to establish a metaphysical or rather metahistorical connection between the Jewish phenomenon and the course and meaning of world history, or the universal trends of the age. This treatment of the Jewish issue as a case *sui generis* reflects again general developments. In the second part of the century, people in Europe had lost all taste for those sweeping generalisations and vast systems which the Romantic Age loved so much, and as a reaction a positivist analytical mood won dominance. Most national ideologies had started earlier in the century with the idea of a universal mission, with the conviction that their own nation or national history was an essential 'moment' in the evolution of mankind. The idea of mission so dear to the Jewish assimilationists, and in his own way to Hess, was a replica of the Mazzinian idea of *Roma Terza*, of the Fichtean ideology of *Urvolk*, the vision of Poland as the Christ of the nations, and the Russian Pan-Slav claim to some pristine purity and unadulterated excellence, destined to save the rotten West.[23] Only in the case of the Gentiles the mission was a justification for fostering a unique national identity in an independent state, while to the theorists of religious reform and assimilation among Jews it was precisely an argument against political nationalism and statehood, although –

a fact mostly overlooked by Jewish nationalists – not for giving up all Jewish distinctness.

The great German historian, Friedrich Meinecke, traced the evolution of German nationalism as a development from '*Weltbürgertum*' (world-citizenship) to '*Nationalstaat*'.[24] All nationalisms of Europe, with perhaps the exception of the oppressed nationalities of Tsarist Russia, had by the 1890's shed their association with universal ideologies or a European revolution. The nation had become an end in itself, and as such was free and even called upon to subordinate everything else to its well-being and to resort to any Machiavellian policies calculated to increase its power, without owing any account to any other nations or general causes, indeed even to accepted morality. As we shall see, that was emphatically not the conclusion of Herzl.

In the 1890's the Socialist movement in Europe was, in spite of the existence of the Second International since 1889, not a single camp with a supreme headquarters, but a loose federation of national parties. Not only did the Socialists prove unable to come to a genuine agreement – let alone, as events in 1914 were to show, carry it out – about united action to prevent war, but the Fabians in England, Bernstein's revisionists in Germany, and the moderate Socialists in France increasingly stressed the importance of a distinct national tradition in the evolution of their respective brands of Socialism. They accorded legitimacy to a war of national defence, and were indeed prepared to advocate imperialist expansion designed to spread civilisation and to create new possibilities for their own working class with the help of new markets. Was it really right and wise – some German social-democrats would ask – for us to leave the field entirely free to British imperialism, and thus incidentally surrender the votes of good, although somewhat patriotically befuddled voters at home to the vociferous promoters of national and imperial grandeur? Lenin had as yet hardly begun to preach his brand of proletarian internationalism to the Russians. It is often forgotten that up to 1917 Bolshevism was regarded in the West as a marginal Russian affair. It was only the 1917 revolution that resurrected the myth of the imminent world revolution guided from a supreme headquarters.

This Jewish 'isolationism' of Herzl's is one of the reasons why the texture of his *Judenstaat* is from the philosophical point of view so much thinner and poorer than that of Hess's *Rome and Jerusalem*. The lack of Jewish contents in Herzl's make-up deprived his pamphlet also of that warmth and limpidity which concrete experience, image and metaphor, recollection and reference – all present in Hess – might have given it. All the same, it is written with blood and white-hot passion, but, *horrible dictu*, it was also written to the rhythm of an utterly alien melody, as Herzl himself testifies:

> During the last two months of my residence in Paris [1895], I wrote the book 'The Jewish State'. I do not recollect ever having written anything in such an elevated frame of mind as I did that book. Heine says that he heard the wings of an eagle beat over his head while writing certain verses. I do believe that 'something also beat' above my head while I wrote that book. I worked at it every day until I was completely exhausted; my only relaxation in the evening consisted in listening to Wagner's music, especially to 'Tannhäuser', which opera I went to hear as often as it was performed. Only on those evenings when there was no performance at the Opera did I feel doubts about the correctness of my thoughts.[25]

Was Herzl unaware of all that Wagner stood for since the publication of that incredible pamphlet *The Jews in Music* well over forty years earlier?

The *Jewish State* became one of those brochures which, like Rousseau's *Social Contract*, Siéyès famous pamphlet, and the *Communist Manifesto*, set rivers on fire. Admittedly, and that is of course the secret of their phenomenal success, those were flaming torches which fell upon dry straw and not upon damp rubbish.

The *Jewish State* consists of two parts: an analysis of anti-Semitism or rather of the Jewish position as affected by it, and a blueprint for getting organised for settlement in the future Jewish territory: obtaining international support and creating the sinews for transporting and settling the immigrants in the way suggested by Herzl.

It would be an exaggeration to claim startling novelty or
original depth for the analysis of anti-Semitism in the *Jewish
State*. The treatment of the subject is more of a symptom than a
new message. In the first place, it reflects the personal experience of
Theodor Herzl, not as a unique case, but as an example. There was
the assimilated Jewish intellectual suddenly emerging as a Jewish
nationalist. The fastidious individualist who had previously been
affecting a mocking nonchalance, who was not merely free, but
also rather contemptuous, of facile, unthinking enthusiasms for
undifferentiated and crude isms and slogans, suddenly transformed
into a prophet, or if one likes a monomaniac, who will never tire
and never give up, brave the scorn of esteemed friends as well as
the most heart-rending failures, and compulsively refer any
fleeting impression or casual incident to his *idée fixe*. There was no
suggestion of a volcano, of steel or of the manager of man and
servant of causes in the earlier Herzl. What had been Herzl's
ambition before his conversion? To be a successful writer.

There is a most revealing confession in Herzl's diaries written
down almost exactly two years before his death.

Sometimes it happens that a man of worth is active in several fields.
Then he is certain to be recognised only in the field that is peripheral to
the real centre of his personality. Thus, for example, I have become
world-famous in a sphere where I have accomplished next to nothing
intellectually, but have merely displayed a mediocre political skill, attainable by anyone with a grain of horse sense, in a matter which only
blockheads cannot find crystal clear – there, in the Jewish question. I
have become a renowned propagandist. But as an author, particularly
as a playwright, I am held to be nothing. I am merely called a journalist. And I feel, I know, that I am by instinct a great writer, or was one,
who failed to yield his full harvest only because he became fed up and
discouraged.[26]

This *cri de coeur* of a tired man wistfully looking upon his past
and committing to paper a secret thought may be taken as another
proof of the extent to which Jews value the things of the spirit and
spiritual creativity above everything else. I can recall quite embarrassing incidents with famous Jewish leaders who had gained
not merely a niche in history, but an immortal place in it, un-

burdening themselves or off-guardedly dropping remarks which unmistakably revealed their sense of frustration at not having become scholars, authors or theoreticians, and an envy of intellectual mediocrities infinitely inferior to them. Of course this is a charmingly and touchingly Jewish trait.

Ludwig Lewisohn has in his very penetrating essay on Herzl suggested that Zionism was to Herzl a liberating experience which lifted him out of the frustrations of an *écrivain manqué*, a mediocre playwright and unsuccessful artist. This seems to me only a half truth.[27]

I believe Herzl's frustrations as an author were directly or through the mediating mechanism of association connected with his experience of anti-Semitism. Weighed down by both, he was for a long time unable to master either intellectually. A cerebral type, although capable of deep and fine feeling and animated by a romantic imagination, Herzl lacked the artistically creative daimon. His compositions, whether the sparkling feuilletons-essays, or the plays and short stories, were contrivances, not outpourings in heat. They might entertain, titillate, but they would not carry and sweep. It is difficult to say whether lack of roots in a closely knit milieu was not at least one of the reasons for that inadequacy. It takes a very great artist to turn rootlessness, ambiguous situations, and frustrations into the pure gold of art. There are not, however, many Kafkas about. Even Schnitzler, Herzl's successful Viennese author-friend, does not represent truly great literature, and one could not claim real originality and force for the pleiad of Jewish novelists who wrote in German earlier in this century, Jakob Wassermann, Werfel, the Zweigs and others. But more relevant, it seems to me, was Herzl's inability to sort out the difficulties, account for the reasons and reconcile himself to the fact that he lacked overwhelming creative genius as a writer, as we can see from his late confession. Where, when, in what way did he just miss that something essential? What slipped through his fingers? Had he only persevered a bit more ...

The same goes for anti-Semitism. Even a superficial acquaintance with the pre-Zionist Herzl suffices to show how intensely preoccupied he was with the phenomenon of anti-Semitism. That

so learned a man as Dühring should be capable of such horrifying
views on Jews shocked Herzl to his depths. There was no more the
consolation, resorted to by Jews in the earlier decades of the
century, that Jew-baiting was a medieval relic, a ruse utilised by
cunning clericals or feudal reactionaries for their selfish ends, something on the way out as the light advances. Moreover, like so
many educated Jews who lack any system of inner defences in the
form of positive Jewish experience, and who love and admire
Western civilisation with all their hearts, and indeed are completely
saturated with its values and modes of thought, Herzl could not
help viewing the Jews from outside, with the eyes and the yard-
stick of the Gentiles. The Jews have to engage in duelling. They
should observe the rules of medieval chivalry. In not doing that,
they show themselves to be lacking in courage and dignity, not
quite up to the requirements of the universal code of honour.
More significantly still, Herzl again and again returns to the point
that the Jews had a surplus of mediocre intellectuals, as if under-
scoring the anti-Semitic argument that the Jews were not endowed with creative gifts, but got along with glib and facile
improvisation – probably to Herzl a way of self-castigation. Did
not the anti-Semites scoff at the feuilleton, of which Herzl became
an acknowledged master, as a spurious Jewish kind of art, con-
coction and not creation? We may recall the half-despairing,
half-triumphant conclusion of Herzl's play *The New Ghetto*,
and still more to the point is Herzl's fantastic plan of a deal with the
Pope. On a beautiful Sunday morning all Jewish children in
holiday attire, with garlands of flowers on their heads, are mar-
ched up by their parents to the gates of the cathedrals as the church
bells toll. They are then ushered in for baptism, while the elders
remain outside, for they themselves would not – on a point of
honour – renounce their identity in exchange for full recognition
as equal citizens. As soon as the next generation of Jews have gone
through the ceremony of baptism, the priests in all the churches
read out a solemn condemnation of anti-Semitism by the Pope.
And that would put an end to a centuries-old predicament.[28]

Herzl gives the impression of a man suffering from a toothache.
He is told he must not touch it, but touch it he must. Herzl

manages to live down one anti-Semitic incident, and for a time encountering no similar unpleasantness, he begins to feel that after all one should not lose one's sense of proportion and be unduly weighed down by an occasional rudeness of a drunken bully. Then he suddenly and utterly unexpectedly on walking out of a beer cellar hears the 'Hep, hep!' call, and the shock is still greater than the last, and the malaise deepens. Why and how, and for what reason? And what is to be done so that such an honourable, highly cultivated man as he, who has never done any harm to anyone, should not be subjected to such indignities?

We all know the effect of the Dreyfus affair on Herzl. That France – 'the second fatherland', as Moses Hess repeatedly called it in the wake of Jefferson, of every enlightened person in the world, and especially, in view of France's pioneering role in granting emancipation, of every Jew wherever he be, and a country in which Jews formed a tiny minority only and were thoroughly assimilated – should give rein to such a frenzy of anti-Semitism, with the blessing of some of the greatest lights of the *Académie*, was indeed calculated to become a traumatic event to a man like Herzl.

But the Austro-Hungarian background was in my opinion still more important in gradually preparing that disposition which under the impact of the Paris shock evolved into a farouche obsession. The more democratic that ramshackle, multi-racial Empire grew, the more untenable became the old dynastic structure. Democracy involved not merely universal suffrage, but also national self-determination. The only linchpin of the Empire was the House of Habsburg, and its cement was the mutual hatreds of the races and the impossibility of severing them in a way that would satisfy each one, and also enable it to have a viable existence from the economic and strategic point of view. In an age of democracy and nationalism, it was extremely difficult to work up enthusiastic loyalty for a royal dynasty and an emotional response to its medieval-feudal symbols. The semi-religious humble loyalty of illiterate peasants – to a large extent of Slavonic stock – to the God-anointed apostolic Emperor-King had given way to nationalist zeal. On the other hand, the ethnic group which had for centuries formed the core and governing elite of the Empire, the Germans, had turned into a dangerous solvent in a way that was destined to have the most far-reaching and most disastrous effects on the world in general, and upon the Jews in particular.

With the growth of democracy the Austrian Germans began to feel that they were doomed to be swamped by the larger numbers of Slavs, whom they had ruled and despised for so long. The parliamentary system based on the counting of heads and on equal vote to all appeared as a mortal enemy. This gave rise to elitist-racist tendencies and agitation for a union of the Austrian Germans with the German Empire (through a disruption of the Habsburg Empire) into a vast state, powerful enough to crush the Slavs in between and on the periphery.

It is one of the great ironies of history that as a reaction the doctrinaire Austro-Marxists were driven to preach the unity of the Habsburg Empire, on the basis of very wide cultural autonomy for each ethnic group upon the model of the Jewish *Kehilla*. Their reason was that the disruption of the Empire by nationalism would be taken as proof that isolationist nationalism was stronger than international working-class solidarity, and nationalist separatism more real than the idea of a universal proletarian revolution, and politics more potent than economics and class struggle.

The Austrian Jews were in a peculiar position. All their interests and instincts were for the maintenance of the unity of the Empire. The supra-national pluralism of the easy-going and indulgent Empire was infinitely more favourable to them as individuals and as a community than the status of a minority within a homogeneous nationalist state. Jews were extremely prominent in the Socialist as well as the liberal leadership of Austria. It was this orientation as well as their role as competitors in the social-economic sphere that made the Jews the butt of German hatred, and turned the Austrian Germans into bitter anti-Semites, whether of the racialist Schönerer variety or of the Christian-Social brand of Leuger. Tragically enough, Austria's Jewish intelligentsia, with the exception of that of Galicia, was almost entirely German in language and culture, which was not of course calculated to endear it to the other nationalities of Austro-Hungary. A man like Herzl, who grew up in Budapest and was technically, like Max Nordau, a Hungarian, having settled in Vienna only when he was at the threshold of manhood, evinces in his writings neither interest in nor sentiment for the Magyar Kingdom. He is an Austrian *tout court*. For indeed, the Jews were the only Austrians, or if one likes, Austro-Hungarians, of the Empire.

The surrealist realities of Austria, a country whose situation, it was said, was desperate, but never serious, engendered three types of response: Hitler, Freud and Herzl, if one may be forgiven for invoking the three names in the same breath.[29]

Freud, as indeed also pre-Zionist Herzl, may be taken to represent the liberal Jewish frame of mind in Vienna around 1900. Its mouthpiece, the *Neue Freie Presse*, Herzl's newspaper, owned and run by assimilationist Jews, had won for itself a world-wide reputation for quality. Every issue of the journal was a feast for reflective readers and lovers of exquisite style, wit and elegance. But although it could boast very extensive international news coverage, and informed and penetrating comment on all events, it was not a militant organ at all. It was in fact prouder of its feuilleton than of its leading article. It cared more for opera, theatre, literature – all of universal appeal – than for party struggle. It was fundamentally apolitical, and it had a most curious way of dealing with phenomena and issues which disturbed it: ignore them. We know that the word 'Zionism' was never mentioned in its columns, although one of the paper's leading lights and its literary editor was running himself literally to death as its founder and head. We find a wry comment on this in Herzl's diaries. He was back from one of the Zionist Congresses where he had been worshipped like a king, and under the glance of his editor he sneaked into his room at the editorial office like a furtive little clerk who had overstayed his leave.

Ignoring Zionism! *Die Neue Freie Presse* never printed the word social-democracy, its liberal Jewish editor boasted to Herzl. That seems rather odd – reflects Herzl. I have not examined the old files of the great newspaper to find out, but one would in the

light of this be prepared for the fact that the word anti-Semitism
or the names Schönerer and Leuger were never or hardly ever mentioned. That was the way liberal assimilationist Jews everywhere
continued to behave for a long time. Charles Péguy, the
Catholic-Socialist Dreyfusard, says in his moving *Notre Jeunesse*
that the Jewish *haute bourgeoisie* in France would have liked nothing
better than to swallow the Dreyfus case and let the innocent man
die on Devil's Island, so that there be no noise. But men like
Bernard Lazare and others would just not let them.[30]

Now was this only ostrich-like cowardice? The late Namier
coined the abbreviation OTI – 'The Order of Trembling Israelites'. That the Jewish attitude did not betoken great courage needs
no proof. But it seems to me there was also something else, and
indeed something deeper, behind it. In one sense the cultivated
and well bred Jewish liberals tried to behave like civilised people
who would not allow foul language or bad manners in good
company, and when witnessing rudeness and coarseness pretended
not to see. In a deeper sense liberal rationalism and fairmindedness
simply refused to acknowledge irrational evil as real. Do not bother
about it, do not draw attention to it, do not provoke it by taking
it seriously. It will die of inanition. Then there was the deep, deep
Jewish sense of justice, which simply recoils from the spectre of
naked force and brutal violence, pure instinct and uninhibited
aggressiveness, and is simply unable to understand it. Whether this
is due to a special Jewish calling, as Ahad Ha'am wished it to be, or
is the reflex of a weak and persecuted race, which can only exist
in a civilisation based on respect for the rights of others, it remains
a fact that it is there. The liberal Jews were utterly incapable of
understanding such a defiant evil as Hitler. This is why for so long
they would not take him seriously.[31]

By the same token Jewish liberals could not but be individual-
ists. Any invocation of the sanctity of a national or religious
tradition, any appeal to the supremacy of the collective entity or
the pre-determined nature of a racial pattern, was in its implications highly inimical to Jews who desired nothing but equality and
assimilation.

While Hitler learned his diabolical lessons about the primacy of race and blood and instinct from Nietzsche, Houston Stewart Chamberlain and the Viennese anti-Semites, the Jew Sigmund Freud eschewed any interest in race and group, ideology and party, and turned to the individual man *per se*, to probe so deeply and so unflinchingly into the innermost springs of his being, to seek the mystery of his aggressiveness and perversion. All interpreters of Freud agree as to the neglect of the social group in his teaching. But controversy is still raging as to whether Freud was after all an optimist or a pessimist, whether he intended to offer a message of cure, or whether he really wished to convey the hopelessness of the human death instinct and perverse aggressiveness; whether he believed in the triumph of rationality or despaired thereof. Without claiming any competence to resolve this thorny question, I would venture to suggest that Freud himself was undecided in the matter, and a careful analysis would, I believe, show, how his vacillations corresponded to the experiences he went through, with – understandably enough – gloom marking the last phase of his heroic life.[32]

Herzl devotes no space in his writings to the nationalities struggle which was the most real issue in Austria and threatened to disrupt the Empire, having succeeded even in splitting the united Social-Democratic party of Austro-Hungary. But there can be little doubt that it brought home to him the reality of the group. Moreover, the fact of the Jew being attacked from all sides and by all nationalities, highlighted the *sui generis* nature of the Jewish predicament: its universality, and he hardly dared to go on – its hopelessness.

With all his awareness of the reality and significance of the entity, Herzl's Jewish nationalism derives from liberal and individualistic categories of thought. Yes, the Jews are a people, one people. Not because of a national spirit, a historic heritage of blood, but because the nations refuse to admit them as equals. They are a people, one people, but it will be more correct to say they have to become a people. The accent is upon national resolve, a sense of pride and purpose, finally organisation and recognition by others. This is a wholly rationalist, atomistic, political, almost contractual conception of a nation. It is reminiscent of American, and as my friend Professor Yehoshua Arieli would have said, American future-minded nationalism:[33] we resolve to be a nation – a model nation, let it be added. Those who must and want to go to their own state, Palestine, if that be the territory, determine to be Jews, although in their country they will like the Swiss continue to speak their former languages (for can you buy a railway ticket or box of matches with prophet Isaiah's Hebrew?). Those who would prefer to stay behind would presumably be opting for total assimilation, although Herzl does not state this in so many words. In brief, nationality is a matter of individual choice and decision. Herzl's rather grudging consent to communal educational activities and *Landespolitik* in the Diaspora in general was an expression not of his wish to cultivate Jewish identity wherever it be for its own sake, but of a search for means to strengthen Jewish consciousness and organisational cohesion in the struggle for independent statehood.

The lack of full clarity and consistency in Herzl's view of anti-Semitism is very meaningful. The wounded pride is the beginning of everything. But beyond that Herzl does not seem to be sure, no more than Freud in regard to the problem of evil, whether anti-Semitism was a relic, an excrescence that could be removed, only it would take too much time, and the Jews have had more than their fill of humiliation in the West and are driven by pogroms and hunger in the East; or an incurable disease, one of those perversions inseparable from the human condition. At times Herzl seems to reduce it all to a social problem – Jewish competition in the free professions. He appears to believe in the possibility of a kind of deal with the anti-Semites: you say there are too many Jews in your country, and granted the circumstances and your mentality the Jews are too numerous for you to bear them, let us therefore agree: we help you in taking out the superfluous Jews, and you help us to get a place for them, and a state of their own. Alas, time was to show that no bargain was possible with real anti-Semites. But this Theodor Herzl, deeply steeped in European fair-play liberalism, could not even contemplate.

As I have said, there are quite a few inconsistencies in Herzl's attitude, but they are easily explicable.

The Jewish predicament revealed to Herzl something of the abyss, of the ultimate intractable unreasonableness and horrible beastliness of man, yet in his vision of the solution of the Jewish question there is nothing apocalyptic or catastrophic, no war, no clash of rights, no human sacrifices, no gnashing of teeth, no dreadful break-through. It is a commercial transaction as far as the preparations are concerned. The passage to Palestine is a pleasure trip, without as much as sea-sickness. Settlement in the country is depicted as almost a Fourierist Arcadia, with congenial company of *Landsmannschaften*, fine airy dwellings, wonderful technology and gadgets and not much physical effort. That kill-joy Ahad Ha'am was quick to seize upon the reference in *Altneuland* to the Jews' experience in their new country as a possible lesson to the American Negroes, once they decide to return to Africa and establish themselves there as an independent nation. The Herzlian recipe was as suited to Jews as it was to Negroes: a wholly abstract utopia, not so much based on principles of morality as upon labour-saving devices and enlightened self-interest.[34]

There is the other inconsistency. Herzl never tired of insisting that the misfortunes and humiliations of the Jews were due to their political weakness. Rich and powerful as they were as individuals, they counted for nothing politically, because they were atomised, unorganised and represented no power, and in this world of power politics pleas for justice and appeals to conscience had no effect. We had nothing to offer in return. In all his dealings with monarchs and potentates Herzl was always deeply conscious of the need of a *quid pro quo*: Jews would offer money, support, services, etc. At the same time, the Jewish state of the future is depicted in *Altneuland* as a neutral state, hardly a state at all, just 'a Jewish Society', internationally guaranteed like Switzerland, with no army and no foreign policy. And the Arabs, unmentioned in the 'Jewish State', barely noticed in his diaries, appear in *Altneuland* as willing and eager to join the 'Jewish Society', because of the material benefits accruing to them. And of course the idea of the Charter was based upon the hope of international endorsement by all the Powers. This conscious wish of Herzl's to lift the Jewish-state issue out of international politics and the rivalries of the

Powers, baffling as it is, can only be explained as the liberal recoiling from the facts of irreducible conflict and from the spectre of force as the ultimately decisive factor in politics. Have not most of us behaved like this for decades in regard to the Arab issue? And surely this is Herzl's version of the Messianic faith in the ultimate and inevitable triumph of good, which had propelled Lassalle and Hess, and indeed all Jewish liberals and Socialists, for so long.

At this juncture we may ask how Herzl looks from the vantage point of seventy years after. A utopian? A prophet? A child of his time?

People are inclined to dismiss as fantastic the three main points of Herzl's practical programme. He hoped to buy from the Sultan the 'Charter' for Palestine. He believed he could get the rich Jews – then, when he had learned his lesson, Jewish subscribers in general – to foot the bill. He envisaged a mighty Jewish effort to transport within the shortest possible time all the willing immigrants and settle them in Palestine – under the aegis of the two national Jewish organs, the political – the Society of Jews – and the financial or economic – the Company of Jews. On a closer look at the realities of the late nineteenth century, Herzl appears less a utopian in regard to his international orientation than in his evaluation of the Jewish people.

IV

There was nothing fantastic in the idea of obtaining a concession from the autocrat of Turkey, and, as events were to show, from the Powers that were to divide up the dead corpse of the Empire. Turkey had a cord around her neck in the form of her international debt. Her main sources of revenue were not merely pawned, but actually supervised and run by representatives of foreign creditors, backed by their respective powerful governments. The expression, 'the Public Debt of Turkey', was never absent from the newspaper columns of the day and constituted an international issue for many decades. In a sense, Turkey could call nothing her own. That state of affairs at the end of a long process of internal decay, utterly cruel harassment by foreign powers, and continuing secession of one Balkan nationality after another at the end of bloody revolt and with the help of European powers, made the corruption at the top utterly hopeless. The North African domains of the Caliph – Egypt, Tunis and then Tripoli – were lost in a manner as injurious to Ottoman interests and pride as possible. In each case state bankruptcy invited European loans, and of course interference. Unhonoured promissory notes, impediments placed in the way of the foreign creditors, and finally bloody incidents paved the way for foreign occupation – by the British in Egypt, the French in Tunis, the Italians rather belatedly in Tripoli. The idea of the Jews' offer to redeem Turkey's international debt in exchange for a concession of Palestine, under some form of Turkish suzerainty – provided the money could be raised – was not at all fantastic. No one, least of all Turkey, bothered at that time about the rights of natives to self-determination in Asia and Africa. Palestine was held by the Turks by the right of conquest. And then, if Turkey had been prepared in the 1830's to cling, as the Sultan put it, to a serpent for fear of being drowned (by Mehmet Ali), and to invite the Russian navy and troops to the Bosphorus, why should she refuse aid from a politically innocuous factor? And if mighty Britain could put a premium upon the good will of world Jewry, and even Wilhelm II in his letter on Zionism to the Grand Duke of Baden, such sympathy was surely not less important to the tottering Porte. Owing to fair treatment throughout the centuries, Jews were well disposed towards Turkey. At the time of the Bulgarian uprising against the Sultan, British anti-Turks and anti-Semites, like the historian Freeman, publicly accused Disraeli of pro-Turkish sentiments and anti-Russian bias owing to his Jewish prejudices.[35]

Neither were Herzl's ideas on colonisation absurd in the context of colonial history, especially in the age of imperialism.

British and Dutch rule in India and in South East Asia began and was carried on well into the nineteenth century by state-supported chartered trade companies, enjoying the widest political, administrative, judicial and fiscal, and indeed military powers. All

North American colonies were established by Royal Charters granted to a group of settlers or individual entrepreneurs. The race for and partition of Africa was carried out by individuals, sometimes single-handedly, sometimes at the head of tiny bands of followers, some of them idealistic explorers, others nationalist visionaries, some of them adventurers, others men of greed. Cecil Rhodes, whom Herzl tried in vain to contact through his many Jewish associates, is only the most famous example of an empire-builder. He had his counterparts in other nations, in men who came to Africa with deep sympathetic understanding, like Savorgnan de Brazza, Auguste Pavie, Karl Peters, and above all that amazing German-Jewish adventurer Emin Pasha (his real name Eduard Schniczer), companion of General Gordon of Khartoum, the only officer to fight his way through with a small detachment, while Gordon and all his soldiers were massacred by the Mahdi. Emin went on to become the ruler of an entirely isolated Equatoria and to be then 'rescued' by Stanley.[36] White settlement in Kenya and the lands of South Africa had provided some lessons in organised and planned colonisation on a half-private, half-state basis; the international agreement on the Congo, which handed over the administration of that unhappy country to the King of the Belgians in his private capacity must have been known and remembered by Herzl.

It would be quite anachronistic to mistake the attitude to colonialism in the mid-1960's for the attitude most people had seventy years ago. The anti-imperialist ideology had as yet hardly made itself heard. J. A. Hobson's *Imperialism* appeared only in 1902, and his disciples, Lenin, Rosa Luxemburg, Hilferding and others had hardly started writing on the subject, when Herzl died.

Where Herzl showed himself a complete utopian was in his belief that he could get a few dozen Jewish plutocrats to put up all the money, and, after obtaining the Charter, to put the Jews on the boats, arrangements for the sale of property left behind and settlement in the new homes having been happily and easily concluded. The amazing thing then is not so much that Herzl could have nourished such sanguine expectations and could so badly underrate the factor of Jewish inertia, but that with all that, he did not give up after his high hopes had been so cruelly and humiliatingly disappointed. His tenacity of purpose commands the deepest veneration. It was sheer greatness. Where did the feuilletonist, who had been gliding through life, with that light touch, so easily bored, and always in need of new impressions, get his steel?

In his admirable *Life of Herzl* Dr Alex Bein quotes a letter written by Herzl in 1901 to his faithful follower and friend Dr Mandelstamm:

I have run myself ragged and I haven't obtained a hearing from the wretched crew which controls the money. Fire and brimstone must rain from heaven before those stones are softened. It is something utterly unheard of, and 50 years from now people will spit on the graves of these men for the fact that I should have been almost through with the question of the Sultan, and that I should have been held up because I could not get the miserable money. But of course we can't make a display of our rage and pain, because then the Sultan would become aware of our weakness, and I must do my best to hold him off, to gain time, trying meanwhile to squeeze water out of stones and scrape gold from the mud. Yes, it should be the easiest thing for me now to drop the whole business and to issue a proclamation: 'Thus it is, Jewish people; in five years I, a poor, helpless journalist, have reached the point where I could conduct business with the Sultan himself. But you've left me in the lurch; you are nothing but a rabble – the devil take you! I'm through with worrying about you'.³⁷

To the comfortably established and rationally analytical people of his day, Herzl must have looked like one of those '*simplificateurs terribles*' who reduce highly complex issues to a few crude theorems, and are, if not crazy quacks, dangerous demagogues. Those ardent Zionists who believed in gradualism and organic growth and cultural work were simply angered by Herzl's insistence that there should be no piecemeal colonisation, without and prior to the Charter. They could hardly hide their opinion that there was a certain charlatanism in Herzl's magic wand approach.

Adolf Böhm, whose history of Zionism,³⁸ available only in the German original and not going beyond 1924, to our shame still

the only Zionist History of academic standing, has already
compared Herzl's idea of a sudden break-through – through
diplomatic action – with the early Socialist vision of a violent
revolution that would make a clean sweep and enable men to
start all over from scratch. Did not some Socialists in the early
days object to taking part in the elections to a national parliament,
and still more to sitting in coalition governments with bourgeois
parties? Was not Lenin opposed to philanthropic activity among
the workers, and did he not fight the 'economists' and trade union-
ists in Tsarist Russia because, in his opinion, they were weakening
the revolutionary resolve of the proletariat, and postponing the
Day of Judgement *sine die*?

The dignity of the Jewish people mattered to Herzl most. The
Charter was to be the signal of recognition on the part of the
nations of the Jews as a people, and not a motley of beggars. The
Charter was to serve as a tremendous inspiration to the Jewish
masses. It was to raise their self-respect, offer them a sense of
purpose, indeed a myth – in Herzl's words a flag, which when
lacking the aura of myth was only a rag. It may well be that
Herzl, who had no spiritual-cultural Jewishness to fall back upon,
needed all that more than men like Ahad Ha'am, Weizmann and
Ussishkin who could be proud and full-blooded Jews without such
a tonic, and who did not share the fundamentally non-Jewish
dependence of Herzl on external symbols. It may well be that a
Herzl weighed down by the consciousness of difficulties, given to
analysing carefully all the pros and cons, would never have taken
off at all. Ahad Ha'am's carping and cavilling were sufficient to
make one give up.

But there was another reason for Herzl's refusal to allow for
slow infiltration into Palestine without international guarantees
and a clear definition of the ultimate goal. In those very days
when he was knocking at the gates of the Sultan and making his
way through the labyrinths of Ildiz Kiosk, the world press was
full of stories of the ghastly atrocities committed by the Turks on
the Armenians. Herzl was mortally afraid that a defenceless
Jewish minority, which had settled there in the teeth of Turkish
prohibition, could be wiped out overnight. He may have under-

rated the power of concrete though piecemeal and gradual achievement. In his pride he felt a deep aversion for the old Jewish methods of oiling the palms of officials, arranging things behind the counter, sneaking in when unobserved and bowing the head before or pretending not to perceive brutal insult.

There is an ironical and tragic paradox in the fact that while resolved to treat with the leaders of the world, emperors and kings, princes and ministers, on terms of equality and in the light of the day, in his capacity of representative of the Jewish people, Herzl was at bottom compelled to resort to the very, very old Jewish methods of backstairs diplomacy. Reverend Hechler, who managed to obtain for Herzl access to the Grand Duke of Baden and then Wilhelm II himself, was a religious crank. Nevlinsky, who enabled Herzl to establish contact with the unspeakable Ministers of Abdul Hamid, was a shady figure, half-blackmailer, half-spy. And then the man who eventually arranged for Herzl the audience with the Sultan, the famous Professor Vambery of Budapest, was 'a seventy-year-old Hungarian Jew who didn't know whether he was more Turk than Englishman, who wrote books in German, spoke twelve languages with equal mastery, and had professed five religions, in two of which he served as a priest ...' and 'through these many religious intimacies ... has naturally become an atheist.' Wherever he went, Herzl had to oil palms.[39] His reports on his dealings with the fantastic blackguards and thieves in the Turkish government are delightful vignettes, little masterpieces. While feeling out of breath on reading about the infinite crookedness of these viziers, diplomats and courtiers, the reader is filled with incredulous admiration for the upright and fastidious man's skill in managing and indeed outwitting the thieves.

In perspective, Herzl's efforts with Jewish millionaires and the rulers of nations appear quixotic indeed. But if Herzl was chasing after mirages, the princes of the world themselves do not strike one as models of responsible conduct, and their acts as the result of well thought out plans and solid assessment of data: the initial enthusiasm of a Wilhelm II, the most powerful man of his time, evaporating so quickly; the Sultan calling in Herzl to negotiate with him, while he had in fact already concluded a deal with a

French group of bankers, and wanted to use Herzl as a scarecrow; and Herzl deep at heart afraid that after all Abdul Hamid may agree to grant the Charter, and he, Herzl, will not be able to raise the millions to pay for it.

But this was not what the masses saw or wanted to see. Starved for leadership, yearning for majesty, not having had either, and having had to put up for almost two thousand years with Rabbis, *Rebbes* and *shtadlanim* as a substitute, they responded with a thrill to the new Moses, who looked every inch a prince, possessed a perfect sense of decorum and a dignity that was as royal as it was charming, and who – as they fondly believed – could hobnob with emperors and kings, and had magical powers at his command. In so far as it had not given itself up to the universal revolutionary ideal, the Eastern European Jewish intelligentsia had for the most part by then not only renounced any hope of becoming integrated into the majority nation, but had developed an intense national pride. The masses on their part found themselves in that inflammable state which is created by the discrepancy between the growth of a sense of dignity and the realities of worsening conditions of existence, with religion no more a prop or consolation: a situation which at all time engenders revolution. While the Jews had become so conscious of the rights of men, their position was more and more threatened by the competition of millions of peasants and dispossessed gentry flocking into the towns and by rampant chauvinism; and the amateurishness of the Hovevei Zion was hardly an answer to the situation.

And so it happened that almost against his own wishes, Herzl, no democrat, and certainly no Socialist, who started out with the idea of doing everything for the people, but not with and by the people, became, when rebuffed by the Hirschs and Rothschilds, the founder of a mass movement and a mass mystique. The diplomat ended up by creating in the first place an organisation. It was then given to the man who had no interest in the cultural side of Zionism to release tremendous creative energies in the spiritual field. The technocrat, whose social ideas did not go beyond mutualism, and cooperativism, inspired after his death a labour movement which in idealism, intellectual daring, social experimenting, practical ability and sheer success has hardly been equalled by any other labour movement in the world. It was all due to the power of a great idea.

From the vantage point of 1966 in Israel and in the Jewish diaspora Herzl stands both vindicated and repudiated. The Balfour Declaration, the Palestine Mandate and the UN decision in 1947 were all Herzlian realisations in content and in spirit. They would not have been achieved without that mighty instrument Herzl had forged, the Zionist Organisation, eternally vigilant, most resourceful and always there to take advantage of every opportunity to further the Zionist aims. And of course, there would have been no UN decision had there been no six hundred thousand Jews in Palestine in 1947, with hundreds of settlements, a closely knit institutional framework, cadres of armed men, all brought to Palestine or created there in a gradual dogged, practical effort, it is only fair to say – under the protection of the power which first came forward with the offer of a kind of Charter, when Herzl was still alive – the Uganda Plan – and then in 1917 gave its pledge of support for the Jewish National Home.

Hardly a Zionist leader felt so acutely the ground burning under the Jewish feet as Herzl did in his last few years: witness his readiness, under the impact of the Kishinev pogrom, to accept Uganda. Yet, intensely conscious as he may have been of the progressive deterioration of the Jewish position in Eastern Europe, the author of the *Judenstaat*, the plea to humanitarian sentiment and enlightened self-interest and of the idyllic utopia *Altneuland*, never envisaged the Jewish State as coming into existence through blood and iron, against a background of a catastrophe without parallel. Nor was Herzl able to visualise a Jewish State as a besieged city, an armed camp, surrounded by implacable hostility. When speaking of the 'Jewish Question', a term never mentioned these days, Herzl and other Zionist prophets had in mind the Jews of Central and Eastern Europe, certainly not the Jews of the Oriental countries or for that matter of the West. Not one of them in their worst dreams could have foreseen that there would be no Eastern-European Jews to settle in the Jewish State, once established.

In 1966 a phase in Jewish history may appear as having reached crystallisation in a kind of post-Herzlian posture. The State of Israel has solidified into a structure which only forces from within are likely to effect (if we discount hostile external pressures), for no large-scale influx of immigrants and no new break-through may be expected in the foreseeable future.

We are told, on the other hand, that the word 'Jewish Question' (or *Galut*) does not apply to the vast majority of the Jews outside Israel. Where they live now, in the New World, all are, in a sense, strangers and newcomers in the same way as Jews. The US or Brazil have been built by immigrants of all races, and total disruption would follow if one racial ingredient were to begin to claim superior ownership rights and deny it to others. An Auschwitz against the Jews there is sure to be followed by Auschwitzes against others. All the nationalisms of the New World are future-minded, and untouched by the fascination with the higher glory of an exclusive heritage. It is admitted that there may still nevertheless persist some difference between say, a Jew and an Irishman or Italian in the US, and the Jew may less readily be taken for granted as an American like anybody else, and that the Jew may feel less sure of himself and less at ease in his claims. But then, it is said, pressures and malaise, alienation and ambiguity have in fact always been the Jewish condition, and if these were to be conjured away, nothing specifically Jewish would be left.

And this is why, the same people continue to say, the Israelis have been losing their Jewishness. The old Messianic missionary claim, shared by Reform rabbis as well as by Moses Hess, is now being restated in a rather dismal, ultra-modern way. The Jews, we are told, are in fact the standard-bearers of the mankind of the future, its most sensitive nerve and barometer. In the modern urbanised, disembowelled, mechanised world all men are increasingly more alienated, rootless, if you like, pilgrims. In short, they are all on the way to becoming Jews. This time the appointment of the Jew with humanity, however, will take place not in paradise, but in hell.

There is one enormously important and mysteriously uncertain quantity in the Jewish position in 1966, and that is the Jewry of

Soviet Russia. That Jewish community holds perhaps the key to the Jewish future. As far as one can see, the Russian Jews are the only factor that may break the thickening crust and set things on the move again in Israel, and as a consequence in world Jewry, once they are allowed to join their brethren in the Jewish State in order to find a home and a way of expressing their Jewish identity; the hopes pinned on universalist Messianism having been so sadly disappointed.

1966

NOTES

1. Theodor Herzl, *Der Judenstaat; Versuch einer modernen Lösung der Judenfrage* (Leipzig: 1896); English translation by I. M. Lask, *The Jewish State; An attempt at a modern solution of the Jewish question.* (Tel Aviv: 1954.)

2. Ferdinand Lassalle, *Nachgelassene Briefe und Schriften*, ed. Gustav Mayer (Stuttgart: 1921–5), Lassalle to Theodor Creizenach, 1843, pp. 72–6.

3. *ibid.*, Lassalle to his father, 13 May 1844, p. 90.

4. *ibid.*, Lassalle to his father, 12 June 1844, p. 102.

5. *ibid.*, Lassalle to his mother, 30 July 1844, pp. 106–13.

6. *ibid.*, p. 110.

7. Na'aman Shlomo, *Ferdinand Lassalle: Deutscher und Jude* (Hanover: 1968); David Footman, *The Primrose Path: A Life of Ferdinand Lassalle* (London: 1946); Herman Oncken, *Lassalle: Eine Politische Biographie* (Stuttgart–Berlin: 1923).

8. Isaiah Berlin, *The Life and Opinions of Moses Hess* (Cambridge: 1957), p. 10.

9. Moses Hess, *Moses Hess: Briefwechsel*, ed. Edmund Silberner (The Hague: 1959). *ibid.*, Hess to Auerbach. 2 September 1841, p. 80.

10. Sidney Hook, *From Hegel to Marx* (University of Michigan Press: 1936).

11. Moses Hess, *Rom und Jerusalem: die letze Nationalitätsfrage* (Leipzig: 1899) First Letter, p. 1, translated by Maurice J. Bloom, *Rome and Jerusalem: A Study in Jewish Nationalism* (New York: 1958).

12. Oncken, *op. cit.*, September 1860, p. 17.

13. J. L. Talmon, *Political Messianism: The Romantic Phase* (London: 1960); Hans Kohn, *Prophets and Peoples: Studies in Nineteenth Century Nationalism* (New York: 1961).

14. Edmund Silberner, *Moses Hess: Geschichte Seines Lebens* (Leiden: 1966), pp. 353, 396.

15. J. L. Talmon, *The Unique and the Universal* (London: 1965); Hans Kohn, *op. cit.*

16. Hess, *Briefwechsel*, Hess to Auerbach, 11 December 1840, pp. 67–8. Moses Hess, *Rom und Jerusalem*, Letter Five, p. 21, 'Du bist ein Jud'.

17. Karl Marx, *A World Without Jews* (New York: 1960). Translated by Dagobert Runes; Solomon F. Bloom, 'Karl Marx and the Jews', *Jewish Social Studies*, Vol. IV, 1942.

18. Moses Hess, *Rom und Jerusalem*, p. 50, in *Zionist and Jewish Writings of Moses Hess* (Hebrew Translation) (Jerusalem: 1954); Nahum Sokolow, *History of Zionism 1600–1918*, 2 vols. (London: 1919); Nathan Gelber, *Aus Zwei Jahrhunderten: Beiträge zur neueren Geschichte der Juden* (Leipzig: 1924).

19. Moses Hess, *Rom und Jerusalem*, Letter IV, pp. 38–9.

20. Jules Michelet, *Introduction à l'histoire universelle* (Paris: 1962); J. L. Talmon, *Political Messianism*, pp. 242 ff.

21. Hess, *General Writings* (Hebrew Translation) (Jerusalem: 1956) 'The Letter on the Socialist Movement in Germany', pp. 67–9.
22. *Heinrich Heine, A Biography*, ed. E. M. Butler (London: 1956) p. 192.
23. Martin Buber, *Drei Reden über das Judentum* (Frankfurt: 1920); J. L. Talmon, *The Unique and the Universal*, Ch. I 'National Brotherhood and International Confraternity'; J. L. Talmon, *Political Messianism*, pp. 265 ff., 272 ff.; Hans Kohn, *Pan-Slavism* (New York: 1960).
24. Friedrich Meinecke, *Weltbürgertum und Nationalstaat* (Berlin: 1923); Rohan Butler, *The Roots of National Socialism 1783–1933* (London: 1941).
25. Theodor Herzl, *Zionistische Schriften*, Vol. I (Berlin: 1898) p. 14.
26. Theodor Herzl, *The Complete Diaries of Theodor Herzl*, ed. Raphael Patai, tr. Harry Zohn (New York: 1960) Vol. IV, 4 June 1902, p. 1283.
27. Theodor Herzl, *Theodor Herzl: A Portrait for his Age*, Introduction by Ludwig Lewisohn (Cleveland: 1955).
28. Alex Bein, *A Biography of Theodor Herzl*, Translated by Maurice Samuel (London: 1957) p. 94.
29. C. Shorske, 'Politics in a new key; An Austrian Triptych', *Journal of Modern History*, 1967, Vol. XXXIX, No. 4.
30. Charles Péguy, *Essays on Jewish Nationalism and Social Revolution with a portrait of Bernard Lazare* (Paris: c. 1948).
31. *Studies of the Leo Baeck Institute*, ed. Max Kreutzberger (New York: 1967).
32. Ernest Jones, *The Life and Work of Sigmund Freud* (Middlesex: 1964); Norman Brown, *Life Against Death* (Connecticut: 1961).
33. Y. Arieli, *Individualism and Nationalism in American Ideology* (Harvard: 1964).
34. Theodor Herzl, *Altneuland* (Berlin: 1921); Theodor Herzl, *Old-New Land*. Translated by Paula Arnold (Haifa: 1960); Alex, Bein *op. cit.*, p. 407.
35. Robert Blake, *Disraeli* (Oxford: 1966); W. F. Monypenny and G. E. Buckell, *The Life of Benjamin Disraeli*, 6 vols. (London: 1910).
36. William Langer, *An Encyclopaedia of World History*, 4th edition (1968), pp. 869, 865.
37. Alex Bein, *op. cit.*, Herzl to Mandelstamm, 1901, p. 369.
38. Adolf Böhm, *Die Zionistische Bewegung bis zum Ende des Weltkrieges* (Berlin: 1935). The nearest approximation to a scholarly history of Zionism is Ben Halpern, *The Idea of the Jewish State* (Cambridge Mass.: 1961).
39. Alex Bein, *op. cit.*, p. 342.

3

Israel Among the Nations
The Six-Days War in Historical Perspective

I

One does not have to be a committed Zionist to recognise that the establishment of the State of Israel has been the most remarkable and most constructive achievement of the Jewish people as a corporate entity for the last two thousand years, and one of the great feats of universal history. Since this essay is written in anything but a mood of self-congratulation, it is only fair to begin by highlighting the outstanding features, familiar though they be, of this vast and inspiring panorama.

In no time at all, relatively speaking, the Zionist movement succeeded in focusing the interest, the emotions, the passions, and the will of members of widely dispersed and very heterogeneous Jewish communities throughout the world upon what had for very long been nothing more than a mere vision. It was able to set up on a completely voluntary basis a whole network of institutions – a government, a national assembly, an administrative apparatus, and an army – long before Jews had even settled in the territory over which they would ultimately achieve political sovereignty. The movement won the Platonic and sometimes even ardent sympathy of wide sections of Gentile public opinion in many countries, and then, through a masterly exploitation of propitious circumstances in a fluid historical situation, obtained formal pledges of assistance from great powers and recognition of its claims by the highest international bodies. It undertook and triumphantly accomplished the task of building, without resort to force, a national-territorial community out of immigrants who came from different climates, cultural traditions, and economic conditions; it established self-governing towns and villages, agriculture and industry, and local organs of self-defence – all this in the teeth of obstruction of all kinds, culminating in determined chicanery and armed resistance by the indigenous Arab population. It laid the foundations for a new civilisation, based on an artificially revived language, and on an endeavour to throw a bridge across the centuries into the remotest past. It undertook at the same time social experiments requiring the most strenuous idealism and avant-garde daring.

Faced at last with the ineluctable necessity of marshalling all the moral and material resources for a national liberation struggle, the Zionist movement was able to organise civil disobedience, underground activity, terrorist and guerrilla operations, while simultaneously conducting an intensive diplomatic campaign on the world stage. It was then called upon to go through the supreme test of fighting the invading armies of half a dozen states. Notwithstanding the permanent armed siege under which the new state has since had to live for all the twenty years of its existence Israel has remained a genuine and effective democracy, the only one within a radius of thousands of miles, and strong enough to sustain itself in spite of deep internal divisions. Its record in education and culture, without being spectacular, has been quite respectable, and its successs in transforming a motley of what could almost be called races into a coherent modern nation has been highly impressive. Finally, there is the incredible feat of arms – the famous victory of June 1967 over four combined Arab armies.

The historian looks to other movements of national liberation for terms of reference and points of comparison. The national aspiration of a normal people struggling for independence turns on a relatively simple issue, aggravated and complicated as it may be by practical circumstances: the expulsion of foreign rulers. In such instances the moral case is so self-evident as to need no proof or elaboration. Not so Zionism. I am not only referring to the obvious fact that the Jews had neither territory nor nationhood

in the conventional sense when they embarked on the Zionist
venture. I have in mind the moral dilemmas which the very Jewishness of the Zionists could not but make extremely acute. Believers
themselves in the right of national self-determination, they could
pursue it only at the cost of conflict with Arabs claiming the
same simple right. In analogous fashion, though fundamentally
anti-imperialist and passionately democratic, the Zionists had no
choice but to look for help to imperial powers. Many a Jewish
youth stood bewildered in the cross-fires of those days – between
the demands of the religious conscience and those of secular
power politics; between messianic nationalism on the one side,
and messianic revolutionary universalism on the other.

The failures or sins of which Zionism has been guilty in this
respect call – I wish to submit – not for censure alone, but also for
compassion as unavoidable tragedies. This sustained, strenuous
effort – awe-inspiring in its single-mindedness, astonishing in its
global strategies, and often heart-rending in the moral dilemmas
it was called upon to confront – was carried out in the midst of
the greatest calamity that has ever befallen a people, and brought to
fruition on the morrow of the most horrible blood-letting that any
group has ever experienced. Dull must be the man, Jew or Gentile,
who would fail to respond with a thrill to this most powerful
assertion of the will to live in the shadows and the agonies of
death; to this triumph of the human spirit over the deepest
degradation and wretchedness.

On the strength of a long and close familiarity with the history
of national movements, admittedly restricted to Europe, I would
venture to claim that Zionism was the richest of them all. In
Zionism we find all the salient features of each rolled into one:
the aura of ancient myth and the vision of renovation which
constituted the unique appeal of the Greek war of independence;
the theoretical, not to say metaphysical, elaboration of national
ideology in nineteenth-century Germany; the missionary idealism
of the Italian *Risorgimento*, coupled with consummate diplomatic
skill and finesse; the dogged romantic desperation of the Irish and
the Poles; the cultural and literary renaissance of the Slav peoples;
the social radicalism of many a national liberation movement in

Asia and Africa. The wonderful gallery of great and colourful personalities thrown up by Zionism will stand comparison with any of the finest and ablest national leaders among the nations: Herzl with Mazzini, Weizmann with Cavour or Masaryk, Ben-Gurion with Bismarck or Piłsudski, Jabotinsky with Nehru, Buber with Fichte, Bialik with Mickiewicz and Petofi, Aharon David Gordon with Gandhi. Israel has also exploded many of the most rooted and widely held fallacies about Jews. The great Theodor Mommsen was sure that the Jew lacked all talent for politics, just as Ernest Renan had little hesitation in lending his immense authority as a Semitic scholar to the idea that Jews possessed no aptitude for philosophy, science, and the arts. Which Gentile only half a century ago had any doubt that the Jews could not fight, were all cowards, and knew nothing of military honour? Israel has changed all that to the point where a French shopkeeper in June 1967 could express his surprise that Poland could have been so quickly and so completely beaten by the Germans in 1939, 'when there were so many Jews in Poland in those days'.

Israel has been seen as the fulfilment and ultimate dénouement of Jewish history, but it has also been seen as the greatest deviation from the course of that history. It may be altogether too metaphysical a pursuit for the scholarly historian to try to define the 'true essence', the 'authentic spirit', or the 'preordained direction' of a millennial history spun over such diverse epochs, civilisations, and regions, and to describe developments which do not conform to that 'authentic core' as deviations, false starts, perversions, heresies, or *culs de sac*. We all know that these speculations are so often the fuel of political ideologies. All of us are by now also sufficiently dialectical in our thinking to view revolution as both the coming to a climax of the old, and the transmutation of that longstanding reality into an opposite state of affairs.

There is nothing absurd or illegitimate in the view that the establishment of a political and warrior state in some way constitutes a repudiation of a long Jewish tradition. According to this philosophy, pre-exilic Jewish statehood was a tribal phase to be outgrown, and outgrown it was, with the result that the Jews came into their own for the next two thousand years as a strictly religious confraternity, an entirely apolitical civilisation. Continuing this trend of thought, one would conclude that Zionism was an assimilationist movement *par excellence*. Its inspiration was the envious desire to emulate the example of 'all the nations', to be like them, and the modes of action to which it resorted were alien to a tradition of nearly two thousand years.

But while it is true that to some extent Jews ended by imitating the Gentiles, it seems no less true that the Gentiles followed in the footsteps of the Jews. It was under Judaic inspiration that the peoples of Europe turned into confraternities of believers in the Middle Ages. They made their way to nationhood in modern times also by largely following the teachings of Judaism. Modern European nationalism was born when educated Europeans began to be ashamed of the title of subject, and came to aspire to the dignity of citizen; at the same time they began to identify themselves first and foremost as members of a nation, and only in the second place as sons of a Church. But before nationalism became conscious of its secular and to a certain degree anti-religious character, there was a period during which militant religious evangelism was spilling over into nationalist pride.

The Jewish example was of considerable importance in that process. The image of the people of God fighting God's battles, of the Maccabees defending the true faith, of Elijah smiting the idolatrous heathen and backsliding Israelites – all this inspired the Hussites of Bohemia and Moravia; the Spaniards waging war against heresy and carrying the cross over the ocean; the Puritans, Cromwell, and John Milton. The idea of having been chosen by God for a special universal mission was taken over from the Jews. Even the essentially secular ingredients of the nationalism of a later day were of Jewish provenance: the myth of past glories, the trauma of failure and defeat, and the dream of a marvellous restoration of ancient greatness through some revolutionary break-through, combined, in the case of nationalities oppressed by peoples of a more powerful culture, with anguished loyalty to an indigenous spiritual heritage.

These sentiments became potent and propelling political forces when they were fused into one by the overarching idea of sovereign statehood as the sole guarantee of their effective integration and assertion. In the wake of triumphant nationalist movements all across Europe, this non-Jewish synthesis of Judaic ingredients was thrown back to, and seized upon by, the Jews. Thus the politicisation of national Jewish messianism was a consequence of foreign influences – as is clearly shown by the fact that every one of the historic statements of Zionist philosophy came in the form of a response to the victory of some national movement. Rabbi Judah Alkalay wrote his tract advocating Jewish colonisation of Palestine under the impact of the Greek war of independence and the emergence of Serbian nationalism. Moses Hess's astonishing little book, *Rome and Jerusalem*, was composed in the heat of general enthusiasm engendered by the unification of Italy. Leo Pinsker's *Auto-emancipation* was stimulated not only by the pogroms of 1881, but also by the establishment of the state of Bulgaria. It appeared so logical, indeed so inevitable – first the glory that was Athens is resuscitated, then Rome begins rising from the dead, and now Jerusalem's turn to be redeemed has come.

There was another and more concrete way in which Zionism was tied to European nationalism. The position of the Jews was made difficult by the latter and, in the countries of greatest Jewish concentration and strongest internal cohesion, untenable. It may be anachronistic to speak of pluralism in pre-nineteenth-century Europe. Still, class differentiation, cultural diversity, regional peculiarities, and religious splits made for some kind of pluralism, and it was away from this that modern nationalism, as an all-embracing creed, was bound to lead. The Jews became a test case of the ambiguity besetting the modern nation-state. There was the conception of the state as the outcome of a social contract among men – atoms emerging from the state of nature and resolving to live together under laws of their own devising, reserving to themselves all the natural liberties and rights, and ceding to the state only what was necessary for the administration of the commonweal and the defence of those very rights. At a very early stage this conception was counterbalanced by the idea of the state as an irreducible organic entity growing out of blood, dispositions, and folk-ways, myth, and destiny, memories and urges, which were supposedly prior to and more decisive than the conscious resolve of abstract individuals to band together for a limited number of purposes.

The separate Jewish tradition and communal cohesion, taken for granted in the *Ständestaat*, a society composed of communities, were challenged by the philosophy which frowned upon group loyalties of any kind as a danger to the individualistic social order. On the other side, those Jews who out of genuine conviction or out of a readiness to pay the price required for emancipation, gave their enthusiastic adherence to this liberal order, were decried by the upholders of organic nationhood as solvents and germs of disintegration, out to undermine the instinctive certainties passed on in the blood and in the perennial traditions. Liberal individualism, cosmopolitan finance capitalism, *laissez-faire* economics, were made to appear as agents of Jewish decomposition, representing the abstract and the universal, rather than the concrete and the place-bound. Yet the same Jews who were such eager upholders of universalism either could not or were not allowed to give up their group identity, and the universalist values and modes of being they propagated were condemned as instruments of a conspiracy to dominate the world.

For decades Jewish liberals were able to dismiss such teachings with a shrug of the shoulders. They would not stoop to defend themselves against that last residue of medieval superstition and prejudice, the rear-guard action of forces upon which history had already pronounced its verdict of doom. By 1880, however, these ideas were suddenly and simultaneously being espoused by mass movements in a number of countries, sometimes finding highly sophisticated expression in metaphysical theories, but more often in virulent agitation and outbreaks of riot and violence. Many Jewish liberals were shaken to the core. It was not only that they felt menaced personally. Their pride was deeply wounded, and their faith in the rationality of man and the inevitability of progress suffered a terrible blow. Thus Herzl, overwhelmed by the orgy of irrational anti-Semitism occasioned by the Dreyfus Affair in France, argued that Jews must no longer wait for their salvation upon the eventual triumph of right. Indeed, since the

Jews had been cast into the role of an irritant, they would be rendering a great service to the cause of general progress if they evacuated themselves, especially from Eastern Europe. That was even more emphatically the view of Borochov. Both Herzl and Borochov visualised the future Jewish State as having precisely the kind of regime to which the Jewish irritant was proving an obstacle in Europe – to Herzl liberal-social democracy, to Borochov a Marxist utopia emerging out of the healthy class struggle from which the Jewish problem in Europe acted as a distraction. Despair, wounded pride, the wish to assert human dignity – such were, once more, the motives which propelled these men whose personal situation was reasonably comfortable and who had never undergone the Jewish experience as a living and natural one. Their Jewish nationalism was thus re-active and not a spontaneous reality achieving self-awareness. But the seed sown by these alienated outsiders fell upon the fertile ground of the unbroken Jewish experience in Central and Eastern Europe, which, in the domain of the spiritual, was at that very moment evolving from religious into secular and national self-awareness, and in the political and socio-economic domains was being subjected to strains and stresses of growing intensity.

The historian is fascinated by the interplay of the inevitable and the contingent in human affairs. It is not true that there are no alternatives in history. Yet when he views long chains of events and long periods of time retrospectively from the vantage point of an ultimate dénouement, the historian is weighed down by the fatalistic feeling that after all what finally happened had to happen that way and no other. Infinitely painful as this may sound, Jewish history in Eastern Europe, when surveyed from the heights of the second part of the twentieth century, appears to have been leading for generations ineluctably to catastrophe. But of course the catastrophe did not have to be Auschwitz; no one in his worst nightmares could ever have envisaged Auschwitz. Yet clear-sighted men like Herzl and Jabotinsky, and in guarded terms Weizmann himself, understood the danger, and when they spoke of an 'evacuation' they were bitterly attacked by fellow Jews for implying that there was no room for Jews in countries where they had lived for centuries, sometimes – for instance in Hungary – longer than the 'host' nation itself. In fact, the burden of the Bund's implacable opposition to Zionism was the charge that Zionism accepted the arguments of the anti-Semites.

As a consequence of the great expulsions in the late Middle Ages from England, France, Spain, Portugal, Southern Italy and parts of Germany, the bulk of the Jewish people found themselves in the dawn of the modern era concentrated in the territories between the Oder and the Dnieper. Of course significant things continued to happen to Jews and they continued to pursue important activities outside the Pale as well – in Northern Italy, Holland, Palestine, Turkey. In Germany, especially, Jewish tradition, developing from generation to generation, became the matrix of great battles of ideas from the days of the Enlightenment until well into the twentieth century: one need mention only the struggle for emancipation, the grand dialogue between Reform and Tradition, the sustained effort of self-identification through internal and external polemic, and last but not least the great intellectual endeavour, *Wissenschaft des Judentums*. Nevertheless, it is no exaggeration to say that in the main the history of the Jewish nation in modern times – before the emergence of a self-sufficient American Jewish community and of the Palestinian Yishuv – was the history of the Pale.

For centuries the territories of the Pale constituted the under-developed part of Europe. Primarily agricultural, and feudal for a considerably longer period than Western Europe, the countries of the area had no real middle class. A large and often impoverished, but extremely self-conscious and exclusive gentry faced millions of horribly poor, illiterate, oppressed and downtrodden serfs. In the middle were the Jews. Even if they had wished to give up their Jewish identity, there was really no one with whom they could assimilate: the nobility was too high, the peasantry too low. So they remained a civilisation apart. The three or four empires – the Russian, Austrian, Turkish, and, to a much lesser extent, the German – on the western fringe of the Pale were all multi-racial states. The various tribes were kept apart by social and religious barriers, while the dominant group in each case lacked the cultural force (or, if one prefers, a sufficiently strong bourgeoisie and an adequate urban life) to attract and assimilate the politically weaker nationalities. The various peoples of the area were thus swept up by nationalist passion before they had had the time and the opportunity to develop a middle class. To an even greater degree than in Germany, nationalism here was deformed by the absence of those virtues, values, and institutions which a flourishing, dominant, and self-assured bourgeoisie has bequeathed to the West: the rule of law, the ethics of reciprocity, respect for the human personality, civilised intercourse – all embodied in municipal self-government, the parliamentary system, and the freedoms of the individual citizen.

Threatened by the higher cultures of the dominant groups, very unsure of themselves and of their own national-cultural heritages, these peoples drew their inspiration not from the social-contract and natural-law philosophies of the West, but from the German ideas of organic *Volkstum* and racial uniqueness. The Jews, whose culture was higher and more ancient, and who in the nature of things were also more attracted by the cultures of the dominant groups and the greater opportunities afforded by those cultures, were bound to appear to the weaker peoples as allies and instruments of their oppressors.

With the decline of feudalism, and the emancipation of the serfs in the Austrian and Russian Empires, the sons of an impoverished gentry together with masses of superfluous peasants flocked from the countryside into the towns. There they found the Jews. Economic rivalry was aggravated by nationalist passion. The newcomers, eager to build a national society with a balanced social structure, saw the Jew as the chief obstacle: an alien, a rival, a threat to national integrity.

Grave as these strains and stresses were before World War One, they assumed the dimensions of acute and unabated crisis between the two Wars. Russian Jewry had in Tsarist times been subjected to discriminatory legislation, administrative chicanery, and waves of government-sponsored pogroms designed to divert the attention of the masses from real social evils. Nevertheless, multiracial empires – not even excluding so entirely chauvinist a one as Tsarist Russia – usually have a dampening effect on nationalistic militancy. With the break-up of the old empires in 1918, a succession of nation-states emerged from the ruins. Some had never enjoyed political independence before; some had lost it centuries earlier; others, like Rumania and Hungary, were so enlarged or so diminished as in fact to be reshaped beyond recognition. These new nations were driven by fierce nationalism, the more fanatical, the less self-assured and externally secure they were. Their hereditary foe and traditional oppressor, Russia, had changed from an old-fashioned despot into the standard-bearer of world revolution – a stance calculated to attract not a few of the citizens of the new young states, and to offer Russia a good reason to expand, seemingly not in order to subjugate, but in order to liberate and redeem. Hence the bitter anti-Communism of these states, a sentiment that needed no particular incitement from Western capitalism.

Socially and economically weak, feeling threatened by external danger, and lacking any democratic experience, the new states were driven to make the oppression of minorities into a basic policy. Although the Jews of Poland and Rumania – unlike the Ukrainians, Hungarians, and Germans – had no separatist ambitions, they none the less came to bear the brunt and to feel the fury of the neurotic nationalisms of Eastern Europe more than any other minority group. Other minorities lived in certain border areas; the Jews, because they lived almost exclusively in the towns, where they often formed a majority, were ubiquitous. As the commercial class, and 'aliens' to boot, they were subjected to punitive taxation. They were considered usurpers, if not parasites, and an impediment to national consolidation: a foreign body when cultivating their own identity: a menace to the purity and integrity of the national creative genius when attempting to participate in the spiritual life of the nation. They were above all regarded as actual or potential Communists, and therefore enemies of the state. In those early days Communism triumphant in the Soviet Union appeared to be carried by the visionary qualities and zeal, the organising talent and technical expertise of the Jews. That message which fifty years later was to become the gravest menace to Judaism seemed to many at the time – in a development disquietingly reminiscent of the evolution of the relationship between Judaism and Christianity – to be a Jewish message.

And indeed, knowing themselves to be undesirables, conscious of the determination of the government and majority population to make conditions so unbearable to them that they would be forced to emigrate, with economic opportunities constantly shrinking, with no access to government posts, public works, and services, no wonder the Jewish youth of those countries felt that their existence was unreal, transitional, a kind of preparation for some future reality – redemption through Zion or through the coming World Revolution. All this explains why Nazism and Fascism elicited so ready a response in Eastern Europe and how Hitler could find accomplices in that part of the world when he embarked upon his genocidal programme against the Jews. In the darkest days of Auschwitz one could hear in Poland voices expressing thanks to Providence for solving the Jewish problem in a way which the Poles could never have contemplated. The greater the tribute due to those Poles who risked and sometimes gave their lives to save Jews.

It was the intensification of the Jewish plight together with the convergent growth of Jewish national consciousness that gave an irresistible impetus to Zionism. Neither of these two factors would have been effective without the other. Plight without ideology would have reduced the Jews of Central and Eastern Europe to a mob of wretched refugees, whereas ideology gave them the dignity of a hard-pressed nation on the march. Yet aspiration alone, without the propulsion of necessity, would hardly have been sufficient. The tragedy lies in this: that when the combined force of the two factors grew into the power that moves mountains, and move them it did, the bearers of that force were no longer there to claim the sunny uplands. They were dead. The State of Israel arose out of the holocaust, too late for the dead – and perhaps not only for them.

Historic inevitability and historic contingency: catastrophe and statehood were both inevitable and preordained, while the physical annihilation of millions of potential citizens of the

Jewish state was an awful contingency, which in turn – as we shall see – became the source of another type of inevitability.

II

The Jewish Movement of national liberation derived from a thoroughly liberal-humanitarian impulse. It was at the same time driven on by intensely anti-liberal forces. The climate in which it was destined to realise its aspiration was nothing short of apocalyptic. Above all, it was condemned to come into conflict with another national aspiration, which clash – let us have the courage to face the brutal truth – was incapable of resolution in any spirit of democratic liberalism.

It was the misfortune of Zionism to have arrived late, and to have achieved its aim in the nick of time, if not, indeed, again too late. The very close early association with the Russian revolutionary ideology imbued Zionism, especially its left wing, with Mazzinian notions of a united front of all oppressed national-ities struggling for liberation against a common oppressor. Yet by the time Zionism arrived, nationalism everywhere in Europe had developed into a cult of sacred egoism. Zionism expressed and represented a yearning for a home for the oppressed and for those who wished to be themselves – has there ever been a nobler aspiration? Yet the planet had by then been divided, and there were no longer any empty spaces. The home to which Zionism naturally aspired was inhabited by another people, the Arabs, and ruled by a third nation, the Turks. All of mankind's history has been a history of invasion, conquest of nation by nation, deportation of populations or their absorption by others, not to speak of extermination. At the turn of the century such things had become both objectively and subjectively impossible, most of all to Jews. They were destined to become possible and horribly inevitable again half a century later. Herzl saw the Jewish problem as an international problem, as a matter of general concern to all nations. What he would have liked best was an international agreement and international machinery, with money provided by Jews and, if possible, also by European governments, for the resettlement of Jewish immigrants. There was no escape in practice from an association with some Great Power, which might have been, in this sinful world of ours, suspected of being more mindful of imperial interests than of humanitarian challenges. When Herzl began his rounds in quest for a powerful ally, finding access to Wilhelm ii, Joseph Chamberlain, Abdul Hamid and others, Imperialism seemed at its zenith. The rule of the white man over all the coloured races had seemed a pre-ordained and blessed fulfilment – the more so for the fact that such imperial powers as Great Britain and France represented advanced political regimes and progressive social systems. But white hegemony and European self-assurance received a strong jolt in the form of the resounding victory of Japan over imperial Russia in 1904 (which was the year of Herzl's death). For the first time in modern history, a coloured race had succeeded in defeating one of the great white powers. In retrospect we can see that event as the beginning of the end of Western imperialism. The Japanese victory triggered a series of momentous explosions in Asia and Africa: the Young Turk revolution, the revolution in Persia, a little later the Chinese revolution, the radicalisation of the Congress Party in India, and the first rumblings of Arab nationalism in the Levant.

Nothing was calculated to please the Zionists more than the spreading of the League of Nations umbrella over the Balfour Declaration and British rule in Palestine. Representing, as it did, an international decision to help the homeless Jews, it seemed to do away with the spectre of Jews having to fight, and ultimately to displace, Arabs. Palestine was put under a League of Nations mandate after World War One, and it was in response to the growth of Arab nationalism that Iraq and Syria and the Lebanon found themselves in the same status. The Zionists would say that the latter mandates were established to prepare the local Arabs for independence and the Palestine Mandate to facilitate the upbuilding of the Jewish National Home as promised in the Balfour Declaration: could a fairer and most just procedure be imagined? The Arabs, however, would interpret matters differently: if Iraq, Syria, and Lebanon were entitled to independence, so too were the Palestinian Arabs.

The State of Israel came into being some twenty years later at a time when the process of decolonisation was already in full swing (in fact, the withdrawal of the British from Palestine in 1948 was modelled on their withdrawal from India a year earlier). It is more than doubtful whether a few years later the majority necessary for the UN resolution on the partition of Palestine could have been obtained at all. Few, if any, of the new Asian and African states, which were due to be admitted to the UN soon after, and which now maintain friendly relations with Israel, would have been prepared to vote for the establishment of a Jewish State before having had an opportunity to see Israel at work not as a society of colonial planters, but as a society of workers and producers, and to derive benefit from its services and example.

The exit of the white man from Asia and Africa and the arrival of the Jews into that nodal point where the two continents touch is a coincidence with tremendous symbolic overtones. Its significance for Israel is further deepened by the fact that the re-emergence of vast ancient civilisations like China, Japan, and India, and the rise of a large number of new nations, are bound to make for a relative decline in the weight of the Jewish ingredient in the sum total of human civilisation. The races of Asia and Africa were not brought up on the Bible. They cannot be expected to respond to the magic names of Zion and Jerusalem in the way Bible readers do. They have never been preoccupied or obsessed with the Jewish phenomenon: they have never admired, feared, or persecuted the Jews. Their record is clean of anti-Semitism, but it is also empty of Jews. Hence their proneness to equate Israeli Jews with white intruders.

The Zionist-British relationship bears the mark of 'too little and too late', and of an ambiguity which burdened the Jews with guilt without at the same time granting them the sweets of sin. It is no mean irony that while the Balfour Declaration may have looked like a deal between imperial Britain and the Jews, disguised on Britain's part by high-sounding idealistic formulae, the entire history of the Anglo-Zionist partnership was one of a sustained effort on England's part to escape the obligations and the logic of that solemn pledge. There has never been agreement on what that pledge really contained. Nor, for that matter, do we really know, in spite of the innumerable reasons given by or attributed to the British government, why the Balfour Declaration was even issued – as Christopher Sykes, the son of Sir Mark Sykes, one of the architects of British policies in the Middle East during World War One, points out in his perceptive *Crossroads to Israel*.[1] The late British Empire was acquired, it is said, in a fit of absent-mindedness; so, too, the Balfour Declaration seems to have been issued by a group of men who did not know what they were doing.

The statesmen of 1917 may have been confused, inattentive, muddled, idealistic, or shrewd; they may have been moved by humanitarian sentiment, by strategic considerations, by the wish to gain the sympathy of American Jewry for the Allied war effort, or to wean the Russian Jews away from Bolshevism, by the desire, finally, to cut the French out of Palestine. It is difficult, perhaps impossible, to know. But certainly no one gave precise thought to the ways in which the Balfour Declaration should be implemented. And in any case, contrary to popular belief, surprisingly little attention seems to have been paid to the idea of turning Palestine into a bastion for Suez.

Very soon after 1917 and throughout the thirty years of British administration that followed, there was little disagreement among the British, least of all among the men called upon to implement the Mandate in Whitehall and in Palestine, that the association with Zionism was at best a terrible embarrassment and liability. Few, even among those who supported Zionism, – or, more accurately, among those who from time to time could be alerted by the Zionists to prevent another attempt at whittling away the provisions of the Balfour Declaration – did so out of a sense of conviction or a disposition to give a helping hand to something good and desirable. Instead they acted out of a sense of obligation to a pledged word, in a resigned attempt to make the best of a bad job. Lloyd George seems to have been speaking for most of his colleagues when, in 1919, he tried to still objections to Zionism with the confident assertion that Britain's age-long experience of empire would enable her to take on all parties concerned – Jews, Arabs, Christians, the Pope, and the Caliph – and (he did not use the expression, though he implied it) muddle through somehow.[2] Why should the Arabs, who were about to get so much, when for centuries under the Turks they had had nothing, 'begrudge the Jews that little notch'? And, indeed, who were the Arabs? Before 1914, they had hardly impinged upon the consciousness of Europe, except perhaps as another native population with colourful nomadic Bedouins, etc., etc.

One man saw the dilemma clearly, and that was Balfour himself:

The contradiction between the letter of the Covenant and the policy of the Allies is even more flagrant in the case of the independent nation of Palestine than in that of the independent nation of Syria. For in Palestine we do not propose even to go through the form of consulting the wishes of the present inhabitants of the country. . . . The four great powers are committed to Zionism, and Zionism, be it right or wrong, good or bad, is rooted in age-long tradition, in present needs, in future hopes, of far profounder importance than the desires and prejudices of the seven hundred thousand Arabs who now inhabit that ancient land. . . .[3]

With all this, Balfour was most reluctant for Britain to assume the Mandate, and very anxious to hand it over to the United States. England was tired and disillusioned in the wake of the bloodiest of wars the world had seen till then; the imperial urge and the sense of mission were by then too enfeebled for her to take up the kind of challenge Balfour may have had in mind: to plan and execute with the cooperation of Jews and various international agencies a scheme of colonisation and settlement within a fixed number of years. It may well be that had such an approach been seriously attempted, the Arabs, dazed and weak as they still were, would have been placed before a *fait accompli* without any injury to their economic interests. They might then have accepted the accomplished fact, and the long drawn-out agony would have been avoided. But all this is plausible only within the theoretical sphere. As a matter of historical fact, such Keynesian methods as

Five Year programmes, Marshall plans, Four Point proposals, etc., were still beyond the ken of most people in the West. The British administration in Palestine had not been intended and was not equipped for such undertakings. Its greatest ambition was to keep the peace somehow and to get the essential services running, harassed as it was by the opposing claims of the Jews – impatient, arrogant, intent on forging ahead – and the Arabs – sulky, riotous, and aggrieved.

Was the Arab Jewish conflict inevitable? Can one put one's finger on sins of commission or omission, on points of no return, and say that had this or that happened or not happened, been done or not been done, things would have taken a radically different course? The more I ponder these questions, the more confirmed I become in the grim conclusion that although in detail, in style and tone, the Jews might have acted more wisely or more tactfully, it would not have made much difference in the final analysis. The same cannot be said about the Arabs. On very many occasions they could, by making concessions, have arrested or very significantly slowed down the growth of the Jewish National Home so as to prevent its transformation into a Jewish State. By adopting an attitude of absolute and total intransigence, they reduced the Yishuv's alternatives either to giving up Zionism or to carrying out its programme to the full extent in the teeth of Arab opposition. Since no give and take was possible, since even such modest forms of Zionism as a measure of immigration and settlement encountered maximum resistance, there seemed no choice but to aim at maximum strength. God had hardened the heart of Pharaoh.

The Arab policy of total and uncompromising denial of any Jewish right to a National Home was punctuated by outbreaks of violence and riot, like those in 1920, 1921, 1929, and 1936. Consistent, proud, and heroic as action of this kind may have appeared to them, it was disastrous to their best political interests. So too was their refusal to participate in the Legislative Council which the British planned to set up in the early twenties, and which might have given the Arabs leverage they did not otherwise possess. If, similarly, the Arabs had been ready to discuss the partition plan proposed by the Peel Commission in 1938 after the

Jews had accepted it, they might have succeeded in bringing about its failure (because it was not really workable); they would then have been in a position to claim a political and moral victory. Finally, had they agreed to let the one hundred thousand Jewish refugees into the country in 1945–46, the Jewish State might never have come into being. In the words of Abba Eban, the Jewish case would have lost its urgency. Had the Arabs not resisted the setting up of Israel in armed combat, there would have been no Arab refugee problem and the territory of the Jewish State would have been much smaller, perhaps too small and with too many Arabs living in it to make it viable.

The stage was thus set for an apocalyptic tragedy, both in the diaspora and in Palestine. Yet few people saw it coming, and fewer still were ready for it when it came. With the hindsight knowledge of what was to follow, the Zionist believer is visited not merely by a feeling of anguish, but also by a sense of embarrassment and shame that up to the days of Hitler those millions of Jews who were soon to perish, and who no doubt had in their majority been seized by the Zionist mystique, should have done so little to settle and build up their National Home for the first fifteen years of the Mandate. There were years in the late twenties when the number of emigrants leaving Palestine was larger than the number of arrivals. What kept the Jews of Poland, of Rumania, of Hungary from boarding every ship and raft in one huge exodus to the Promised Land? I cannot resist the temptation to quote a passage from Friedrich Engels, although I have already done so on another occasion: 'History is about the most cruel of all goddesses, and she leads her triumphal car over heaps of corpses, not only in war, but also in "peaceful" economic development. And we men and women are unfortunately so stupid that we never pluck up the courage for real progress unless urged to it by sufferings that seem almost out of proportion.'[4]

In the absence of a sense of irresistible urgency, deeply ingrained liberal modes of thought held the Jews back from facing up squarely to the implacable fact of irreconcilable conflict. Progressives are always unwilling and frequently even unable to understand that some conflicts can be resolved only by force. Thus it was that many Labour Zionists and others on the Zionist Left could deny any real conflict of interest between Jews and Arabs, and could put all the blame on feudal effendis or religious fanaticism. The Arabs, according to this view, had nothing to fear and much to gain from Jewish settlement. Some in the Zionist movement had visions of a bi-national state. The more starry-eyed even dreamed of acting as the midwife of socialist transformation to the stagnant semi-feudal, ritualistic societies of the Middle East – not through conquest, but by good precept. The Jews were completely sincere when they claimed that they had no intention of unsettling a single Arab. They had not come to take the place of the Arabs, but to create new opportunities, reclaim the desert and the marshes, and settle alongside the Arabs.

After seven years of relative peace, the turn of the decade witnessed the dreadful massacres of 1929, caused ostensibly by an absurd dispute over rights to the Wailing Wall, but in fact by the spectre of a world-wide Jewish plot – the setting up of the Jewish Agency for Palestine, in which large non-Zionist bodies and very eminent non-Zionist Jews were to join the Zionists. The pogroms were followed by committees of investigation whose reports recommended the virtual abandonment of the Jewish National Home policy. This recommendation was embraced with alacrity by the Colonial Secretary in the Labour Government, Lord Passfield, better known as the famous Fabian theoretician Sidney Webb, and his wife, the still better known Beatrice Webb, both prophets of socialism and progressivism, enjoying immense prestige as unrivalled experts in the social sciences. That they should have adopted an attitude of contemptuous hostility to Zionism was particularly galling to the liberal and left-wing elements of the Zionist movement. Not even the letter Ramsay MacDonald subsequently sent to Weizmann, rescinding in effect all steps taken by Passfield, could really heal the trauma.

In Europe, too, the Jews continued to think and behave as though they were still living in the liberal age, which is why the events set into motion by Hitler's assumption of power on 31 January 1933 came as so great a shock. Jews were used to pogroms, to discriminatory legislation, to insults and physical violence, to anti-Semitic theories and slander. But it was utterly unthinkable to them that the government of a great country, and one of the most civilised nations in the world, would – 150 years after the Declaration of the Rights of Man – abolish Jewish equality by a stroke of the pen, and do it with an air of defiance and victory. The theory of catastrophic Zionism suddenly seemed vindicated and was soon to be confirmed in a way which even the gloomiest prophets could never have imagined. The whole of Jewish history began to appear as one long preparation for doom in the diaspora and redemption in the Land of Israel. The messianic movements of the past were no longer seen as marginal episodes, but as the highlights of Jewish history, the great spasms, premature revolutionary outbreaks leading to the Great Revolution. Emigration to Palestine was growing in momentum, raising hopes that the Jews might become a majority within a generation. Embarrassing questions which had earlier been dodged as idly theoretical now began to press for answer. What would or should happen at the moment when the Jews came in sight of their goal, needing only one final push? Would the Arabs and the British look on, or would they make a supreme effort to call a halt, and if so what should the Jews do in response?

The Arabs did indeed make a supreme effort to call a halt. April 1936 saw the beginning of riots and a general strike, which were to swell into a prolonged armed uprising. So strong were the liberal and pacific instincts of the Yishuv that even at that late date the leadership was able to proclaim and for a long time maintain a policy of no retaliation. But the Arab revolt drove home to the Zionists the depth and intensity of the clash, and the difficulties, perhaps the impossibility of winning through the slow organic growth envisaged by Weizmann – one more cow, one more goat, one more acre. This is why so many, probably the majority, seized upon the solution proposed by the Royal Commission on Palestine presided over by Lord Peel – partition of the Holy Land into a Jewish and Arab State. Some saw partition as the only way out of the deadlock; others had vague ulterior motives: let us consolidate what we can, bring in as many immigrants as possible, and then let us see what further opportunities history may occasion.

In any case, the Peel Commission lent a new respectability to the idea of a sovereign Jewish State in the eyes of the Jews themselves – and this at a moment when they were being given increasingly stronger reasons to think themselves persecuted by one half of the world and abandoned by the other. For the world was now divided into countries which wanted to get rid of the Jews, and countries which did not want to let them in. Contrary to the expectations of many, the Nazi regime did not relent after driving the Jews out of all public positions. It continued to persecute the Jews with a brutality that culminated in the November 1938 pogroms. Hitler imposed anti-Jewish legislation upon Italy, the rump of Czechoslovakia, and other countries under his tutelage or influence. Nazi anti-Semitic propaganda was also making inroads in the West where there was no country without a growing Fascist movement. The Western democracies seemed paralysed in the face of Nazism, unable to resist.

Wooed at one time as a community of vast influence and accepted then as an ally of incalculable promise, the Jews had shrunk to the status of hunted animals and unwanted refugees – a circumstance to which the fiasco of the international conference on refugees at Evian bore gruesome testimony. And as their needs grew more desperate, the power of the Jews continued to decline. This decline was both a cause and a result of the rise of Arab nationalism and the formal abandonment by the British of the Jewish National Home policy in the famous White Paper of 1939–40, which put a virtual stoppage to Jewish immigration and land purchase in Palestine.

Humiliated, betrayed, forsaken, the Jews were left almost entirely defenceless before Hitler's genocidal campaign. The world had never before witnessed anything like this campaign. It was not a wave of pogroms by an inflamed mob, not excesses committed by drunken soldiers, not the horrors of revolution or civil war. A whole people was surrendered to assassins with the sole stipulation that every member of it, every man, woman, and child, healthy or sick, normal or paralysed, should be put to death, individually or collectively, by the bullet of a thug or in specially built human abattoirs, after being starved, tortured, flushed out from every hiding place and brought to the factories of death from the remotest corner of Hitler's empire. The Allies were far away, and claimed to have only one obligation – to hasten the day of general victory. There was no judge to appeal to for redress, no government to turn to for protection, no neighbour from whom to ask for succour, no God to pray to for mercy.

Despair to the point of madness gripped the Yishuv. The gates of the Jewish National Home remained shut and sealed, while desperate fugitives drowned at its very shores. By degrees the resolve hardened that there must be one place in the world where Jews could be masters of their own fate, where they would not have to rely on others from whom in any case they could expect neither help nor justice, and where if they had to perish they would go down fighting to the last man and not like sheep led to the slaughter-house. The State of Israel assumed the dimensions of the great reparation for an untold wrong, the only way of asserting the Jewish right and the Jewish will to live, and as the only instrument and guarantee of corporate survival.

III

The story of the final break-through to Jewish statehood was a great epic. Against the background and under the impact of an apocalyptic catastrophe, in the shadows of a veritably Dantean hell, the despair of the Yishuv transformed itself into the kind of divine and creative madness which not only stills all fear and hesitation, but also makes for clarity of vision in a landscape bathed in a lurid, distorting light. The climate changed visibly. Situations and actions considered only yesterday unthinkable, impossible, crazy, began to appear possible, logical, natural, desirable, imperative: fantastic risks, violence, sabotage, terror, war. Only a short while before, a community cherishing law and order, the decencies of life, civilised intercourse, had recoiled from Jabotinsky's teachings of blood and mud as the setting for the struggle for national independence, and had felt horrified by the slogan of his more extreme followers: 'In blood and fire Judea fell, out of blood

and fire she will arise.' Of course, only a minority became terrorists. But the vast majority no longer had the conviction or the
heart to oppose them.

It is idle to argue which factor was more decisive for the final
outcome. The terror brought urgency, drama, and myth. But of
course it would have been unavailing if not for the towns and
villages, the economy and the institutions which slow and arduous
toil had patiently and lovingly built up. In that respect both
Weizmann and Jabotinsky stand vindicated. Yet even these two
factors together do not tell the whole story of the break-through.
There was the irresistible pressure of the survivors in the former
concentration camps in Germany and Austria, their numbers
swelling daily with the arrival of fugitives from Eastern Europe;
there were the ships carrying illegal immigrants, intercepted by
the British on approaching the shores of Palestine; there was the
half horrified and half guilty sympathy of world opinion, finding
expression in active assistance from official quarters; there was the
diplomatic offensive in the United States, where the Jewish
community was propelled by the feeling that but for the grace of
God they too might have ended in Auschwitz, and the passionate
conviction that the memory of the dead martyrs and their own
power imposed upon them a historic responsibility which they
dared not shirk.

The methods had changed radically; the focal point of the
struggle had shifted from London to Palestine; and inevitably,
indeed one might say symbolically, the rudder was taken from
the hands of Weizmann by Ben-Gurion. The Jewish people have
never had a more impressive and persuasive apostle unto the
Gentiles than Weizmann. In the gravity and charm of his bearing
and deeply furrowed countenance, he epitomised both the sufferings and the majesty of an ancient and unique people. Few men of
the Gentile elite could resist the magic of that peculiar mixture of
prophetic idealism and ironic scepticism, profound moral seriousness and addiction to facts, felicity of phrase and metaphor and
contempt for rhetoric and pose, intense sensitivity to others and
the self-sufficiency of a powerful and idiosyncratic personality.
But Weizmann belonged to the pre-1914 age. He could appeal

to the reason and enlightened self-interest of cultivated persons; he could tap buried sentiments of compassion and love; he could stir visions. But he could not electrify or intoxicate crowds. He abhorred the tricks of the rabble-rousers, and the world of the irrational was entirely beyond his ken. Lawlessness, violence, terror were to him not only morally reprehensible and utterly at odds with the Jewish spirit, they were squalid and repulsive as well.

But if the subhuman was alien to him, so were the superhuman resources of heroic madness and despair. Subject to fits of depression and paralysing lethargy, he longed to get away from the thick of things into the quiet of laboratory and study. He loved his people with unequalled depth and tenderness, yet how harsh and biting he could be towards his fellow Jews. Wholly identified with the cause, he would none the less never give up his private world.

Weizmann's political orientation was entirely Britain-centred. It derived from his great faith in, and admiration for, British character and institutions, and rested upon his proven ability to influence upper-class British statesmen of a romantic cast of mind. Once the British had made up their minds that the association with Zionism must be terminated, Weizmann's usefulness was at an end. He simply had no alternative policy: neither another great power to lean on (for America would not assume direct and complete responsibility) nor a different strategy for dealing with Britain. When a British Foreign Secretary, Ernest Bevin, warned the survivors of Auschwitz not to push themselves to the head of the queue, and sneeringly attributed American support for Zionist demands to an unwillingness to take in more Jews, Weizmann could find no words to answer him.

Weizmann was, to borrow Isaiah Berlin's[5] epithet, the great exilarch who led his people back to the Promised Land, and he will always be remembered as the architect of the Jewish National Home. But it is Ben-Gurion's name that will forever remain associated with the final break-through to statehood. In speaking of Ben-Gurion, I can only repeat an evaluation I ventured some eight years ago that he will take his place among the half-dozen most decisive figures in Jewish history. So completely identified has Ben-Gurion been with the Yishuv from the moment he landed as a youth of eighteen at Jaffa from the small Polish town of Plonsk, that every facet and period in his life is indistinguishable from some aspect or phase in the history of the Yishuv itself: agricultural labourer; Socialist-Zionist publicist; trade-union organiser; soldier in the Haganah and the Jewish Legion during World War One; Mapai leader and General Secretary of the Histadrut; member of the Zionist Executive and Chairman of the Jewish Agency; Prime Minister; and, retired elder statesman who would not retire and would refuse the self-chosen role of a Cincinnatus in the desert, the virulent head of an opposition party, the lonely old man left behind by momentous events and even by his own party, the pathetic still-born child of his declining years.

Ben-Gurion has no loyalties other than Zion. A supremely political being who has shown himself to possess uncanny intuition in most concrete situations, he is also a great visionary whose vision transcends the here and now, expanding into past and future. To be sure he is a *grand et terrible simplificateur*, for whom two thousand years of diaspora history might just as well be erased from the record, and who denies the title of Zionist to anyone who does not settle in Israel. But in that crucial moment when men no less good than he grew hesitant and lost their nerve, his unclouded clarity of vision, his unerring instinct, his ability to make decisions made the providential difference. Having identified himself so wholly with the cause, he was able to fight for it with relentless ferocity and a ruthless disregard of those who took another view or wavered and vacillated. His faith was infectious, his resolve inspired confidence, his passionate words swept crowds: statehood as the goal, a national uprising as the method. It was now or never, for no such situation as the one created on the cessation of hostilities in 1945 would ever return, and in the desperate tug of war between Jew and Arab, with the British ranged behind the latter, any faltering meant for the Jews being hurled into the abyss.

Ben-Gurion as national leader was the architect of this policy, holding in his hands the reins and the levers of power, and if not initiating all actions, at least sufficiently in control to prevent actions like those of the Irgun and the Stern group from undoing his own efforts; yet it was still given to Weizmann to play his own inimitable role even after all the bridges with Britain had been blown up. It is enough to recall the appearance of the great old diplomat before the United Nations Commission on Palestine and his contacts with Truman which issued in the assigning of the Negev to Israel and the immediate recognition of the new state by Washington. These services were performed in the now-or-never spirit of Ben-Gurion's own absolute resolve that there must be no retreat into Trusteeship schemes as suggested by the Americans, and no weakening before Arab threats and neutral pressures.

The State of Israel came into being within the borders of 1949 as a result of an armed uprising, an international enactment, and a victorious war. When we look more closely, we discover here the very pattern followed by many national liberation movements in history. Except during the post-war period in black Africa, no new nation has ever been formed nor has any old enslaved people won independence without undergoing an ordeal of fire – in the first phase, rebellion, and in the last, war. It would seem that only through struggle, suffering, and violence is a people held to have proved that it deserves to be recognised as a nation, and even then, after it has compelled recognition, the rising nation almost invariably has to continue its fight for safer frontiers, as was shown most strikingly in the 1820's by the Greeks, and by the Italians a few decades later. The international concert steps in after the facts have already been established by the rebel nation, very often in an attempt to stem the tide and, by acknowledging accomplished facts, to prevent further facts from being established. Almost invariably the rising nation has to continue its fight for real security. The Greeks, the Italians, the Poles have all gone on fixing the borders of their country with the sword, in disregard of formulae and definitions laid down by international agreements.

But the war between the Yishuv and the invading Arab armies that broke out upon the establishment of the State of Israel can also be seen as a part of a more immediate pattern – as the belated spasm of the tremendous convulsion which had racked the world for the preceding six years and more. The flight of the Arab refugees thus appears as an episode in the enormous migration of populations, with millions driven and driving others across Europe

and the vast expanses of Asia and Africa – the largest such migration for many centuries, and of which the Jews were the most
helpless victims. So airily detached a view of millions of cases of
individual tragedy and personal suffering may sound inhumanly
harsh. But the historian has no answer to the question of why,
in the great conflicts of nations and classes, innocent people suffer
and uninvolved persons are wronged.

IV

'*Qu'elle était belle la République sous l'Empire*' was the saying in
the early days of the Third Republic in France. 'Beautiful was the
Revolution under the Tsars'. Might we with equal justice say how
wonderful the Jewish state was under the Mandate?

The dream and the reality, the myth and the facts: revolution,
liberation, independence, victory are the myths which lift men
out of and above themselves, upon which they focus all their
passions and energies. The vision must be made supernaturally
glorious, for otherwise men would be unable to summon the
necessary resources to suffer, struggle, and die. Since reality cannot
possibly come up to these expectations, disenchantment is inevitable. Once the single-minded concentration on the all-embracing
goal is relaxed, men return to their selfish petty concerns, and all
the problems and difficulties which had been brushed aside or
forgotten in the great emergency reassert themselves with a vengeance. Poverty, endemic civil war, bitter social strife, assassination, backwardness in every sphere were the answer to the dreams
of the Greeks and enthusiastic philhellenes about a renaissance of
the most gifted, eternally youthful and miraculously creative
nation. The visions and transports of the Italian *Risorgimento*,
actually badly bruised by repeated humiliating failures on the
field of battle, were followed by the dispiriting pettiness and
meanness of political life, against the background of the huge
Southern morass. A blanket of obscurantism and provincialism
descended upon the Ireland of the great rebels and the meteoric
writers. Poland between the two wars was a sad comment upon

the fate of the messianic nationalism of its poets and prophets. Bismarck's Reich was the most powerful nation in the world, but it was drunk with the arrogance of power and squeezed dry of that idealism and those flights of the spirit which in earlier days won the admiration of the world. And what a swampy place present-day India appears to be. But a much more disquieting reflection forces itself upon the contemplative historian. Is it an accident that those countries in which missionary universalist idealism found its loftiest expressions at an earlier age – Italy, Germany, and Russia – eventually became the seats of the most perverse regimes – Fascism, Nazism, and Stalinism?

To these examples, Israel represents a heartening contrast, an illustration if not of complete fulfilment, then certainly not of irretrievable failure. If Israel has by no means escaped an erosion of vision and promise, it has at least so far been saved from perversion.

I spoke earlier of nationalism as marking the primacy of national consciousness over religious self-identification. But nationalism, like revolutionary socialism, is also a secular religion. Independence and statehood were not conceived by the aspiring as a utilitarian instrument for satisfying mundane needs or gratifying the urge for power and the ambition for a spectacular place in the sun. Nationalism generally involved a sense of mission, which postulated dedicated service to a universal ideal – of liberty, of the spirit, of ethical rebirth. The hankering after lost glories, coupled with tribal self-idealisation, made the believers feel that they were about to recover their true being, the pure, authentic self which bondage, disunity, and evil influences had buried and caked with filth. The restoration of independence was to be the pre-ordained hour for a totally new start: the redeemed nation would turn its back upon the mistakes, errors, and routine selfishness of the older nations, and would guide itself entirely by the light of reason and justice. At the same time it would maintain the brotherhood steeled in battle, and bring into their own the pristine qualities of the race.

The more so, as usual, the Jews. Simple gratification of individual needs and group desires could never become the declared aim of a Jewish state. Imbued from the beginning of their history as a people with the idea that they must accept a particularly heavy yoke of responsibility because they were charged with the mission of serving as a light unto the nations, the Jews were incapable of finding meaning in a life strictly devoted to the here and now and lacking any transcendental significance. For so long aliens to the normal rivalry for political power, moreover, the Jews had entirely lost any understanding of the urge itself. Hence the distrust and indeed contempt for coercion, militarism, and even the virtues of the warrior.

They fed upon each other, the hatred for the squalor and degradation of the ghetto, and the dream of restoring the rustic simplicities and heroic glory of Biblical times. The air of late nineteenth-century Russia was thick with populist notions and scorn for the over-ripe rotten West, and in Germany enthusiastic youth was abandoning itself to the revitalising magic of nature. Not a few Jewish intellectuals became quite hypnotised by openly or obliquely anti-Semitic theories which depicted the Jew as the representative and germ-carrier of cosmopolitan rootlessness, modern alienation, the type of analytical sophistication which kills spontaneity and authenticity of instinct and feeling, and of course as the only begetter of oppressive capitalism, sordid money-making, hypocritical cunning, and urban degeneration. To all this the Zionist ideal of a communal return to the soil constituted an answer. As for those young Russian Zionists who responded with fervour to the Socialist challenge, they had to answer the charge of fellow revolutionaries that by trying to take themselves out of Russia and going to Palestine, they were deserting the world revolution. The deeper, then, became the resolve of the Socialist Zionists to build a model society in their National Home.

Political needs thus seemed to coincide with utopian demands. After all, settlement in Palestine was never a commercial proposition. Not only was there precious little profit in it for the individual. The reclamation of the land, the creation of a society of toilers and the collectivist methods were all necessary to achieve independent nationhood and a balanced social structure, and obviate the danger of becoming a planters' economy in a country with plentiful cheap labour. This idealistic social endeavour is sure to remain the most distinctive, most original, and most precious aspect of the Zionist effort in Palestine. Other nations have won signal victories on the battlefield; heroism and martyrdom have been the marks of many a national movement of liberation. But that ferment of social ideas, that intensity of feeling, that sustained dedication to a chosen way of life, that wealth of experiments (the Kibbutz, the Moshav, the Histadrut) in the field of social organisation – all this is probably without precedent, especially when we consider the exiguous number of men and the paucity of assets with which everything had to work itself out.

An egalitarian puritanical society emerged, combining in a fine blend the virtues of individual self-reliance and an enthusiastic readiness to join in cooperative endeavour. This has been the main secret of every success scored by the Yishuv – in agriculture, in the struggle for survival and growth, and finally in armed combat. Indeed, nothing has contributed more to the repeated victories over the Arabs, who, owing to Oriental traditions and the heavy hand of Turkish despotism, have lacked both sets of qualities.

Such, then, was the religion of the young Zionists in Eastern and Central Europe. The ideals, the achievements, the myth of Labour Zionism were all of their making. It may be doubted whether these ideals could have been maintained in a modern technological state for any length of time. What is quite certain is that the holocaust destroyed the cadres of potential immigrants required for their continued realisation. Hitler lost the war, and no doubt Hitler hastened the establishment of the State of Israel. But Hitler also won a far-reaching victory in depriving Israel of the most precious reservoir of manpower and moral strength to be found in the Jewish world.

For decades before the emergence of the State, arguments had been raging in the Zionist camp on the issue of selective versus indiscriminate immigration. Those who dreamed of a utopian society naturally favoured the former, while those who were weighed down by the predicament of the diaspora and were in haste to achieve statehood clamoured for the latter. But the holocaust robbed the debate of all meaning, turning Israel from a country of choice primarily into a place of refuge.

First to be brought in were the survivors of the Nazi massacre in the DP camps and in Eastern Europe; then came the Oriental Jews from the Middle East and North Africa, partly under duress as refugees, partly in response to an inner urge and Zionist inducement. Neither of the two types of new immigrant had much training, aptitude, or taste for the utopian collectivist endeavour. Having led a hunted existence in the years of the war, or having experienced Communist regimentation, the survivors of the Hitler period wanted above all to enjoy the blessings of privacy and security. As for the Oriental Jews, they had not for the most part gone through the mill of Socialist teaching. Besides, the family and clan of the patriarchal tradition were still a living reality to those who came from tribal societies and bronze-age civilisations. Romantic, Rousseauist-Tolstoyan slogans of 'back to the land', the philosophy which glorified the university graduate who exchanged his pen or scalpel for a spade or a hammer, became irrelevant when the country was suddenly swamped with hundreds of thousands of newcomers who could handle nothing else but a spade, and when rapid industrialisation and modern organisation put a premium on high technical training and university education. An extremely egalitarian society, based on voluntary teamwork, changed almost overnight into a managerial society, split into those who manage and those who are managed. And the split was along social, cultural, almost racial lines: Westerners versus Asio-Africans.

The Oriental Jews represent an ancient civilisation with a dignity and loyalties of its own, invisible as those may sometimes be to the superficial and impatient outsider. But these are not the values of a modern technological society. Responsible Israelis, anxiously aware of the problem, have made intensive efforts, especially in the field of education, to narrow the gap between Westerner and Oriental. But the facts of life are very stubborn, and even the best-intentioned and best thought-out programmes take a long time to bear fruit, whereas in the modern world, and especially in Israel, time is in very short supply.

Confronted with all these difficulties, Israel has in at least two vital matters been blessed with good fortune. There has been no serious, certainly no effective, attempt on the part of the Oriental Jews to organise themselves into a separate political party. Any such attempt would have been fraught with grave dangers from demagogues and rabble-rousers. As it is, incidents of riots in the course of twenty years can be counted on the fingers of one hand, in spite of housing and unemployment problems. It must also be added that the existing political parties, preponderantly of European origin, have displayed an admirable sense of responsibility. (This includes the opposition party Herut, which finds itself in the anomalous situation of having a Polish leadership and a largely Oriental, particularly Yemenite, following.) The second stroke of good fortune has been the fact that there is no religious militancy among the Oriental Jews, for an alliance between the militant Orthodox of West and East would have imposed an unbearable strain on Israeli society. Traditional and observant though they tend to be, the Oriental Jews are not motivated by any proselytising urge, and when left free to practise their own brand of Judaism, they do not care what others do. Nor do those of their young who, under the impact of detribalisation, drop out, feel any need to fight the faith they have abandoned.

V

The inevitable transformation of the pioneers of yesterday into the managers of today has brought into sharp relief the antinomies which arise when a great faith, heroic memories, and a beautiful myth are carried over into the context of a changed reality. The more sincere and firm the idealism of the past, the greater the danger of hypocrisy and even reactionary attitudes in the present. There is the natural unwillingness to see that what was service yesterday is today power, that what was then sacrifice has now become privilege, that what was voluntary confraternity has become coercive hierarchy.

The political parties in Israel are a good example of how this corrosive process works. The parties have every right to look back with pride upon their past. They came into being long before the establishment of the State, not as loose congeries of men becoming active on the eve of an election in order to line up voters behind a given candidate, but as tightly knit confraternities pledged to a strenuous way of life: some were virtually monastic orders. Zionism encouraged a multiplicity of such confraternities in the belief that the Jewish National Home stood to gain from ardent competition among them. Thus the Zionist parties (not, incidentally, unlike the Socialist parties in Germany and Eastern Europe), each embodying a *Weltanschauung* and a system of ethics of its own, evolved whole networks of cultural, social, economic and educational institutions – in short, they assumed the character of self-sufficient societies. Upon the establishment of statehood, the Israeli political parties were not only fully organised and well provided for, but fully armed. Mapai controlled the Hagana, Ahdut Avoda had very close links with the Palmach, the Irgun was the army of Herut, and Mizrahi could always summon the hosts of the Lord. The parties thus took over the State to such an extent that it became possible to say with a good deal of truth that Israel was a country where the parties owned the voters rather than the other way around.

In the days of the Mandate, immigration certificates were distributed according to the so-called party key – that is, in proportion to the numbers of enrolled members. The party key continues to be consulted today in the division of spoils and jobs. Proportional representation is the inevitable accompaniment, cause and result of such a philosophy and such a practice. This in turn makes coalition government an unavoidable necessity. Together, proportional representation and the coalition system work to encourage the parties not to bury but to emphasise and even invent political differences. Coalitions are precarious, majorities are weak, and the power of blackmail possessed by small splinter groups considerable. No wonder that Ben-Gurion, who experienced a full measure of political bazaar haggling, became a bitter enemy of proportional representation and a preacher – to no avail – of the virtues of the constituency system.

This state of affairs is calculated to enhance the power of the party machines, to favour the higher age groups, to discourage nonconformism. It is not surprising that the Knesset should have probably the highest age average of any parliament in the world, especially in the left-wing parties, and that a politician who has passed fifty should count himself and be counted by others as among the young revolutionaries. The same state of affairs also explains the dearth of original political thinking in present-day Israel when compared with the daring and originality displayed in the great debates of old.

Following the Six-Days War, the three Socialist parties – Mapai, Ahdut Avoda and Rafi – fused into a United Labour Party. On the face of it, this is a promising development. On the other hand, it raises the spectre of the perpetuation of this governing party in power, since it threatens to rule out for a long time the emergence of an effective alternative in the form of a middle-class party. Rafi came into existence as a force pledged to fight the corruption that comes from holding power for too long, to replace outworn clichés with critical thinking, and nostalgia with modern empirical methods. It remains to be seen whether the Rafi component will prove able to revitalise the united party or will lose its combative urge in the comfortable embrace of the mother.

The erosion of aspiring idealism as it comes into possession of power is most strikingly illustrated by the kibbutz. This most original and most impressive achievement of Zionism has exhibited very little creative energy in the last twenty years, while maintaining a very strong hold on the life of the country. Although the kibbutz movement comprises only about four per cent of the population of Israel, roughly half the Ministers, probably a third of the Knesset, and a very large number of generals, ambassadors, directors of government departments and public agencies are at least nominal members of a kibbutz. One hastens to add that a quarter of the soldiers, and especially officers, who fell in the last war, were sons of the kibbutz. If ever there was a ruling elite, and moreover one not based upon wealth, this is it. It was only natural for the State to tap the finest human material in the country for the most responsible and exacting tasks, but in doing so the State skimmed off the cream of the kibbutz population, leaving the less dynamic elements to carry on.

The State has diminished the functions and status of the kibbutz in many other ways as well. The kibbutz movement made an incalculable contribution to the struggle for independence, but as though to confirm Hegelian dialectics, it was thrown thereafter if not on to the rubbish heap of history, certainly on to the margin of events. Unequipped for the task, and for ideological reasons reluctant to open its gates to all and sundry, it played no part in the great effort of the ingathering of exiles. Besides, the post-1948 immigrants showed little eagerness to knock at its doors, and the few new recruits from among Israeli youth could hardly compensate for the exodus of so many old members into the society at large. The glamour of the kibbutz was being stolen by other institutions – army, State, civil service, science and technology, all of which were crying out for highly trained personnel and claiming the ablest and best.

No longer in the centre of the stage, almost forgotten and rendered irrelevant, in spite and partly because of the success of its leading cadres, the kibbutz sank into a malaise. Many began to wonder whether after all the kibbutz was not a transitional phenomenon rather than a form of life with a permanent role to play, apart from serving as a home and refuge for those whom it suited.

On a broader canvas the problem of the kibbutz in the State of Israel epitomises the problem of the State of Israel within contemporary world Jewry. The exhaustion of the sources of *aliyah* in the countries from which the Jews needed and wished to get away on the one hand, and on the other, the lack of any appreciable immigration from the countries where the Jews have a choice, constitutes Israel's gravest and in every way most decisive problem. Although little was said openly at the time, nothing shook the Yishuv more than the fact that when a classical Herzlian situation arose in Algeria, with a whole community moving out of a land inhabited by Jews for two millennia and more, most of the Jews preferred to settle in France instead of joining their anxiously waiting brethren in the Jewish State. Zionist philosophy had depicted the creation of the State and the ingathering of exiles as the climax of Jewish history, the great watershed, the great fulfilment. As it became clear that Western Jews had no intention of moving, Zionism began to appear in the eyes of many as only an episode, an aspect of modern Jewish history, not its final vindication – in the last analysis, the solution to a temporary problem of a part of the Jewish people overtaken by an extraordinarily horrible calamity. Israel, then, was a refuge but not *the* Jewish National Home, heir to the Jewish civilisation of the Pale but not the medium for the energies and peculiarities of the millions of Jews all over the world. Zionism on its face had called for the 'normalisation' of the Jew, but it could never bring that about. An abnormal people, the Jews are driven. Strive they must, justify themselves in their own eyes and in the eyes of others they must. They are unable to take reality as it is for granted. They are hypnotised, now as always, by the idea of ultimate meaning, final dénouement.

When the fact that no more Jews were to be expected began to sink in, the feeling of having reached an impasse, of facing a *cul de sac*, took hold of the Yishuv. Relations with the Arab states were at an unbreakable deadlock. The economic situation was grave. The number of emigrants leaving the country was growing, among them young men born and bred in Israel. Most Israelis were seized by panic at the reports of the fast advancing assimilation of American Jewry. One could hear voices predicting that in two generations no Jews would be left outside Israel, not even in Russia.

No longer the vanguard of the Jewish people and its spearhead, the Yishuv was now experiencing the cold winds of isolation: a ghetto hemmed in by implacable enemies, pledged to drown it in streams of blood. What was it all worth? For whom were they toiling? The self-questioning mood was giving rise to a general crisis of identity. Was there any such thing as a distinctive Jewish culture worth preserving? And would Israel ever be able to create anything in that sphere that would have so strong an appeal as to wean highly sophisticated Jews in the advanced countries away from assimilation?

Young Israelis would react with impatient scorn to the old Zionist slogans, treating them as cant and humbug. At one end of the spectrum, the Canaanites preached dissociation from diaspora Jewry and its traditions, a loving communion with the facts and values growing out of the soil and landscape, a return to pre-Judaic realities, and an attempt to fuse with the non-Jewish inhabitants of the area into a single old-new race. At the other end there were calls for a repudiation of secularism and a return to an observant mode of Jewish life as the only way of staving off complete assimilation and eventual apostasy.

This spreading malaise joined with traumatic memories of Munich and Auschwitz to make the diplomatic crisis triggered by Nasser's closing of the Straits of Tiran in the spring of 1967 look like proof of a paralysing loss of nerve. The government was fumbling and stumbling. Israeli emissaries were knocking at the doors of the chancelleries of the Great Powers for help which would clearly never come. The enemy seemed to hold the initiative and to be defiantly and systematically tightening the rope around the neck of Israel.

The fantastic victory that came so unexpectedly in June violently propelled the Yishuv into a diametrically opposite mood. The Six-Days War was a display of incredible vitality, fighting spirit and sheer talent, and it activated a new sense of destiny in the Israeli soul. All at once Zionism became immensely meaningful again.[6]

VI

But meaningful in what sense? By Israel's having obtained the longed-for goal of peace on the basis of a genuine recognition by its neighbours as a natural and integrated component of the area? Or by having conquered all of the promised territory and imposed its presence with superior force on an unreconciled foe?

The former was the prevailing mood in the early days after the war. People did not think of 'reaping the fruits of victory'. They wanted to believe that 'this time the Arabs have learned their

lesson' – that they cannot destroy Israel. 'I do not want any Arab
territory' – I was told in a private conversation two or three days
after the victory by the late Prime Minister, Mr Levi Eshkol. He
was happy that 'at last we have something we can bargain with',
meaning conquered territory for peace.

There is likely to be much argument in the future between
historians as to whether Israel was to blame for not coming forward on the morrow of its triumph with a bold, imaginative and
magnanimous offer, instead of waiting for the famous telephone
call from Cairo (and Amman), or whether the Arabs deserved
condemnation for closing all the avenues of a give and take through
the Khartoum Conference resolution, which repeated all the
traditional litany of grievances and reiterated with additional
vigour all the vows and bans of never, never.

One is constantly told by Israeli Ministers that the Government
has passed on innumerable messages to the other side, with sufficiently clear hints for its imagination to grasp that a favourable
bargain could be got. Much the same is being said by Hussein and
to some extent even by Nasser. Unfortunately, what one side
considers as the absolute minimum for its security is seen by the
other as a pistol held at its head. There is then also the obsessive
conviction that diplomacy consists of bazaar haggling, and what is
a far-going concession from our point of view becomes to the
adversary at once a point of departure for asking more. The
Israelis insist on the bitter experience of Arab hostility, the Arabs
decry Israel's effective and victorious expansionism. In its para-
noiac self-centredness neither side gives any thought to the fact
that if one seriously means to start negotiations one has first to
think of what would be acceptable and what not acceptable to the
other side. Since that is not done by either side, both are able to
repeat with good conscience that there was no one to talk to on the
other side, and no one to whom one may give up anything.

In the event, every impediment which stood in the way of any
form of reconciliation before 1967 expanded into an immovable
blockage, and both sides, each in its own way, succumbed to
what appears to be an incurable neurosis. Nasser may not have
actually planned the June war. He may have just glided into it,

egged on by the recklessness of the newly arrived pro-Soviet regime in Syria on the one hand, and Israeli threats of retaliation on the other. The Russians decried the latter as an indication that Israel was in collusion with America – preparing an attack on Syria – a repetition of Israel's action in 1956, only with a different objective and, more important, with a more formidable ally. The overthrow of the pro-Communist Sukarno regime in Indonesia and the more recent success of the military coup in Greece were still fresh in Russian memory. Both actions were attributed by the Soviets to CIA machinations, and now Israeli threats against the new Syrian rulers appeared as part of a world-wide American plot to destroy Soviet influence everywhere. At the same time Jordan radio was sneeringly calling upon the self-proclaimed leader of the Arab world to show his hand or step down. Nasser had to do something. He took his first steps against Israel, moved his troops into Sinai and got rid of the United Nations Force, but met with no resistence. Israel seemed paralysed as if confirming the exaggerated Soviet reports about the far-gone demoralisation of Israeli society. There emerged in the Arab mind the vision of an hour of opportunity for undoing the legacy of the Sinai campaign and wiping out the blot of defeat. And so Nasser took the last and fatal step – he closed the Straits of Tiran. By the end of May 1967 the editor of *Al-Ahram*, Heikal, close confidant of Nasser, proclaimed that the Arabs already had Israel in their net. The great day of reckoning seemed to have arrived.

For decades the Arabs had been obsessed by memories of past glories and prophecies of future greatness, mocked by the injury and the shame of having had an alien and despised race injected into the nerve-centre of their promised pan-Arab empire, between its Asian and African halves, just at a time when the colonial powers had started their great retreat from their colonial possessions in Asia and Africa. To ease their feelings of humiliation the Arabs would attribute all the Zionist successes – Jewish settlement, the victories of 1948 and 1956 – to the machinations of Western imperialism. Israel as the agent or spearhead of the Great Powers became thus the peg upon which to hang all the frustrations encountered by the Arab peoples in their anxious and jealous effort to skip centuries of social, economic and cultural development, and catch up with the well-established and self-assured Western old-timers. The effect had been to make them almost incapable of setting their minds to anything else, or of seeing anything on its own merits and as unrelated to the central grievance. Everything had, as it were, to be suspended until that wrong could be redressed. To make a virtue out of a vice, the Arabs developed the vision of an extreme misfortune turned into the lever of an ultimate fulfilment: in the course of preparing for the joint total confrontation with Israel, the Arabs would create the sinews of their future empire, and the victory over Israel would almost automatically – as in the case of Italy in 1859–61 and Germany 1870–71 – ensue in a pan-Arab empire, an Arab nation one and indivisible, which had also incidentally achieved its social revolution by wresting the rich oil fields from the feudal sheiks and turned them into the rightful inheritance of the nation as such.

It is easy to imagine the shock of the 1967 defeat, which not only destroyed all these calculations and schemes, but also under-scored the humiliation by the fact that Israel's victory was this time manifestly single-handed, and unlike the 1956 Suez (or Sinai) campaign could hardly be attributed to imperialist aid.

The anti-Israel obsession gave rise to a kind of systematic Manichean metaphysic, the focus of an entire philosophy of history, with the Jew as the devil incarnate from the days of patriarch Abraham himself till his assumption of the role of the lynchpin of an American-Imperialist-Zionist world-plot against the Arab world, the Socialist Commonwealth and all colonial peoples.

By an unspeakably tragic irony the Zionism of Jewish exiles marching to the tune 'Oh if I forget thee, Jerusalem' not only created an Arab Zionism, propelled by a similar sense of exile and dream of a return to that very Jerusalem, but imparted the mad obsession with a world-wide Jewish conspiracy to the Islamic world, which however contemptuous of and unfriendly to Jews had in the past not known that essentially Christian neurotic preoccupation with Jewish deicide and the Protocols of Zion, from the dire results of which the Jews sought refuge in Palestine.

Nothing highlights so much the intractable character of the conflict than the fact that what to the Jews appears a *conditio sine qua non* as well as the crowning achievement is to the Arabs something unthinkable – the ultimate humiliation: to sit down and negotiate a peace in a direct give and take. To the Israeli ministers, most of them persons of sound horse sense and warm humanity, although in some cases afflicted by a good deal of self-righteous incomprehension of the Arab cause, such an outcome seems logical and natural. But there is more to it. Deep down in the Jewish soul there is the conscious or unconscious tremendous anxiety to do away with that which has plagued their existence for two thousand years in the diaspora – the lack of simple, unreserved recognition of their right to exist as of right, and not on sufferance. Was not the essence of Zionism the deep longing to be a nation unto the nations in the family of nations? Nothing could therefore be more galling and frustrating than the fact that Israel was the only State in the world to which its neighbours refused the very right to exist, and whose frontiers were hermetically closed even when they were not ablaze. For ultimately all turns upon this point: the presence or absence of a readiness to recognise the State of Israel, or, what it amounts to, the will for peace or the will for war. If the former was there and convincingly demonstrated, questions of borders, refugee settlement, guarantees, even the guerrilla activities, would become secondary and likely to fall easily into their place. If the latter was paramount, then there was only one categorical imperative, 'kill him before he kills you': strategic borders become then all-important, readmission of refugees is tantamount to the introduction of a Trojan horse, and even the signing of some sort of document on non-belligerency by the Arab Governments only a ruse for gaining a breathing pause for another round, in preparation for which the guerrillas would be encouraged to conduct softening-up operations deep

into the neighbourhood of Tel-Aviv, indeed, if possible, into its
very heart.

The other day I fathomed something of the depths of Arab
neurosis. A group of prominent Arabs and Jewish intellectuals,
who had been meeting together at fairly frequent intervals, were
discussing 'the problem' for the n'th time in an atmosphere of
accentuated mutual courtesy and in the common conviction that
history had decreed that we have to live together or we shall
perish together, meaning – I hasten to add – by living 'together'
not a bi-national State but separate Jewish and Arab States, so as to
enable each people to express itself freely as God had created it –
a distinct entity – without any wish for or opportunity of patron-
ising the other, and with no reason to fear being swamped by the
numbers or the superior competence of the other side. A Hebrew
University professor addressed the direct question to our Arab
interlocutors: whether any one of them knew of a single example
in history of victors withdrawing when the vanquished had not
even begun to sue for peace, but vowed day in day out that they
would never make peace, never recognise the victor's very right to
exist, never meet him to negotiate face to face but would continue to labour with no respite for his destruction and annihilation? 'Surely you know also very well that had your leaders
shown the slightest inclination to sit down with us and talk, the
Jews would have been falling over one other in a stampede to
meet you, and you would have got out of them gains which you
could never obtain on the battlefield.' Turning to the soldier
among the Arabs present, a former high officer in the British and
at a later date in two Arab armies, and altogether an attractive and
warm person, the Israeli scholar exclaimed, 'And you for one,
after all, know that the Arabs are in no position to defeat Israel for
a very long time.' The man to whom these words were addressed,
usually highly articulate and eloquent, sat quite speechless and his
countenance showed signs of deep travail. He murmured something about honour, glory, history. He had been plainly touched
on the raw. There came to my mind a recent article by Heikal in

which in a pathetic *cri de coeur* he exclaimed that once the Arabs
had succeeded in inflicting a single defeat upon Israel and in
killing ten-fifteen-twenty thousand Jews, their self-respect
would be regained, and – he hinted – it might then become possible for them to meet the Jews face to face. It seemed like the
case of the impotent who has tried and tried so many times in
vain and is obsessed with the dream of that break-through, after
which he will be able to look men and women straight in the
eye. That the break-through was sure to come the Arabs have the
Crusaders as proof. Admittedly, it took two hundred years for
the Arabs to finish off the Crusaders' Kingdom. Well, had it
not taken the Jews two thousand years to come back to the Holy
Land?[7]

There is ground to fear that a not dissimilar type of impotence is
in the process of paralysing Israel. The Arab predicament stems
from resentment and rage, steeped in a sense of failure. The Jewish
complex grows from a mixture of fear and distrust, on the one
side, and a feeling of power on the other. There is a deep-seated
longing for peace in Israel, and there can be no doubt that were the
Jews to discern some opening, a narrow chink in the Arab wall of
obduracy, the great majority of them would leap forward to
meet the Arabs more than half way. The grave psychological
impediments which continue to pile up may prove however
strong enough to stultify that urge, or at least to prevent the
Israelis from detecting that longed-for 'opening', even if it should
begin somewhere. That process started as soon as the Arabs
closed themselves into a cage with their Khartoum resolutions.
The spirit of generous euphoria began at once to give way to fear
and distrust and to a hardening of arteries in Israel. If the Arabs
were absolutely resolved on a war of annihilation, surely – it was
said – it would be criminal negligence not to maintain the utmost
precautions and stick to the present frontiers, which allow us to
strike at Cairo or Damascus within seconds almost, while the
Egyptian planes cannot reach Tel-Aviv in less than a quarter of an
hour. Who could in such circumstances give up the Jordan ditch

and allow the Jordanian border to be re-established at between twelve and fifteen km. from Tel-Aviv? People began to recall the lessons of history, how every Arab 'no' resulted in greater gains than had been hoped for from an Arab 'yes'. Time was on our side, no matter what pressures the US might exercise – they could not be too strong, since we were, after all, the only safe ally of America in this area, its bastion against Soviet encroachment into the Indian Ocean, and we had never asked US soldiers to fight for us. One must not be scared by threats and abuse coming from Moscow, for the Russians would not send an expeditionary force against us. Nor should we be unduly upset by unpleasantness from the UN Security Council, which was surely dominated by our enemies and was at the same time impotent. The unrest in the occupied territories was easily manageable and the shelling on the Canal or the forays of guerrillas were incapable of even making a dent in Israeli armour. Our pilots enjoyed the shooting down of Migs like pigeons and our armoured units liked the forays deep into Egyptian territory. All that was needed were strong nerves. The usual argument which the Israeli hawks would bring out to 'demolish' the pleadings of the doves would be 'trust the Arabs to help us out in the end'.

As time went on more and more people became receptive to the romantic pseudo-religious mysticism of the various fire-eating and Bible-quoting prophets of manifest destiny, who compare the Zionist endeavour to a revolution which must unfold to its last consequence. It was written in the Book of History that Israel will be restored to the fullness of his inheritance. That inheritance belonged to all generations past, present and future. And the present generation which had been singled out by the Almighty as trustee and executive had no right to give away what belonged to all the generations. The Arabs owned fourteen States, while Israel was to the Jews the poor man's little sheep. The Balfour Declaration and the Mandate had recognised the rights of the Palestinian Arabs as individuals, but not as a sovereign national entity. Sovereignty over the Holy Land was reserved for the Jews alone. The Palestinian Arabs who, in spite of the Israeli resolve to guarantee them their human and civil rights and to grant them equality, preferred to live in an Arab State, were welcome to emigrate.

Would such a policy not constitute an insurmountable obstacle to peace with the Arab countries? This objection the new militants would counter by saying that the Arabs would agree to peace or rather give up war only if they became absolutely convinced that they had no hope of breaking the resolve of Israel. Since any sign of weakness only encouraged them in their intransigence, Israel was bound not to yield an inch. Some extremists have gone even further than this, asserting that peace might not be desirable to Israel at all, and pointing in support of their view to the bracing effect wars have had on the nation, its pride, and its sense of unity.

There is something pathetic, at once touching and repellent, in the desperate quest of the mystical maximalists for means and ways to meet the awful, supremely ironical contingency of the Jews of Greater Israel being swamped in no time by the higher birth-rate of the Arab minority, in other words in their effort to make good the irretrievable catastrophe of Auschwitz. Thus one of the oldest of the new militants exclaims in prophetic ecstasy: 'Two million new immigrants in two years!' Where from? He and his like refuse to recognise any fundamental difference between the closely knit and self-sufficient Jewish communities of former Poland and Rumania on the one hand, and Western and American Jewry, an ethnic group in a pluralist society of immigrants, on the other.

Misreading and exaggerating the significance of the wave of anxious solidarity which swept world Jewry in the days of May and June 1967, when Israel seemed to face its supreme ordeal, they would attribute to an ethnic group in a pluralistic society yearnings for an untrammelled national existence that an older generation of East European Jews went to Palestine to seek. If not from North America, then the millions of recruits – they pray – will come from a Soviet Union seething with anti-Semitism or from South America, menaced by Castroism and Ché Guevaraism. Without voicing such sentiments openly, some hawkish mystics are almost on the look-out for anti-Semitism, such as the Negro anti-Jewish sentiment in the US, on the assumption that 'the

worse the better' – if egged on by fear of persecution, diaspora
Jews will emigrate to Israel. Some set their hopes upon a change of
heart among the Jewish hippies and members of the New Left.
Who knows if their surplus of idealism, when frustrated, could
still be channelled into Chalutsic resolve? A poet of the romantic-
ally nationalist persuasion, but doubtful of the possibility of
enticing many Jews to immigrate, launched a delirious 'appeal to
the Gentiles' – Norwegians, Dutchmen, Danes, Mexicans,
Frenchmen and Italians:

> Let us tell them: come and partake of the wonderful adventure of
> building Eretz-Israel . . . We will share everything with them. We will
> give them our pretty daughters for their wives, and their dark or light-
> skinned women will find men here worthy of the name. We will make
> it easy for them to convert to Judaism, and those who will not wish to
> convert can live here as a sympathetic minority of Christians and
> Atheists, tied to us in heart and soul, as citizens.

The arguments about the danger of a Rhodesian situation developing in Israel divided into two so utterly different societies are
brushed aside by the hawks: their opponents are men of small
faith in their doubts about the ability of Israel to cope with any
problem, and moreover are propagating slanders by insinuating
that Israel will not know how to treat fairly and justly the strangers in its gates.

Apocalyptically minded super-hawks of both sides feed each
other. The Arab ones are determined to provoke Israel to expand
till it bursts, till it is choked with Arab population, saddled with
such insoluble problems and so harassed by guerrillas and sabotage that it is goaded into resorting to savage repression and irrational squandering of strength, to the horror of the whole world.

There are some Jewish super-hawks on the lunatic fringe who
also pray for an apocalypse, which will somehow make the Arabs
vanish into thin air through mass flight and leave Israel safe and
happy for ever after, behind the Jordan river, or who knows – the
Syrian desert, turned into a Chinese wall. The dovish argument
about world opinion the hawks would brush aside as pusillani-
mous and dishonourable. The Jews owe nothing to the world (as

if Zionism could ever have taken off the ground without public sympathy). Had the world done anything about Auschwitz or in the days preceding the Six-Days War?

On a less exalted and more mundane plane, the more sober politicians argue quite plausibly that if peace is very distant, since Hussein cannot make it for fear of the terrorists and Nasser will not make it for fear of losing his leadership of the Arab world, Israel cannot impotently leave things in suspense. One cannot stand still: you either go forward or move backward. Fortified outposts must be established, and they have to be flanked by settlements and supplied with safe and easy lines of communication – the Golan heights, strategic areas in the Sinai, in the mountains on the West bank and in the Jordan valley. Even those who while insisting on strongpoints, disclaim the wish to annex Arab populations in substantial numbers, go on arguing that one cannot leave two economies to go their separate and very different ways. The state of uncertainty about their future – some go one further – prevented moderate Arabs from collaborating with the Israeli authorities, while it encouraged the extremists to assist in or condone the acts of the saboteurs and terrorists. From this there is little distance to the conclusion that annexation would redound to the good of the Arabs themselves and even help in resettling the refugees. And should the Arabs by a miracle agree to negotiate at some future date, nothing would prevent us from pulling back from the outposts in exchange for a real peace – say the moderates; what we will have annexed and integrated into Israel will remain ours – is the the hope of the hawks. Accomplished facts create laws, theories of international law do not establish facts.[8]

This divided mood – between the yearning for peace and profound distrust of the Arabs, consequently disbelief in peace, and the hankering sense of obligation towards the 'potential' citizens of Israel in the diaspora – becomes the source of so much that is equivocal, inconsistent, and is likely to appear hypocritical or even cynical in the eyes of outsiders. Although the official Israeli policy is still direct negotiations with all options open, increasingly more frequent and louder are Ministerial statements about this or that point – usually territorial – not being negotiable, until one even hears that it is better to hold Sharm-el-Sheikh, the God-forsaken desert-surrounded exit to the Red Sea, without peace, than to get peace without Sharm-el-Sheikh.

The divisions in the Cabinet are deep and are openly voiced. But since the need for a real decision is made to look very distant by Arab intransigence, the protagonists are only too glad to postpone the hour of decision so as not to wreck the National Coalition. The latter imperceptibly turns from a means into an end, and indeed becomes a pretext to take no initiative in the pursuit of peace.

This mixture of *hubris* and fear is all-pervading in Israel. One hears people say in the same breath, 'We can reach Cairo within hours; we may be destroyed within half an hour if the Arab tanks break through the narrow neck of pre-June 1967 Israel north of Tel-Aviv.' This ambivalence may be taken to epitomise the general human condition since the intrusion of atomic weapons, but it brings into still sharper relief the baffling ambiguity of the Jewish situation through the ages. The steep and rapid fall from blinding splendour to bottomless misery has been such a constant feature in Jewish history. This makes for obsessive over-anxiety and over-reaction, and for a neurotic determination to make the worst fears come true. One of the most discussed issues in Israel has been, for instance, the question of recognising the West-bank Arabs as a Palestinian Arab entity, with a view to establishing an autonomous Arab State there. Some see in such a plan a way of frightening Hussein into entering into negotiations, others an end in itself and a first unilateral step towards an overall settlement with the Arab world. Strong reasons for and against such a policy have been adduced on practical grounds. There is indeed much justified doubt whether such a statelet would be viable at all. There is then the argument that it would in fact be either an Israeli protectorate or a springboard for militant Arab irridentism. With El-Fatah staking out the claim to speak for the undivided Palestinian nation, opposing any kind of arrangement with Israel, and vowing total destruction of the Jewish State, some Israeli leaders have lately caught fright at the idea of acknowledging even in theory the existence of such a national entity as the West-bank Arabs, lest this offers the enemy a handle to proclaim that the whole and undivided Palestine was the patrimony of the indivisible Palestine Arab nation; as if the fanatical terrorist groups were really in need of additional arguments. Some Israeli leaders got themselves wantonly entangled in pernicious and self-defeating theoretical disquisitions intended to show that the Palestine Arabs were not a nation, oblivious both to the inappropriateness of such theorising in the mouths of people who had fought so hard to be recognised as a nation, and to the fact that to deny a group the dignity of a nation is the surest way to establish it as a militant one. Sterile in itself though such theorising may be, the wounds it leaves are deep. More immediately it means shelving any plan of an Israeli initiative in setting up a Palestine Arab entity as at least a tentative step.

The Israeli attitude to the Four Powers Conference is rooted in this complex of fear, distrust and sense of power. The Israeli Government stubbornly maintains its position that by constituting themselves into a kind of Acropagus the Big Powers are lending implicit approval to the Arab refusal to treat with Israel. They invite, as it were, the Arabs to demonstrate through the intensification of terror and the warming up of the frontiers that they will never negotiate, and that the situation is so explosive that the Powers must curb Israel. This vehement rejection of the Four Powers' intervention by Israel may at least partly be motivated by the understandable, clear or dim wish of the victor to be left alone with the vanquished. It is, however, the Munich trauma that is at the bottom of Israeli intransigence, or at least the not unjustified fear that the Great Powers may just patch up some hasty and precarious cease-fire, in order to be able to show that they have achieved something, but will in fact leave all the embers burning, and through inattention or weariness, secure for Soviet Russia a legal standing for perpetrating trouble for both Israel and the USA. Israel is strong and determined enough to defy all the Powers – the official policy claims.

If the Arab press seizes upon every hawkish declaration as conclusive proof that Israel does not want peace, but desires expansion, the Israeli papers, on their part, select the most blood-curdling proclamations of Arab guerrilla leaders to show that nothing can be done with the Arabs. Both sides leave out the mitigating 'ifs' and 'buts' of the official spokesmen, or treat the more moderate statements of the other side as a ruse, cunning, or just pitfalls and traps.

VII

In brief, with so many good reasons, justifications and pretexts on both sides for doing nothing to bring peace closer, the idea that force is the sole arbiter is growing into an axiom, partial rights and wrongs having become almost irrelevant. But, as Namier said, 'the dead festering past cannot be eliminated by violent action any more than an obsession can be cured by beating the patient.'[9] If anything has been proved by the fifty years of conflict, it is precisely that it is just not true that the adversary 'understands only the language of force'. Instead of bringing him to his knees, despair goads him on to more desperate acts of resistance or aggression. When he has nothing to lose, he can risk everything, because he risks nothing. This has been shown again and again by both Jews and Arabs, not to speak of Vietnamese, Algerians and so many other cases. It would be amusing if it were not so painful to hear Jews expatiating on the special and different mentality of 'our' Arabs in the way anti-Semites were not so long ago philosophising about the innate and unalterable, usually mean, characteristics of the Jews.

Should full scale hostilities be resumed, there is little doubt that the Israeli troops would seize Damascus, enter Cairo, and conquer Amman in no time. But what next? Could they stay there? And even if they could, what would be the point of it? Is there any certainty that a fourth Jewish victory will at last drive home 'the lesson' to the Arabs? Few people in Israel nourish any illusions on this point. Israel may be able to win and win, and go on winning till its last breath, thereby demonstrating the truth of Hegel's aphorism about the 'impotence of victory'.[10] After every victory we would face more difficult, more complicated problems. For as Nietzsche has put it, there are victories which are more difficult to bear than defeat. This ghastly realisation is breeding a quite fatalistic mood: we are doomed to live for ever in a state of siege; a conclusion which comes perilously close to a denial of the most cherished dream and deepest *raison d'être* of Zionism – a safe home, and to an admission that we have exchanged a ghetto of pariahs for 'a ghetto of victors'.

Should this state of war between Jews and Arabs, which has lasted already fifty years continue – and who knows what type of weapons will be introduced into the area in the midst of a world changing with kaleidoscopic speed all the time, and what forces may still intervene in this region – there will be no victors and no vanquished, but mutual general destruction. Those Arabs capable of thinking lucidly, and from time to time one meets such persons, realise fully that Israel cannot be destroyed, and even if that were possible, the Arab countries themselves would be shattered beyond repair before they could succeed in striking a death blow at Israel, so that the victorious survivors would celebrate their triumph on ruins and ashes. Nor could Israel bring a suicidally determined Arab world to its knees without incurring in the process mortal material and moral damage, and having all the values which have in the past won it the sympathies of the best of mankind completely eroded.

There is thus only one alternative to the nightmare of reciprocal destruction, and it is that of reciprocal recognition. The very claim to the totality of Israel's inheritance does much to justify the claim to the entirety of Palestine as an Arab land. Much as one may inveigh against the Arabs begrudging the Jews that little notch, while having themselves so much, the argument sounds specious in a world in which no country, no more than any individual, has divested itself of a part of its territory, its coal or oil to make good the wants of its close or distant neighbours. Jews have been able to exist and prosper only where reciprocity was obtained. Where an exclusive claim based on superior power or supposedly higher right has prevailed, Jews have always been the first victims.

Of course, any discussion of reciprocity must take into account the fact that while the aim of the Israelis, even the extreme annexationist minority, is security, the Arabs have indicated all too frequently their determination to wipe Israel off the map, and no one can blame a people who had experienced Auschwitz for not treating threats of annihilation as rhetoric or metaphor.

But the preoccupation with security, however natural and justifiable, so often becomes a self-defeating obsession. Which state in the world has ever enjoyed absolute security, and particularly now in the age of nuclear, chemical and biological warfare? The axiom of the eternity of Arab hatred and active hostility is suicidal: if these can not be stilled, then every new defeat from the hands of Israel will exacerbate them still further, and the Arab resources in manpower and material are ultimately inexhaustible. The desperate anxiety not to allow Jordanian rule to return to Kelkilya for fear of guerrillas in the neighbourhood of Tel-Aviv may – by preventing any settlement – help the most uncompromising extremists in their effort to sweep away all the moderate particularistic forces in the Arab world and to unite it with the blessing and active help of Maoist China.

There are so many lessons in the history of victorious nations, just out of mortal peril, anxiously and desperately determined to obtain foolproof guarantees against aggression which they feared would be renewed in ten, twenty or fifty years. Through the search for the best they lost the chance of obtaining the good, and brought upon themselves much sooner than feared calamities much greater than those they wanted to ward off from future generations. One is reminded of the frantic efforts of French statesmen and generals after 1918 to obtain guarantees against German militarism, as well as of the insensate and very soon regretted perorations of British statesmen on squeezing the German lemon till the pips burst. The Allies got no reparations in the end, but they helped to conjure up Hitler. Many people who hurled abuse upon Lord Landsdowne for his famous letter to the *Daily Tele-*

graph pleading for a negotiated give and take peace with Germany in 1917, came afterwards to muse ruefully how much better a place the world, and their own country, would have been, had the advice of the former Foreign Secretary been heeded – in all probability a world without Mussolini and Hitler and without Stalin.

The Israeli Army has shown itself so many times more than a match for all the combined Arab forces that one is taken aback by the fears that if this or that is given up or not made secure, Israel is signing its own death warrant. Furthermore, should Arab hostility never relent, but continue to mount, and with it its military ability, what frontiers will ultimately be of any avail? And what kind of security could there be for a country with such a large and determinedly hostile minority within its frontiers, in those wide ditches and high mountains – in an age of bitter national strife all over the world and in the age of jets and missiles! So any measure of real security is in the disposition of the protagonist, and consists in diminishing its grievance and urge for revenge. And as to the obligation towards the potential Jewish settlers in Israel, could one really justify the certainty of continued actual warfare, with all the actual suffering and the unknown disasters in store, for the sake of a hypothetical need for refuge, which might arise if (God forbid) the world is again plunged into the barbarism of the 1930's and 1940's, a state of affairs which would in all probability spell universal destruction. We clamoured for the freedom of Soviet Jews to emigrate to Israel and challenged those Western Jews conscious of their Jewish identity and proud of their ancient heritage to join us here long before anyone dreamt of the present frontiers.

The quest for therapeutic means to replace force hangs upon the anguished hope that there is a fundamental disposition in favour of peace, at least in a part of the Arab world, though terribly inhibited and handicapped by neurotic impediments and over-strained susceptibilities. It follows that nothing should be done that might provoke or hurt these susceptibilities, and nothing should be left undone that might enable the buried better self to assert itself. One clutches at the hope that sufficient and sufficiently influential people in Egypt and in the other Arab countries realise the utter futility and dangerous consequences of a renewed war; that they have become aware of the fact that if the present state of war is continued, the dream of restored Arab glory, with the common cause of Palestine as the cement and lever of pan-Arab nationalism, will reach a sad consummation in Soviet advisers in every government office and technicians in every Arab factory, and in every Army unit, difficult though it be to imagine two races and civilisations less congenial to each other than Communist Russia and the Moslem Arabs.

One should perhaps try to remind the Arab intellectuals of historical parallels. In the sixteenth and seventeenth centuries Spain was bled white, went bankrupt and sank into torpor and impotence at the end of eighty years of war against Holland. Catholic-monarchical Spain could not bring itself to recognise or to treat, except for cease-fire arrangements, with heretics and rebels and usurpers of parts of its Empire, assigned to it, after all, by the Pope himself in 1496. In the end, the proud Spaniards were compelled to sign in 1648 a treaty with a Holland which had in the meantime grown from a handful of desperate rebels and fugitives into a vast Empire, the first financial power in the world, and culturally the most advanced country in Europe.

What misfortunes has the burning but constantly frustrated desire of the Italians to show themselves, to demonstrate martial qualities and win resounding victories, brought upon that so wonderfully gifted, sophisticated and generous nation? The Italians seem to have at last learned their lesson and cured themselves. Both nations, the Arabs and the Israelis, would do well to take to heart the resigned words of wisdom spoken by a thinker who has grown white in the quest of justice, passing through the whole spectrum of ideas: 'past injustice cannot be made good. The sufferings endured by earlier generations obtain no redress.'[11]

The Arabs cannot get a 'just' peace, and the Jews are unable to obtain a 'total' and 'true' peace. All that can be hoped for at present is a stemming of the tide, in the hope of its gradual ebbing away. The expectation that the Arabs will come cap in hand to sue Israel for peace is no longer cherished even by those who had still not long ago believed – or still believe – that time was working in our favour, and laid store on accomplished facts. Were even a directly negotiated and formally signed peace treaty attainable – the Israelis themselves say – the Arab leaders who will have put their signature to it would be assassinated next day, and the Arab Ministers would in any case, like the Germans in 1919, sign it only under duress and with mental reservations and hostile resolve in their heart. By refusing to have anything less than that, and thus perpetuating and perhaps intensifying the present tensions to a boiling point, may we not be helping the guerrilla organisations which however insignificant their military achievements have been, have nevertheless raised a flag, created a myth, become a focal point for the hopes and the activities of the young, and done incalculable harm to the image of Israel in the world? Any kind of arrangement with the Arab governments at this hour, even one short of a treaty negotiated face to face and signed amidst handshakes in the blaze of television lights, would implicitly be based upon the one common interest of all sides concerned, Israel, the Arab Governments, the USSR and the US: preventing the contingency of a total triumph of the extremists in the Arab world and of an incursion of China into the area. But the sands are running out fast. The chance may be lost for that *détente* and deescalation which a common interest – less in peace than in the avoidance of future dangerous complications – may create, leading to *de facto* cooperation despite continued incantations about the unforgotten wrongs suffered and eternal rights possessed by the Arab people. It is today highly unpopular in Israel to recall that such a situation existed between Israel and Egypt for some ten years after Suez. Admittedly it did not prevent the 1967 explosion. But where is the proof that this must happen again? Dangerous as it is not to learn from past mistakes, there is a no lesser peril in being hypnotised by traumatic memories and the obsessive fears of history repeating itself. And have we not shown a supreme ability to meet the dire contingency?

Why despair of the genius of the Israeli army in the future?

There are no more pressing, and in the long run more decisive imperatives, than these two – the checking of the growth of the guerrillas, and the resettlement of the refugees through a concerted action, internationally supported and financed. The success on these two issues would take the sting out of the terrible imbroglio, and enable the sides to slide slowly into peace, should the hope of first establishing the formal peace as a prelude to the particular remedies prove vain.

Of course, if Israel is prepared to go to such lengths to save the susceptibilities and irrational obsessions of the Arabs, she is surely entitled to expect the Arabs to offer similar alleviation to the Israeli deep-seated fears and passions, like the unity of Jerusalem (with some autonomous status for the Arab community in it); some modifications of frontiers – the Golan heights; the right to hold on to strongpoints, such as Sharm-el-Sheikh, if not forever, at least for some years till the need for them has become superfluous in the eyes of all; and, of course, total freedom of passage through the Straits, demilitarisation of sensitive areas, the stationing of UN troops in them under the aegis of the Security Council.

If stemming the tide and defusion be the aim, should we not take another look at the Four or Two Powers Conference on the Middle East, and instead of savagely looking at it as a conspiracy, perhaps try to utilise it in making it easier for the other side to come forward or yield with a minimum of loss of face.

There are liberals in Israel who though aware of the immense difficulties and pitfalls of an imposed settlement, endeavour not to lose their sense of proportion. They recall that hardly ever has such an intractable conflict as the Israel-Arab imbroglio been resolved without the Great Powers Concert intervening and laying down the law. Their intellectual integrity is rather offended – when they think of the treatment of Palestine Arabs in the past – by the incantations of some Israeli Ministers about the right of the parties directly concerned to determine their own affairs, without the tutelage of outside Powers – 'the Middle East is no one's protectorate'. They do not expect the Powers to become angels, forgoing their own interests, or eunuchs impotent to defend them, but set their hopes on the mutually contradictory interests of the Powers cancelling themselves out into some reasonable compromise. The best way for Israel to avoid loss of face through an enforced withdrawal is to come out with a formal declaration of its readiness to initiate withdrawal on specified dates, provided that in the meantime such and such a *quid pro quo* is carried out by the adversary and other agents concerned.

The State of Israel came into being in 1948 through Soviet-American agreements; the Suez crisis was resolved in 1956–7 because the two Super Powers wanted it to be. It is said that in the early days of Israel, Ben-Gurion would instruct a diplomat going abroad to 'do everything possible to please the Americans and nothing to displease the Russians'. That balance could not be maintained for long. Soviet support for partition in 1947–8 was an isolated episode. Although it was greeted with jubilation by Zionist left-wingers, to whom consistent Soviet hostility had been a source of deep chagrin, the motive of the Russians, as it soon became unmistakably clear, had been no change of heart in regard to Zionism. Nor can any such change be expected so long as the US and the USSR are locked in rivalry.

It is impossible under any circumstances for Israel to adopt an anti-American attitude or even to defy American wishes for any length of time in a vital matter. The reasons are too obvious to need elaboration. This is well known to the Russians, and from it they draw extreme conclusions. Russia is surrounded by American bases, and it is very important for her to have allies and friends and bases behind the American bases – in other words, in Syria, Egypt, Iraq. The Russians think in quantities, and thus conclude that even if Israel could be weaned away from America, the strategic value of the large Arab territories, not to mention the oil they contain, makes the Arab world a much more worthwhile ally. The Soviets ask themselves also the simple question: who pays for it? He who pays has the say. Since totalitarian regimes would never allow, in fact could not even conceive, that a group of their own citizens might advocate a foreign policy which differs from or is not dictated by the government, they are bound to conclude that through the intermediary of American Jewry Israel is of course an American puppet and agent.

There are other considerations behind Russian policy as well. In so far as it has been stirring up Jewish sentiment among the Russian Jews, making this 'indigestible' group still more difficult to digest, Israel is resented by the Soviet government as a nuisance and an irritant. The social achievements of the Israeli Labour movement, far from impressing the Bolsheviks, evoke contemptuous hostility: how dare a tiny country like Israel presume to build Socialism better than Russia itself! Similarly the demand to permit emigration from Russia to Israel must appear as an anti-Soviet device, implying as it does a vote of no confidence in the achievements and nature of the regime: one is supposed to be happy in a Socialist regime.

Thus, while not motivated by conventionally anti-Semitic convictions and aims, the Soviet Union is almost objectively, to use its own language, led to adopt policies which, given the murderous hostility of the Arabs and the role of Israel in the post-holocaust period of Jewish history, amount to a definite threat to the survival of the Jewish people.

Particularly horrifying is the Soviet-Arab sponsorship of an updated version of the Protocols of Zion: the Zionist-American-Imperialist world plot, operating not only against Arabs, Asians and Africans, but also against all the Socialist regimes, causing economic difficulties, student unrest, Catholic intransigence. We have travelled a long way from the revolutionary universalism of Marx which recognised neither Jew nor Greek nor Gentile, but only workers and capitalists.

And yet, there is a glimmer of hope that the spectre of China and the inexorable compulsions of modern technology and warfare may still work to bring about a Russo-American agreement to resolve the Arab-Israeli conflict. As a very great power, Russia finds it extremely difficult to do nothing for the Arabs beyond replacing the arms they have lost, and to take Israeli defiance lying down. At the same time there can be no doubt that the Soviet Union will never risk a nuclear war over the Middle East, any more than the United States will. This may induce the two Super Powers to search for a face-saving formula for a Middle-Eastern settlement. Understandable as their anxieties are, the Israelis would do well to pause and reflect whether it be in the long-term interest of Israel to be irretrievably tied to America in the way South Vietnam, South Korea or Western Germany are. It is not only a question of the image of Israel in the eyes of the world, especially the Afro-Asian nations, with whom Israel must live and trade in amity. As France has shown, a Great Power finds it easier to change allies or abandon clients than a small isolated state to win new protectors. The Israelis would be well advised not to bank too much on the 'special relationship' between Israel and the US, always liable to yield to isolationist moods. Nothing would be more dangerous for them than to act on the assumption that they have America in their pocket. The Suez War has shown that they did not even have American Jewry in their pocket. The only hope of a peaceful settlement in the Middle East lies in an American-Soviet agreement, however difficult and distant such a prospect continues to look, and not in the preponderance of Israeli armies backed by the Sixth Fleet.

For the Israeli liberal to be able to come out against the rising tide of anxious and militant intransigency and press his case with any effectiveness, the condition *sine qua non* is that the Arab leaders wish in their hearts to be more gently or more forcefully cajoled. For when all is said and done, Israeli hawkishness is really a function of Arab obduracy and hostile intent. Without some clear and convincing proof that Nasser was prepared to be coaxed – and the latest portents are by no means encouraging – the Israeli liberals would be powerless Don Quixotes. Worse, they would be decried as faint-hearted defeatists, capitulationists, traitors. They would inevitably be reduced to watching fatalistically and impotently the great cruel ironies working themselves out in a seemingly inexorable manner: the heroic exertions and astonishing talents of so hard pressed a nation, with a deep yearning for peace and justice, beating in vain against an unattainable goal, and suffering horrible haemorrhage in the process; a society which started off with so much Socialist idealism and constructive resolve becoming reduced to the position of a beleaguered city, wasting its substance on arms and the best years of the flower of its youth on destruction; a freedom-loving society doomed to engage in the squalid business of spying, policing, suppressing, putting schoolgirls behind bars; a rational people swept by morbid passions and neurotic obsessions; a nation whose deepest desire has been to escape the fate of being not an end in itself, but a function of the existence of others, a problem, a liability, an impediment, an undesirable presence, compelled to treat a neighbouring people in that very manner; a barrel of powder – which all the Powers are most anxious to prevent from exploding – catching fire through some 'untoward' Sarajewo accident. Some console themselves with the hope that there is a Hegelian *List der Vermunft* hidden in all that, and that like the Holland we mentioned before, the nation would come out greater and better from this ordeal. Although twentieth-century gruesome experience of 'final solutions' are bound to have an inhibiting effect on such expectations, one does not dare not to reflect from time to time that most problems are in fact never solved. They are survived, outlived, by-passed, slowly shaken off out of weariness, driven out by more urgent and more pressing ones. 'It is' – writes R. H. Tawney in one of his purple passages, 'the tragedy of a world where man must walk by sight that the discovery of the reconciling formula is always left to the future generations, in which passion has cooled into curiosity, and the agonies of peoples have become the exercise in the schools. The devil who builds bridges does not span such chasms till much that is precious has vanished down for ever.'

POST SCRIPTUM

This essay is going into final printing under the shadow of the dramatic developments of May and June, 1970. Soviet pilots are manning Egyptian air defences, flying over the Sinai peninsula and erecting missile sites on Egyptian territory, creating thus the grave danger of a headlong collision between Israeli and Russian pilots. The firing between Israeli and Arab positions, accompanied by intensive bombing from the air, keeps raising the toll of casualties on both sides. In Lebanon and Jordan a war between Government forces and guerrillas is on.

The scene seems to be set for an awesome apocalypse, for no one knows the ultimate intentions of Russia, especially if she is not made to fear a determined stand on the part of the US. There is no guarantee that things may not slip out of control in a way unplanned or even undesired by any of the protagonists, since there remains no doubt at all that Israel will resist to the last any Russian attempt, whatever form it may take, to cross the Canal.

Far from invalidating the reflections voiced in the body of the present essay, the recent developments seem to add dramatic poignancy to the nightmarish perils outlined in the previous pages, and new urgency to the need for a compromise settlement. One recoils from conjuring up the dangers of brinkmanship, but it may well be that the future historian will in a spirit of Olympic detachment conclude that such a dramatisation of the ultimate peril was necessary to shock the Super Powers into calling and making a halt.

More and more Israelis are beginning to realise that 'politics is a choice between the unpalatable and the disastrous', and some observers believe they detect in the Arab world a greater receptiveness to the idea that a reasonable settlement with Israel would be a much lesser evil than the incalculable consequences of complete Russian domination, unlimited external war and total internal disruption.

In the face of the paralysing effect of both the well founded fears and the irrational passions upon the direct combatants, one is reduced to putting one's hopes for the anguished peoples of the Middle East upon the post-nuclear balance of fear, and the old-fashioned system of the division of spheres of influence. These have after all kept the world from ultimate disaster for the last twenty-five years. They may in time also produce a change of heart in the embattled peoples of the Middle East.

7 July 1970

Index